A DAY IN THE SUN

Outdoor Pursuits in Art in the 1930s

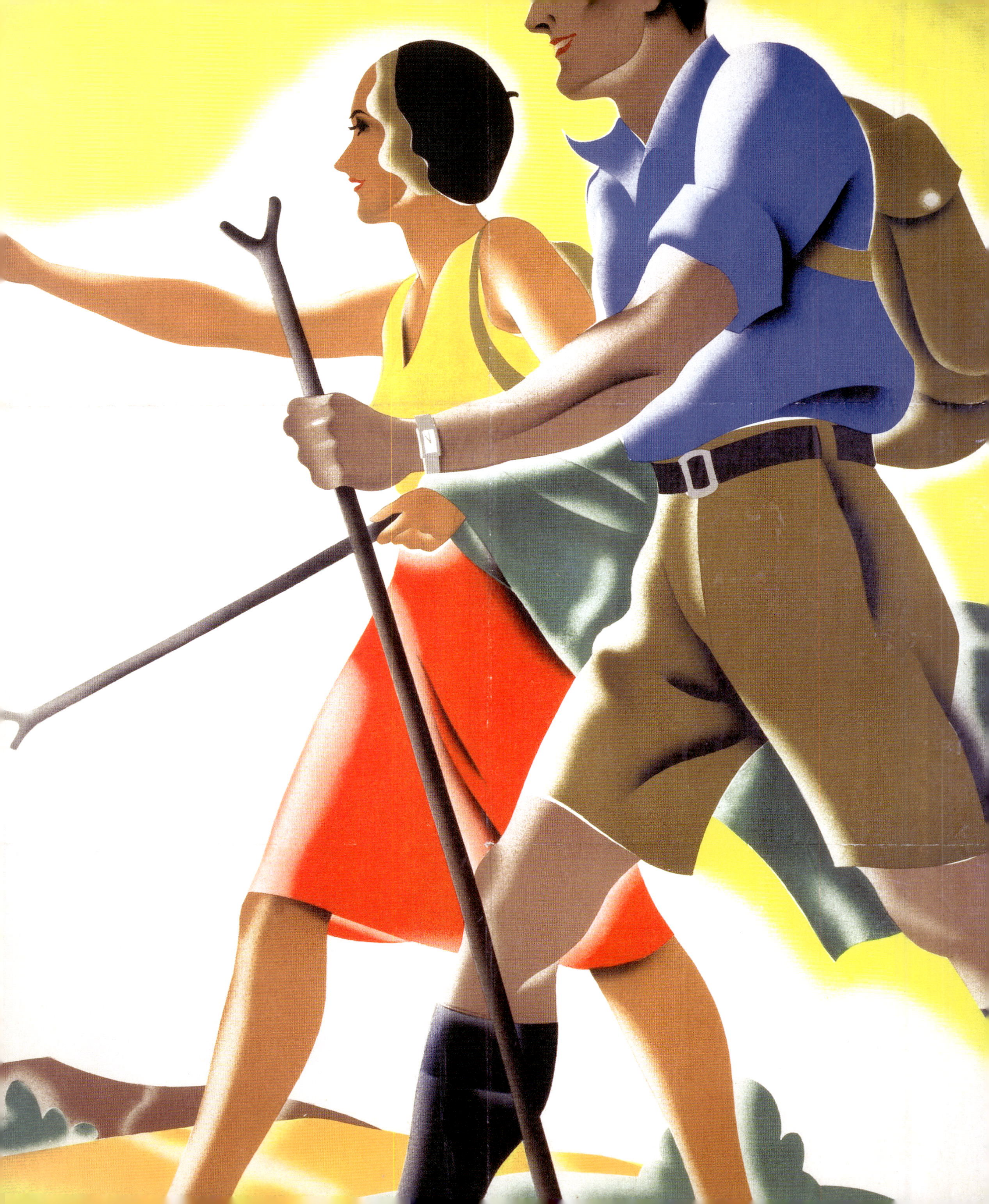

A DAY IN THE SUN

Outdoor Pursuits in Art in the 1930s

Timothy Wilcox

with a contribution by David Matless

DJANOGLY ART GALLERY,
LAKESIDE ARTS CENTRE, NOTTINGHAM

PHILIP WILSON PUBLISHERS

Contents

Foreword

The collective pursuit of leisure and a new discovery of the English countryside through walking, camping and a host of sporting activities was one of the most remarkable social phenomena of the 1930s. Yet, although images of such pursuits are familiar to us from numerous 'new' and social realist paintings produced in other European countries during this period – particularly under the official sanction of the National Socialist Party in Germany – they have until now received very little attention in Britain with perhaps the exception of the striking graphic work produced by artists for Shell, London Transport and the national railways.

This book and the exhibition it accompanies reveal a small group of figurative painters, many of whom were regular contributors to the annual Royal Academy exhibitions, who sought to depict subject matter that was both topical and self-consciously modern. Whereas a number of these artists, such as Stanley Spencer, William Roberts and Dod Procter, have been the subject of one or more retrospective exhibitions and published monographs reassessing their contribution to British art in the twentieth century, several of the names will be largely unknown to a general public and the joy of a project such as this is to bring to wider attention the work of artists who have fallen into relative obscurity or who now enjoy only regional celebrity. The crisp, realist style of painting which characterises the majority of this work has an instant appeal and the power to conjure the period in all its immediacy.

A Day in the Sun is the brainchild of art historian Timothy Wilcox who, recognising this overlooked strand of British art, has researched tirelessly over many years to locate exhibited works and those illustrated in contemporary journals. His essay effortlessly navigates the territory of artistic endeavour set against the wider social and political events that shaped attitudes towards health and leisure in the years leading up to the Second World War. David Matless, Professor of Cultural Geography at The University of Nottingham, has contributed a perceptive and useful introduction.

As always, we are indebted to the many public and private collections who have generously loaned their works to the exhibition and to the artists' estates for granting permission for reproduction of the works in this book. In particular, the National Museum of Photography, Film & Television at Bradford has loaned the large number of photographs from the Daily Herald Archive, and both the Victoria and Albert Museum and London's Transport Museum have made substantial loans of posters to provide a context for the works on canvas.

It is highly appropriate that *A Day in the Sun* should be organised and mounted at the Djanogly Art Gallery built at the beginning of the 1990s on the site of the old Highfields lido which up until its closure some thirty years ago was a prominent and fondly regarded outdoor leisure facility on the edge of The University of Nottingham campus. The exhibition has been organised in association with The Lowry at Salford Quays to which it transfers following its showing in Nottingham.

Neil Walker
Djanogly Art Gallery

The New Outdoors

David Matless

The images brought together in this exhibition convey the emergence of a new outdoors in 1930s Britain. If the weather on this island was as variable then as now, the fact that the phrase 'A Day in the Sun' can form an apt title for this show suggests something of the narratives of hope and/or release which often framed outdoor leisure in the period. On holiday, on a week-end hike, by the sea, the mood would, it was hoped, always be sunny, even if the weather might let you down. New forms of leisure could signify modernity, could be read as signs of an improving world of holidays with pay (more widely available for blue as well as white collar workers in the period and cemented through the 1938 Holidays With Pay Act), of novel technologies of transport and communication, and relaxed moralities of pleasure through the body. Yet car-borne trippers, hikers on hills, and bodies unclothed on the sand could also be a source of concern for those seeking to guard public morality or rural amenity. One person's day in the sun could be another's sign of a nation going to the dogs. The story of outdoor pursuits in the 1930s is a complex one of the negotiation of the innovative and the traditional, the urban and the rural, the conventional and the out-landish. What it was to be modern outdoors often involved moving through such polarities, with terms such as 'moral', 'vulgar', 'new' and 'natural' acting as signposts for commentary on leisure activities.[1] The artists in this show sought in their various ways to figure this new outdoors.

Not all of the outdoor pursuits shown here were entirely novel. People had walked in a landscape or lounged on a beach long before 1930, and all the activities engaged with here have a long social and cultural history. However, a number of senses of novelty congregate around these practices in this period. There is newness in the sense of places being made accessible for the first time to a wider population through new forms of transport, as motor vehicles opened up rural spaces far beyond the orbit of a railway station. Railway companies and London Transport played a key role in fostering leisure in the period, as the posters in this show indicate, but in some ways the very presence of these posters indicate one mode of transport having to compete for passengers against another new way of moving. The car moves down the social spectrum to become an object of middle-class ownership, while buses and 'charabanc' tours open up the country down the social scale. Open-air commentator Cyril Joad suggested in 1934 that the 'motor's capacity for ubiquitous penetration' had created 'a new situation'.[2]

There was also newness in the manner in which these pursuits were styled and depicted. In terms of artistic convention the images here negotiate aesthetic polarities of the modern and the traditional, indeed the modernist and traditionalist, and in doing so serve in part to illustrate the porosity of such categories. This figuration of the outdoors centres on the body in the landscape, by turns active, languid, striding, restful, playful, meditative. The complex cultures of the body in 1930s Britain, and indeed 1930s Europe, are played out in these pictures. Some images, most obviously the photographs taken from newspaper archives but also many of the paintings, work as social observation, extending artistic modes developed in Victorian genre painting and also picking up on the anthropological and documentary gaze turned upon British culture in the 1930s by groups such as Mass Observation. Careful study of these images can instruct the viewer on the possible details of a 1930s picnic or sunbathe; the modern picnic basket in Harold Williamson's *Picnic*, 1938 (fig. 68; cat. 41) or the gramophone discs on the ground of William Roberts' *Sunbathing*, 1936 (fig. 13; cat. 31). If the mode of social observation informing such images is itself part of the culture of this time and place, so too is the idealisation of the leisured body present in many pictures. Depictions of physical fitness, of the health and happiness supposedly brought by outdoor pursuits, chime with another of Cyril Joad's maxims: 'Whence can we derive an education alike of body, of mind and of spirit, so happily as from Nature?'[3] The sense of the outdoors as a source of individual and collective self-improvement was common in the period. Political campaigns for access to closed private land generated conflict and controversy in the 1930s, most notably in the upland landscapes of Derbyshire and the Pennines registered here by Harry Epworth Allen, and a series of voluntary and public institutions sought to foster the open air. The Youth Hostels Association was founded in 1930 and the Ramblers' Association in 1935, assorted youth movements followed the outdoor example of the Scouts and Guides, and in 1937 the Government sought to encourage open-air activity through the National Fitness Council, forerunner of the Sports Council. Strange mixtures of bodily discipline and liberation run through such initiatives, with for many freedom depending upon the ability to conduct oneself outdoors in a disciplined fashion. What Joad termed the 'art of right living', which the 'citizens of the future' might develop through open-air leisure,[4] was set against various characterisations of wrong living by those seeking to promote the outdoor body. Litter droppers, gramophone players, crowds disturbing the peace, all came in for criticism by those promoting a moral geography of new citizens made through new leisure in new landscapes. Such disciplines of bodily conduct, and the spiritual and intellectual cultures of landscape which accompanied them, found an echo in contemporary events in Germany, where for some the enthusiastic state takeover of a longstanding and politically varied outdoor movement in the name of Fascism signalled a warning. For others Germany might be an attractive example of national renewal; such questions are posed in Percy Shakespeare's 1935 painting *On the Rhine* (fig. 52; cat. 35). The ideological appeal of such a body culture of freedom and regulation could however stretch right across the political spectrum, from Fascism to Communism through all points in between. And other body cultures emerged which hinted at more libertarian possibilities, the entire throwing off of regulation and authority in the natural open air. If Lancelot Glasson's *The Young Rower*, 1932 (fig. 38; cat. 14) might be read as the kind of image which could have resulted had Degas been commissioned by the Sports Council, Glasson's choice of a pose semi-clad in the changing room rather than dressed at the oars could, for some, make such a painting less than wholesome. The culture of the naked body, whether sunbathing, sporting or otherwise, moved into complex moral territory, with the erotic and the voyeuristic only ever a short cultural distance away in the new outdoors. The 1930s saw the growth of nudism under labels such as 'naturism' or 'gymnosophy', a pursuit claiming and stressing its own morality, a higher and purer outdoor pursuit of harmony with nature and an untrammelled and non-erotic meeting of humans as nature intended them to be. A day in the sun could, for the naturist, only be fully realised without clothes. The outdoor nudes in this show appear contemporary with such a culture of the naked body aligning health, morality and modernity. The aesthetics of the human body promoted in naturism often drew on ancient Greek models, echoed in paintings such as Walter Hutton's *They See an Oread*, 1933 (fig. 8; cat. 17), where healthy hikers spy a mountain nymph sunbathing. But how are we to suppose these hikers reacted? With delight, surprise, shock? This all too human mythic creature would hardly be marked on their Popular Edition Ordnance Survey map. Or perhaps they reacted with mocking humour. These nudes of the new outdoors are also contemporary with music hall and variety routines about the comedies of nudism, with seaside postcards presenting a rather different corporeality, and with moral objections to the potential overtones and consequences of public displays of flesh. The nude in art strays, as ever, over sharp cultural terrain.

The new outdoors of the 1930s was a complicated cultural landscape, and the images shown here, some by artists whose reputation remains, others by artists since forgotten or who never gained a reputation to lose, remind us of the ways in which painters and photographers pursued such subjects. Walking through the show we accumulate something of the possibilities of this historical new outdoors, and become aware of how something so taken for granted as outdoor leisure is profoundly historical in terms of its social practices and representational conventions. Returning from stores and collections to public view, these pictures make a fine exhibition of themselves.

NOTES

1 On the issues discussed here see David Matless, *Landscape and Englishness* (Reaktion Books, 1998). For studies of outdoor leisure see also Harvey Taylor, *A Claim on the Countryside: A History of the British Outdoor Movement* (Keele University Press, 1997); John K Walton, *The British Seaside: Holidays and resorts in the twentieth century* (Manchester University Press, 2000).
2 CEM Joad, *A Charter for Ramblers, or The Future of the Countryside* (Hutchinson, 1934), p. 97.
3 Joad, *Charter for Ramblers*, p. 150.
4 Joad, *Charter for Ramblers*, p. 158.

A DAY IN THE SUN

Timothy Wilcox

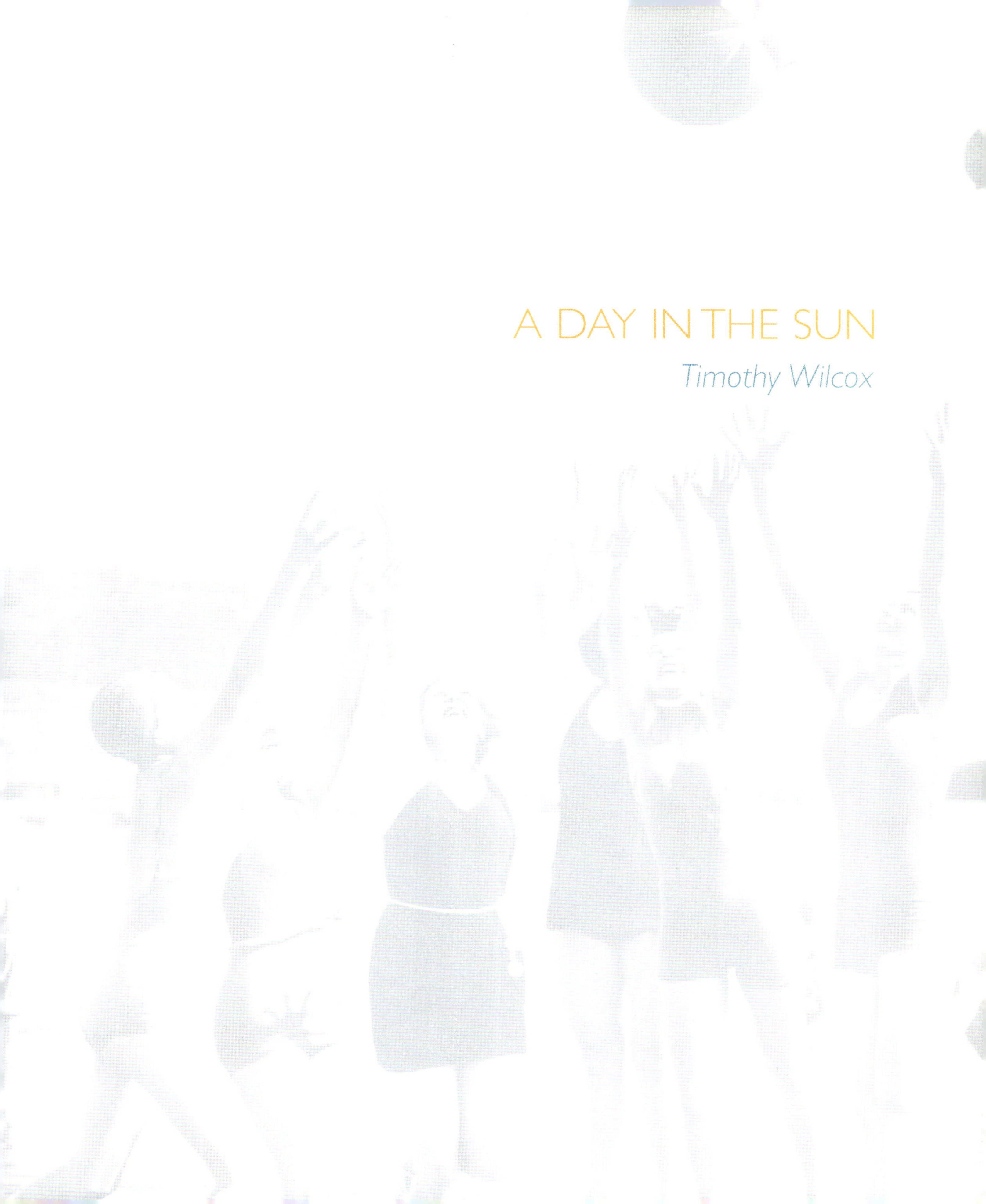

Introduction

Piccadilly Circus, in the heart of London's West End, may seem an unlikely place to celebrate the pleasures of the English countryside. In 1928, when Stephen Bone's mural painting in the central ticket hall was unveiled (fig. 1), it was a hub for pleasure-seekers of a different kind: shoppers, diners, theatre-goers and those attending the new cocktail bars and late-night review clubs which were attracting the attention of the London Public Morality Council. By contrast, Bone's frieze tempted travellers to sample the more innocent amusements of walking, riding, swimming, boating or even simply lounging on the grass with an illustrated magazine. The invitation was sealed with lines from Coleridge, extolling the experience of sea, sky and land.

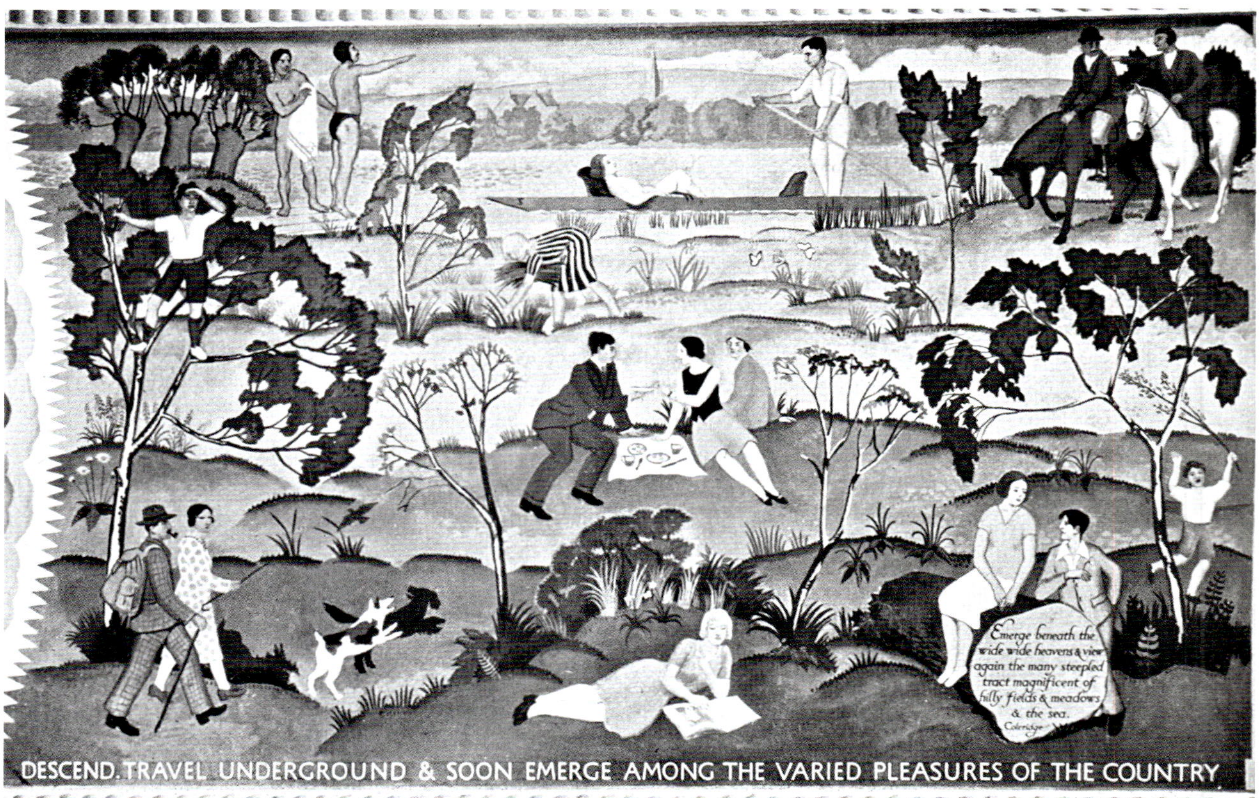

FIG 1

Stephen Bone

Mural Painting in Piccadilly Circus Station 1928

Bone provides a visual compendium of outdoor pursuits, some traditional, like riding, others, like hiking, more contemporary.

Nowadays, any interest in Bone's mural (no longer visible and believed no longer extant) would be likely to focus on the enlightened artistic patronage of London Transport during the inter-war years, under the leadership of Frank Pick. Bone had recently graduated from the Slade School, and was still only twenty-four when he installed the panels. What might pass almost unnoticed, unremarkable because apparently so commonplace, is Bone's subject matter, the terms in which he chooses to describe 'the varied pleasures of the country'. His collection of almost naïve vignettes is of more than anecdotal interest; Bone has created a visual compendium of a popular understanding of leisure that is utterly contemporary.[1]

There is in fact much more at stake here than mere 'amusement'. During the 1920s and 1930s, against a background of strikes, mass unemployment and threatening developments in Europe, the pursuit of leisure emerged as

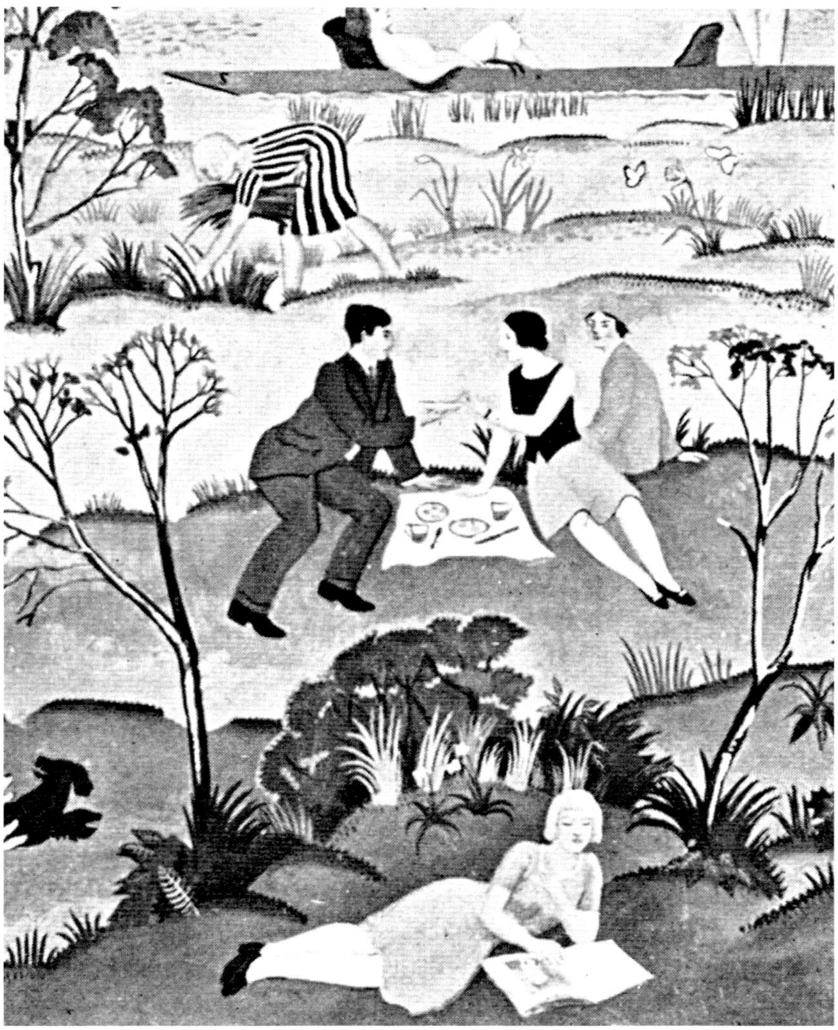

DETAIL OF FIG 1

a major social and political issue in Britain. This went far beyond simple escapism, or a release from the harsh realities of daily life. A profound mental shift was taking place throughout the entire population, one in which work, flourishing industrial productivity and the world dominance of Empire could no longer be taken for granted as the basis of British identity. Prime Minister Stanley Baldwin signalled a reorientation of government policy and the weight of expectation associated with it in 1926 when he recognised the need to provide not only jobs, but also leisure: 'the greater the facilities for recreation, the better will be the health and happiness of the people and the closer will be the spirit of unity between all classes' (fig. 2; cat. 5).[2]

The promise was not only for physical health, but moral health as well. Among the many challenges of the post-war era, the constructive use of leisure came to have major significance. While the movies, gambling and

FIG 2

Anonymous

It's a Pleasure 1938 (cat. 5)

The simple, geometric design, the employment of a range of unposed photographic images and the simple slogan make this one of London Transport's most direct pieces of publicity. It not only takes in a wide variety of leisure activities, it also includes women and children among its subjects.

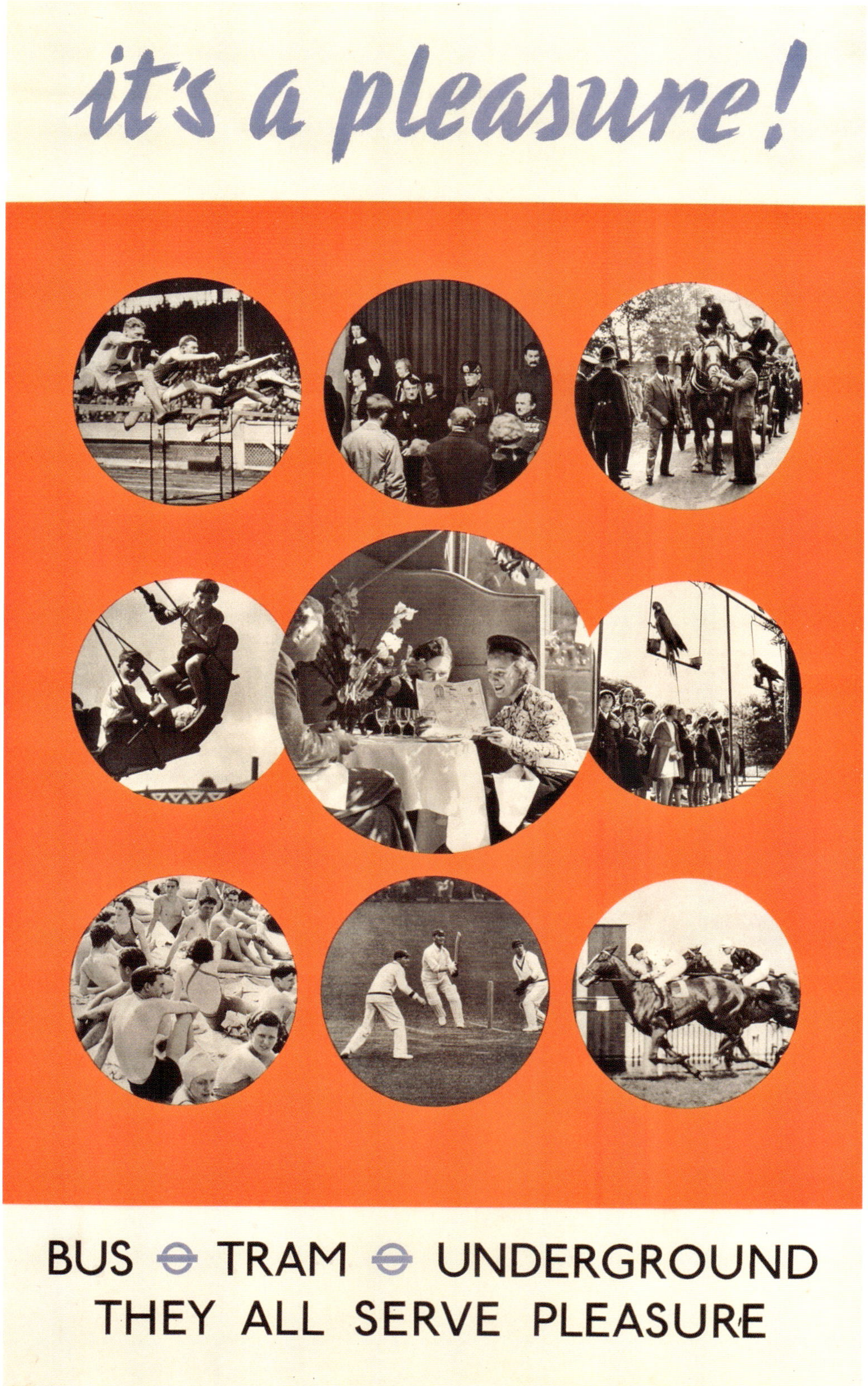
it's a pleasure!
BUS TRAM UNDERGROUND
THEY ALL SERVE PLEASURE

after 1926, the radio, provided for the many, the numbers engaged in more active pursuits grew and grew. The wider availability of a greater range of sports to women, in particular, and to participants beyond the affluent middle classes were one of the defining characteristics of the age: leisure became the very image of modernity.

In the fine arts, and specifically in painting, the inter-war years have generally been seen as a period of retrenchment, succeeded by the gradual emergence in the 1930s of abstraction (and, to a lesser extent, of Surrealism). Paul Nash, writing in 1933, identified these as the two most powerful trends in contemporary art; the group he had recently assembled, Unit One, intended to unite both elements. 'A desire to find again some adventure in art seems more and more urgent to our sculptors and painters and, now, to our architects. This seems to suggest, as well as any

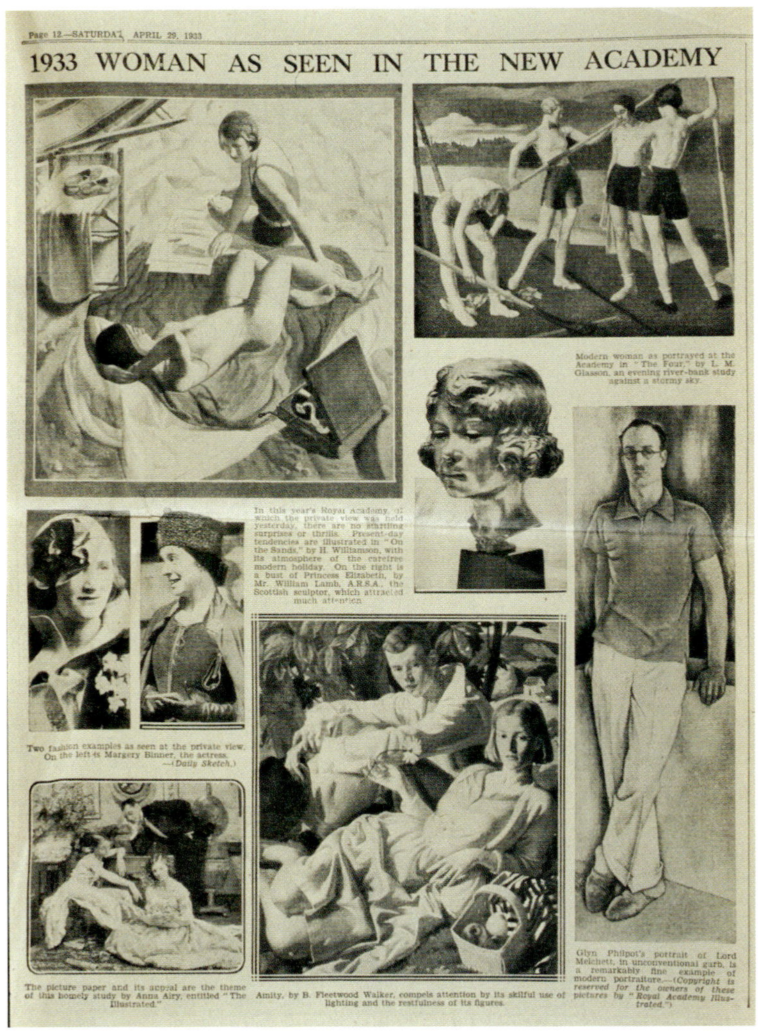

Page 12—SATURDAY, APRIL 29, 1933

1933 WOMAN AS SEEN IN THE NEW ACADEMY

In this year's Royal Academy, of which the private view was held yesterday, there are no startling surprises or thrills. Present-day tendencies are illustrated in "On the Sands," by H. Williamson, with its atmosphere of the carefree modern holiday. On the right is a bust of Princess Elizabeth, by Mr. William Lamb, A.R.S.A., the Scottish sculptor, which attracted much attention.

Modern woman as portrayed at the Academy in "The Four," by L. M. Glasson, an evening river-bank study against a stormy sky.

Two fashion examples as seen at the private view. On the left is Margery Binner, the actress. —(*Daily Sketch.*)

The picture paper and its appeal are the theme of this homely study by Anna Airy, entitled "The Illustrated."

Amity, by B. Fleetwood Walker, compels attention by its skilful use of lighting and the restfulness of its figures.

Glyn Philpot's portrait of Lord Melchett, in unconventional garb, is a remarkably fine example of modern portraiture.—(*Copyright is reserved for the owners of these pictures by "Royal Academy Illustrated."*)

FIG 3

1933 Woman as seen in the New Academy
Daily Sketch 29 April 1933

A spread from a popular newspaper showing how fashions, hairstyles and sunbathing and sport were seen as parts of wider social trends bringing women greater personal freedom.

explanation, the meaning of "the contemporary spirit". It is the adventure, the research, the pursuit in modern life ...'[3] Figurative art as a whole, but especially art based on the human figure, has, from the perspective of late twentieth-century modernism, been seen as traditional by definition, and more or less excluded from serious examination. The works of many of the artists gathered together in this book tell a different story. It is one up to now almost entirely overlooked, but which represents a small but resilient strand in the art of the 1930s: work which was not so radically adventurous as Nash, perhaps, but still showed a commitment to subjects which were overtly modern in subject matter. Many of these paintings were first exhibited in the Royal Academy, then more than ever a bastion of traditional English values. The affinity between the contributions of these painters was recognised at the time to the extent that the pictures of sports, picnics and

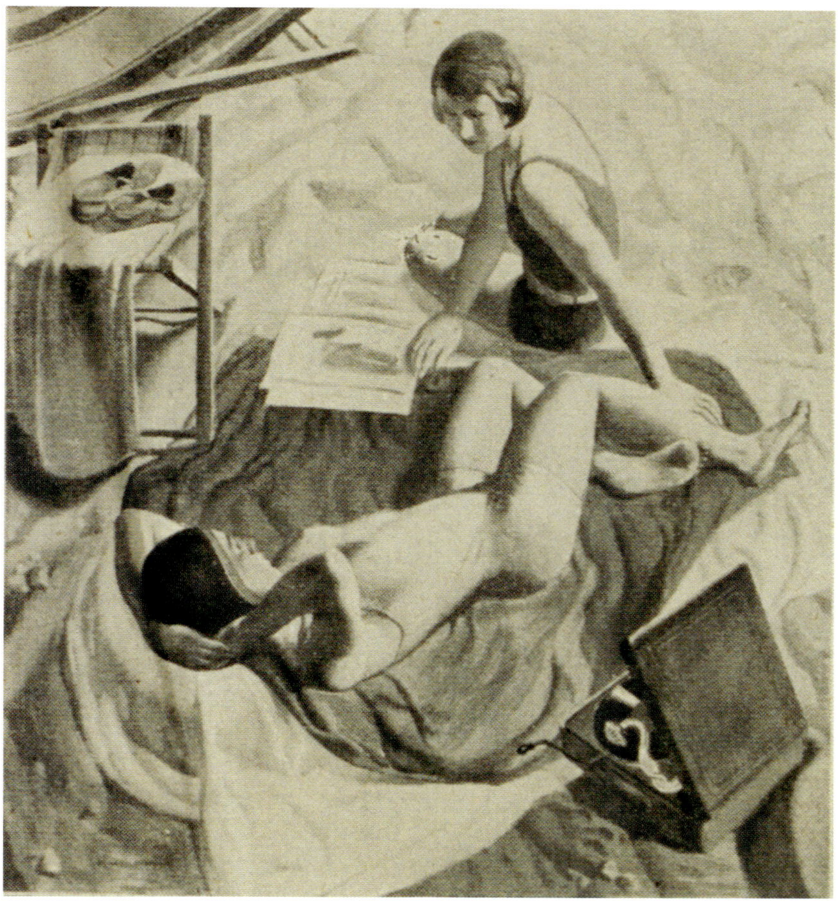

DETAIL OF FIG 3
Harold Williamson
On the Sands

other open-air activities were often reproduced side by side in the annual *Royal Academy Illustrated* and seized on by critics and editors for the regular features in the illustrated press as representing literally 'a breath of fresh air' in the turgid atmosphere of what was still largely a late-Victorian salon. The clear-cut linearity of Fleetwood-Walker, Williamson and Glasson has affinities with a parallel enthusiasm for the neo-classical style in the applied arts; the tempera painters, who really came of age in this decade, showed themselves to be concerned not only with technique and decoration, but with an uncluttered directness of expression. These works provided more than a pungent whiff of the present-day, however. The photo-feature from the *Daily Sketch* of 1933 (fig. 3) shows how, taken in combination, they addressed other topical issues; in this case, the changing role of women, not simply as something to be recorded or commented upon, but as a dynamic force

FIG 4

Mary Adshead
Country Joys on London's Undergound 1927 (cat. 1)

Adshead's first commission for London underground presents an almost aristocratic image of outdoor leisure, before the sense of a popular movement had taken root.

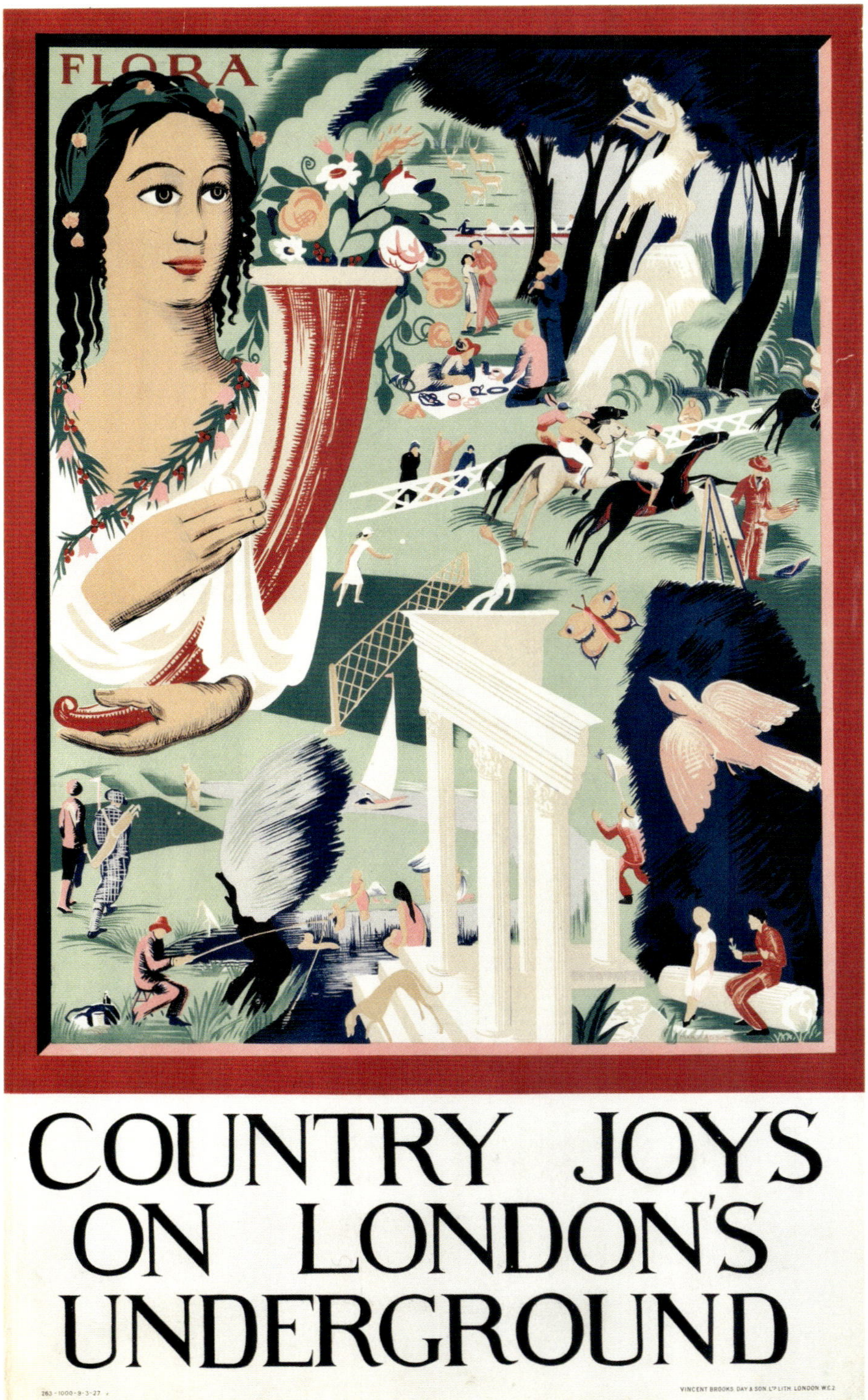
FLORA
COUNTRY JOYS
ON LONDON'S
UNDERGROUND
263-1000-9-3-27
VINCENT BROOKS DAY & SON L^TD LITH. LONDON W.C.2

creating new types of visual images. It is in the nature of the art of this period that most of these images were created by men; the works of the women artists included here, notably Laura Knight (figs. 72, 78) and Mary Adshead (fig. 4; cat. 1), who married Stephen Bone in 1929, are, however, often little different in content or style.

Despite being presented in the predominantly middle-class arena of the Royal Academy, many of these paintings tackle subjects that were popular in a wider sense. Social commentators were well aware that not only did sport have mass appeal but it was an area in which divisions of class, and of race, were being repeatedly challenged during this decade. The inclusion in this book of travel posters and of a small selection of photographs from the *Daily Herald*, a Labour-supporting mass-circulation newspaper, reveals how painting participated in a wider community of images. While certain com-

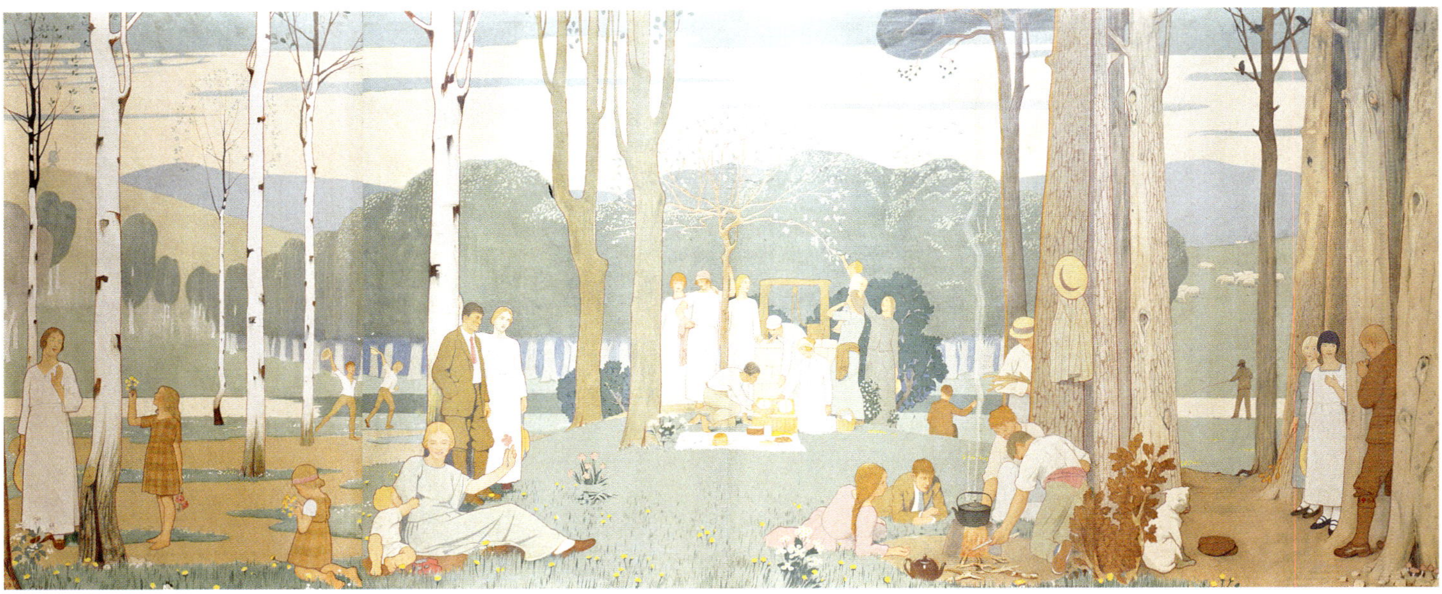

FIG 5

Frederick Cayley Robinson
Summer: A Day in the Country c. 1923–24 (cat. 33)

Commissioned by London Transport in the mid-1920s, Robinson's three-panel poster looks back directly to the great French Symbolist Puvis de Chavannes. The women in their long white robes give the humble picnic something of the air of an arcane religious ritual.

mentators, notably Clive Bell in his book *Civilization,* argued that culture must be exclusive, many of the works of art gathered here embrace their connections with publicity and photography and use this as a sign of their break with the past.[4]

Bone's mural seems to stand on the brink of a new era; an accompanying panel depicting office workers makes plain the message that these leisure activities are now available to the many, not the few, at least in principle. This marks a considerable advance over the 1927 poster designed by Mary Adshead (fig. 4). The range of pastimes depicted is not dissimilar to Bone's, but here they are presided over by a classical deity, with a fragment of a temple in the foreground and a piping faun in the woods; this is leisure for the leisured, culture for the cultivated. Adshead had graduated from the Slade School in 1924 aged only twenty, sharing the prize for composition. The subject set that year was 'The Picnic'. Adshead created a setting like a seventeenth-century tapestry, showing more concern for tradition than for the contemporary resonances of her theme.[5] The picnicking figures in the triptych designed by the symbolist Cayley Robinson for London Transport in 1924 are sombre and statuesque (fig. 5; cat. 33). Here, the very idea of a day out appears an unfamiliar ritual, but one that in a few years' time will be transformed by the sunlight and agile movement that flooded in with the 1930s.

Sunbathing

One of the subjects that was not new in itself, but now acquired a distinctively contemporary resonance, was the nude. Commenting in 1957 on one of his 1931 Royal Academy exhibits, Fleetwood-Walker recalled, 'At the time I painted *The Bane* there was a tremendous vogue for nudes. I painted a lot of them. Nowadays there is not much call for them'.[6] The unclothed figure was released during the nineteenth century from the confines of classicism, and continued to appear most frequently in the guise of a bather, both male and female. *The Bather*, a back view of a woman seated by a pool, exhibited by Harold Knight in 1916, is essentially a continuation of the fleshy Victorian nudes of Watts, yet found its way into the exhibition of sporting art

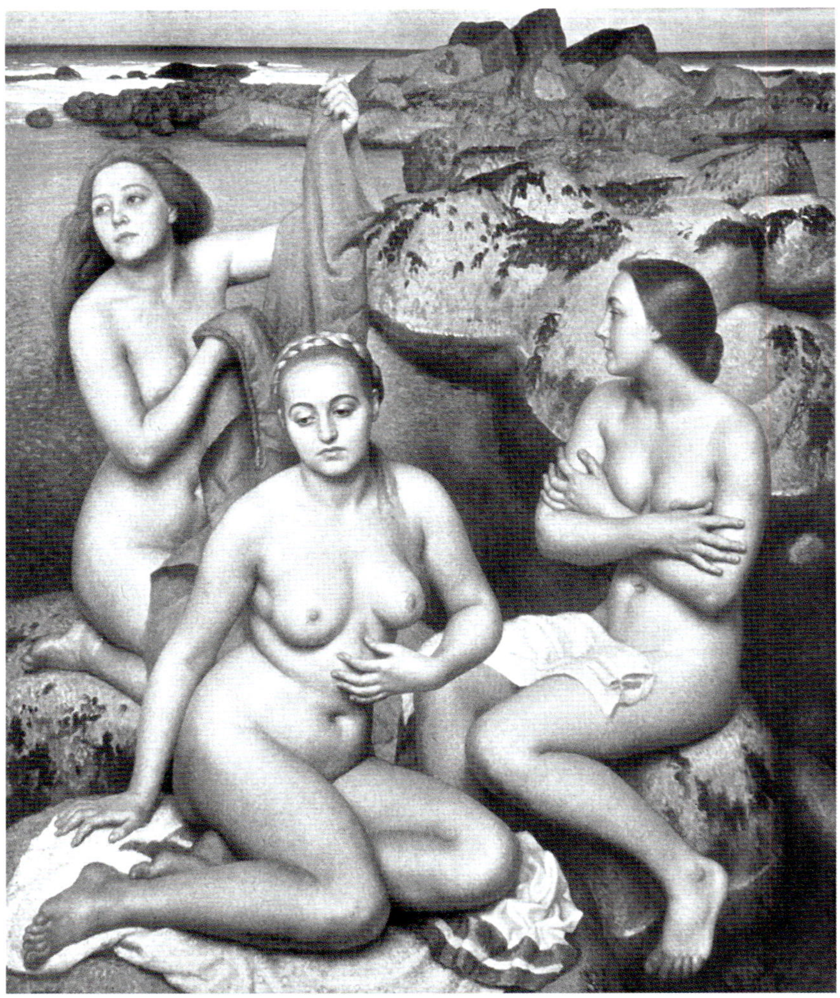

FIG 6

Laura Knight
Daughters of the Sea
(exhibited Royal Academy 1928)

An ambitious painting, marking Knight's election as ARA the previous year. The different body types suggest a woman's sensibility, giving a modern slant to an ostensibly traditional subject.

mounted for the Amsterdam Olympics in 1928, lent by the Laing Art Gallery, Newcastle-upon-Tyne. In 1927 Henry Tuke showed a group of young nude males around a rock pool, little different to subjects he had tackled regularly for over thirty years, but in giving it the title *Sunbathers* he showed a modern awareness. In the past, Tuke apparently insisted that his models remain fair-skinned; this subtly accentuated their youth and lack of experience (in the days when tanned skin was seen as an undesirable effect of outdoor labour); now, at the very end of his career (Tuke died in 1929), this almost hackneyed subject acquired new resonance. Laura Knight, who had painted many partially clad bathers on Cornish beaches, in the year following her election as ARA, 1928, exhibited a composition of three unidealised nudes (fig. 6). Such exposure was not always acceptable; Dod Procter, another woman painter based in Cornwall, was prevailed on to remove a

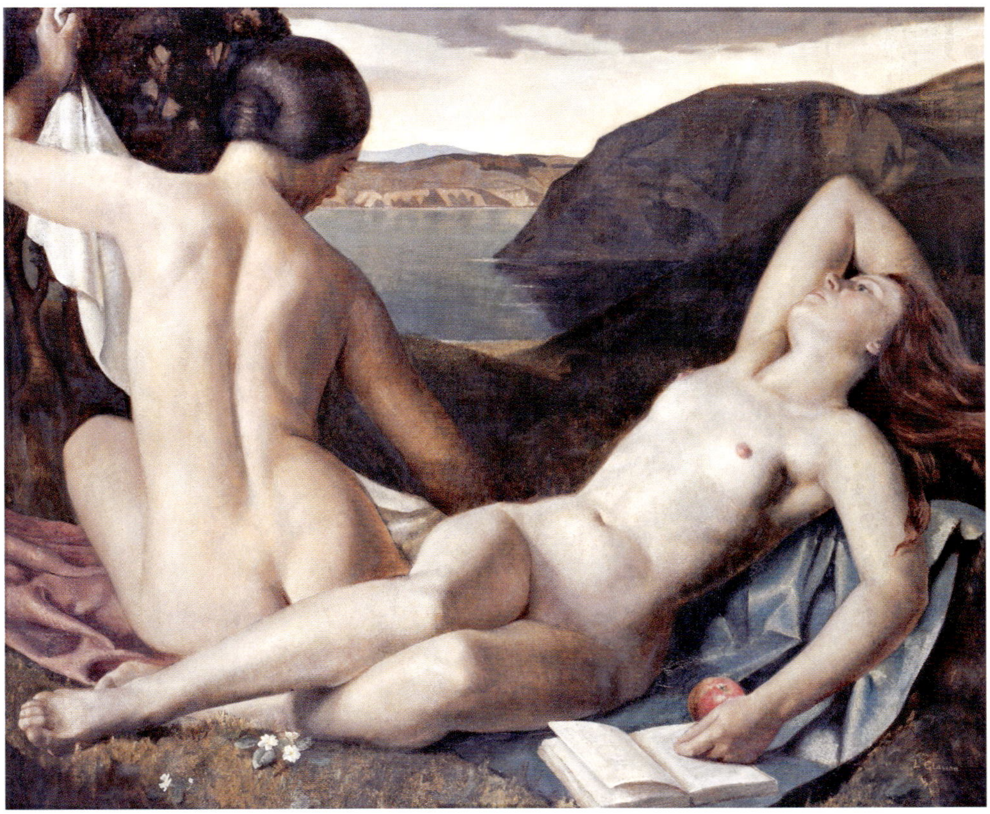

FIG 7

Lancelot Glasson
Repose 1929 (cat. 13)
Glasson is putting his studies in the life-room to good effect in a work which gives a contemporary slant to what is, on the surface, a highly traditional treatment of the nude.

painting of a nude from the 1929 exhibition. It is even reported that the crusading Home Secretary, William Joynson Hicks, closed one West End exhibition on grounds of public decency. Fleetwood-Walker's *The Bane*, bought by an enthusiastic Birmingham brewer, apparently 'startled his friends' so much that in 1936 he donated it to the city's art gallery.[7]

A huge gulf separates these unselfconsciously naked figures from the sunbathers of Lancelot Glasson (fig. 7; cat. 13). The exposure of flesh in public was acquiring a new cultural context, that of naturism. The therapeutic properties of exposure to sunlight and fresh air had been pioneered in Germany as a treatment for tuberculosis since the end of the previous century. Partly for reasons of climate, but also of modesty, the movement had been slow to gain ground in England, but a particularly hot summer in 1928 may have been responsible, at least in part, for a marked rise in its

FIG 8

Walter Hutton

They See an Oread 1933 (cat. 17)

The chasm in the middle of the painting evokes the social and psychological divide between the innocence of the walkers and the risqué behaviour of the sunbather. As the title makes plain, both walkers see the nude; while he strains for a better view, she cowers almost in embarrassment.

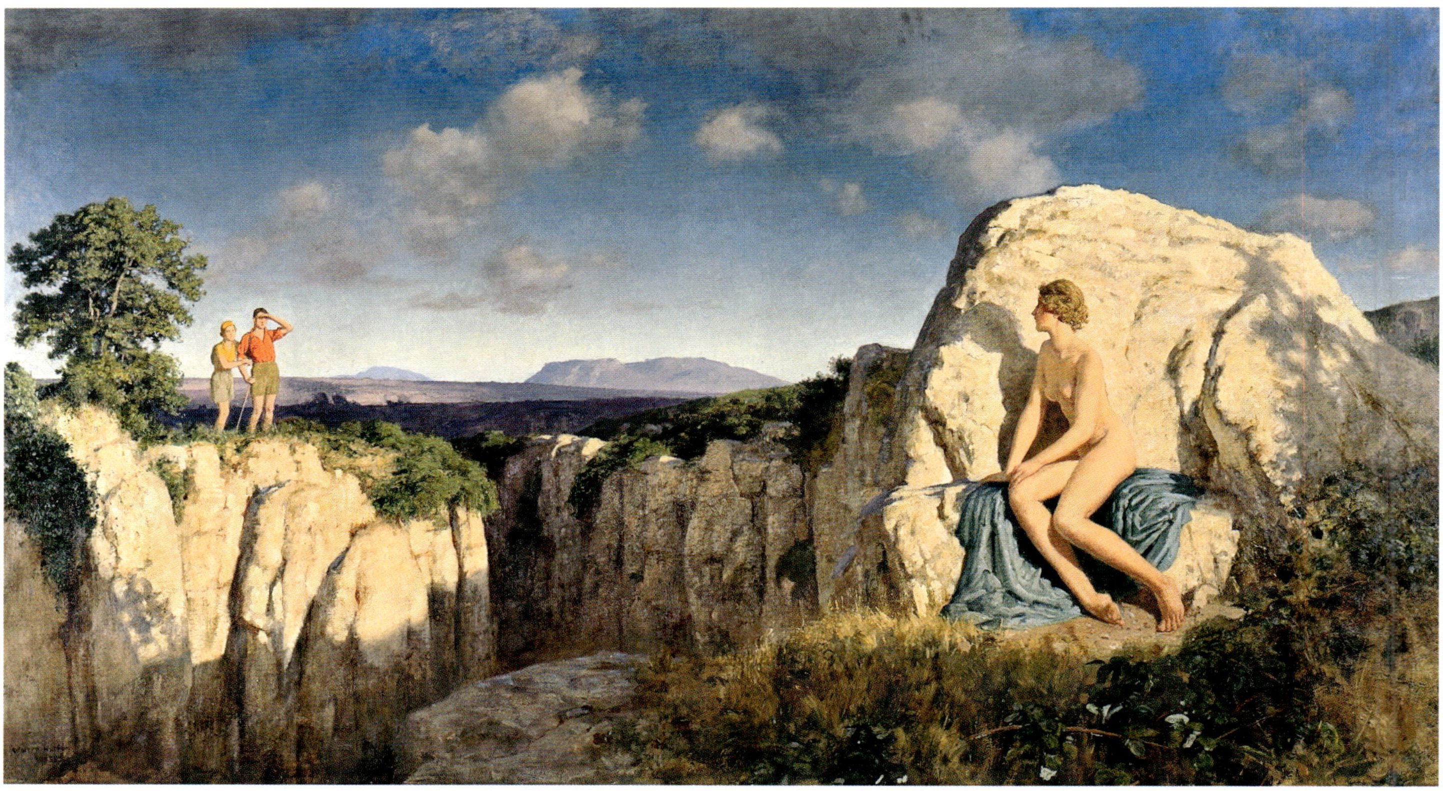

popularity.[8] The modernity of sunbathing and public uncertainty as to its desirability on moral grounds, is captured magnificently in Walter Hutton's Royal Academy painting of 1933, *They see an Oread* (fig. 8; cat. 17) A hiking couple come across a nude sunbather half concealed behind a rock in the middle of open moorland; the proximity of water, which is often presented as a half-excuse for nakedness, is entirely dispensed with here (in classical mythology, an oread is a mountain nymph). The male walker holds his partner back. Displaying a chauvinism typical of the age, the female body, visible to him, is somehow construed as offensive to another woman. Later in the decade, some local authorities sought to introduce bye-laws preventing the wearing of swimwear except on beaches. The display of the body, even partly clad, was deemed an assault on public decency. In Brighton, regulations governed the dwindling size of bathing costumes, but this did not

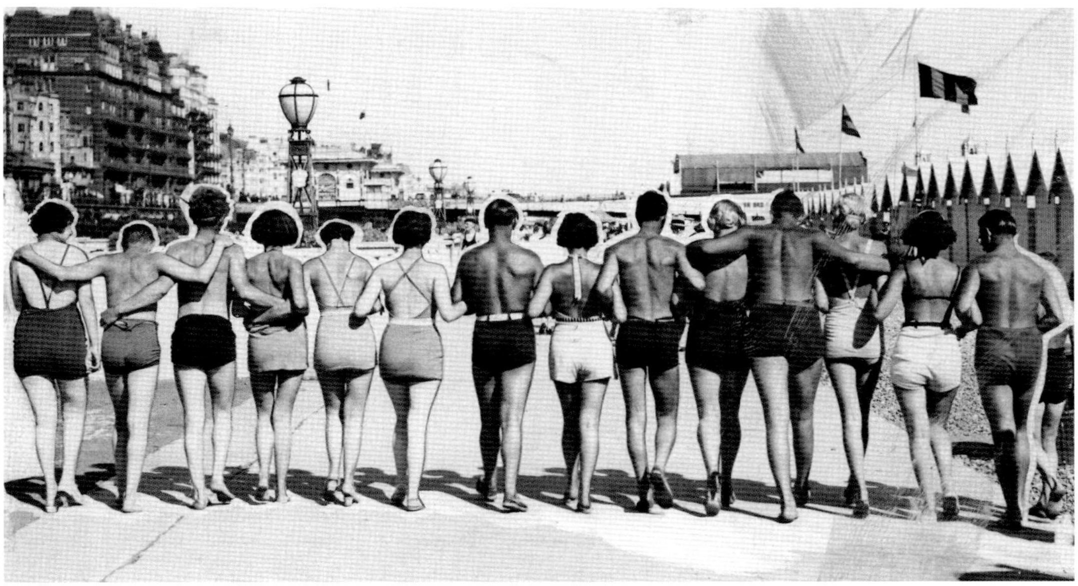

FIG 9

Sunbathing at Brighton 3 August 1935 (cat. 51)

Published just after the August Bank Holiday in 1935, this photo speaks volumes about the sense of liberation and camaraderie a day by the seaside could express.

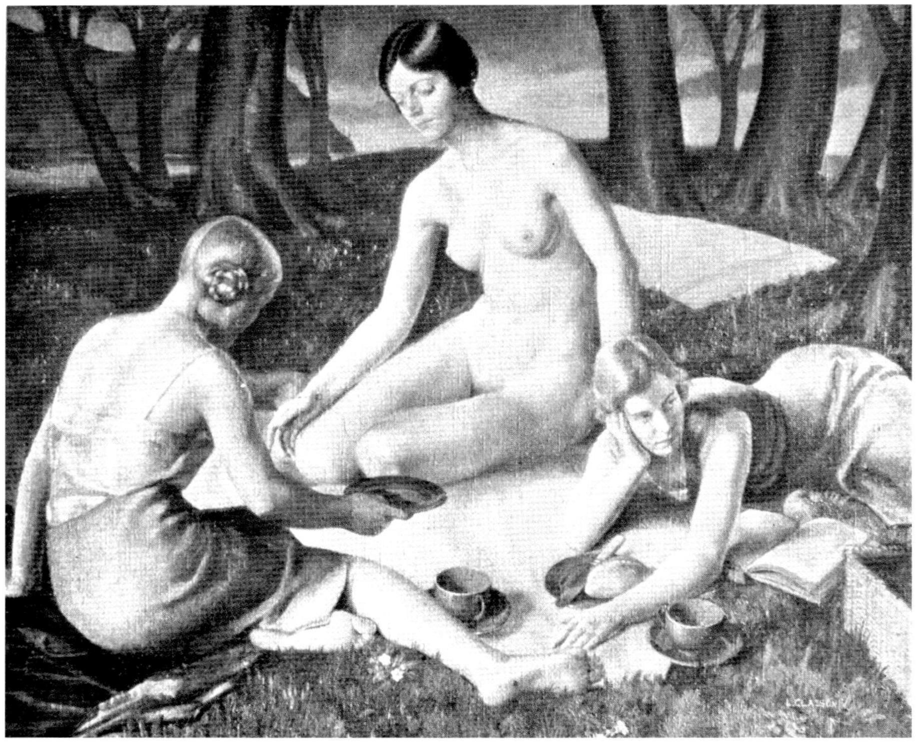

FIG 10

Lancelot Glasson
Déjeuner sur l'herbe
(exhibited Royal Academy 1931)

Glasson reworks Manet's composition of clothed and unclothed figures, but defuses the most shocking aspect of his model by removing any male presence from the scene.

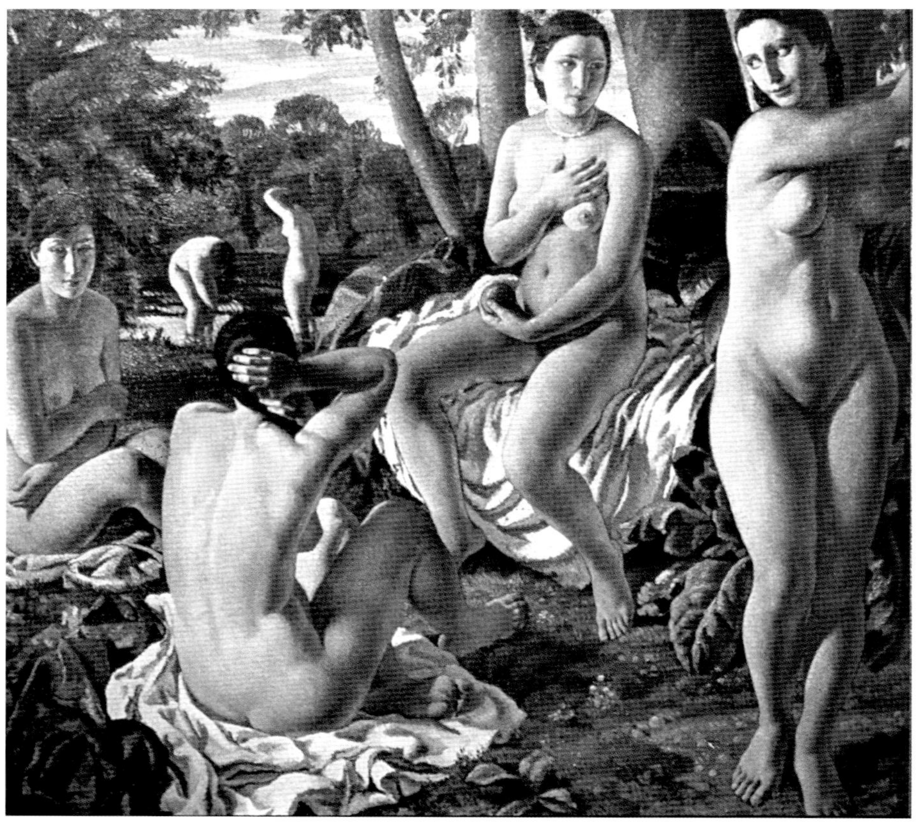

FIG 11

Francisco Vidal
Summer

The work of the Argentinean painter Vidal, reproduced in *The Studio* in 1933, hinted at an international dimension to the recent British revival of the open-air nude.

prevent the parade captured on the promenade in 1935 (fig. 9; cat. 51). The fact that Blackpool and Brighton, the two most famous seaside towns in England, acquired the paintings by Glasson and Hutton almost immediately after their first appearance is far from coincidental. Culturally inclined visitors would find that even the art on display in the municipal art gallery appeared to legitimate the activities of those who never found their way into those calm and orderly spaces.

Hutton's reference to Greek myth was at best a half-hearted attempt to make a rather risqué subject palatable. Glasson, in common with many of the artists included here, had recourse to the history of art in order to give his potentially shocking images an acceptable lineage. Manet's *Déjeuner sur l'herbe*, a *succès de scandale* in 1863, lies behind Glasson's updated version of 1931 (fig. 10), but, even seventy years on, he is unwilling to show his

FIG 12

Dod Procter
The Orchard 1934 (cat. 26)

During the 1930s, Procter was beginning to emerge as a strong, serious artist. Here, she paints more sensuously and gives the figure a far more physical identity than in her well-known clothed recumbent female, *Early Morning*, which had brought her widespread attention in 1927.

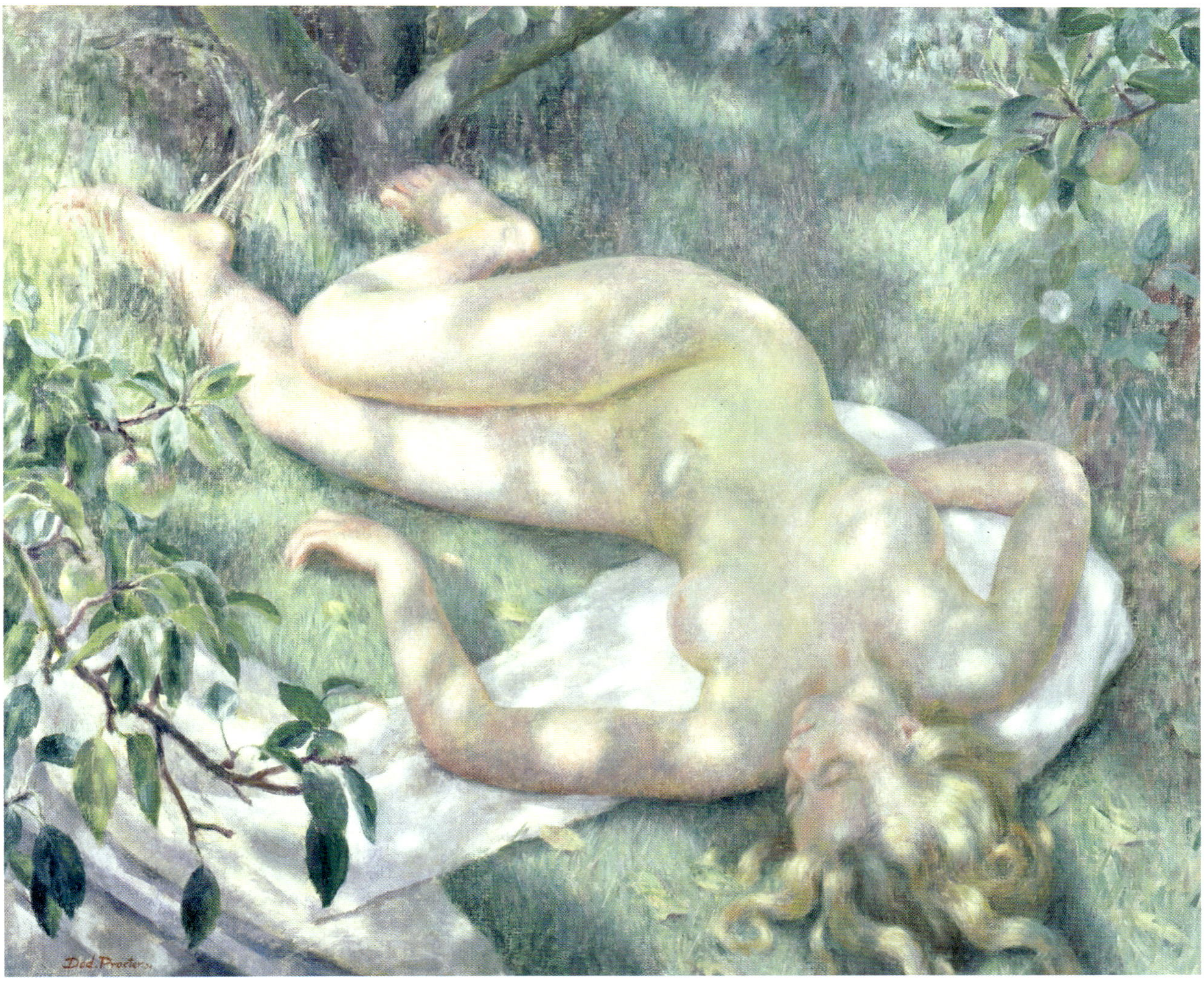

unclothed female in male company. The reference to France, where morals were held to be more lax, was surely also a strategy to defuse potential criticism. In 1930, Glasson showed his female nude *Bather*, with which he had made his debut at the Royal Academy in 1928, at the Paris Salon. He may well have become aware that his work was part of a pan-European movement, apparent in Italy and Germany as well as France.[9] Some evidence of this internationalism was supplied to a British audience by the reproduction in *The Studio* in 1933 of an impressive composition by a young Argentinian, Francisco Vidal (fig. 11). For the mainstream of English art, a late nineteenth-century Impressionist technique still represented modernity; Dod Procter's *The Orchard* (fig. 12; cat. 26) takes Renoir as the model for its sun-dappled flesh, while the pose is distinctly reminiscent of Courbet's *Woman with a Parrot* in the Musée d'Orsay. Acquired for the Tate

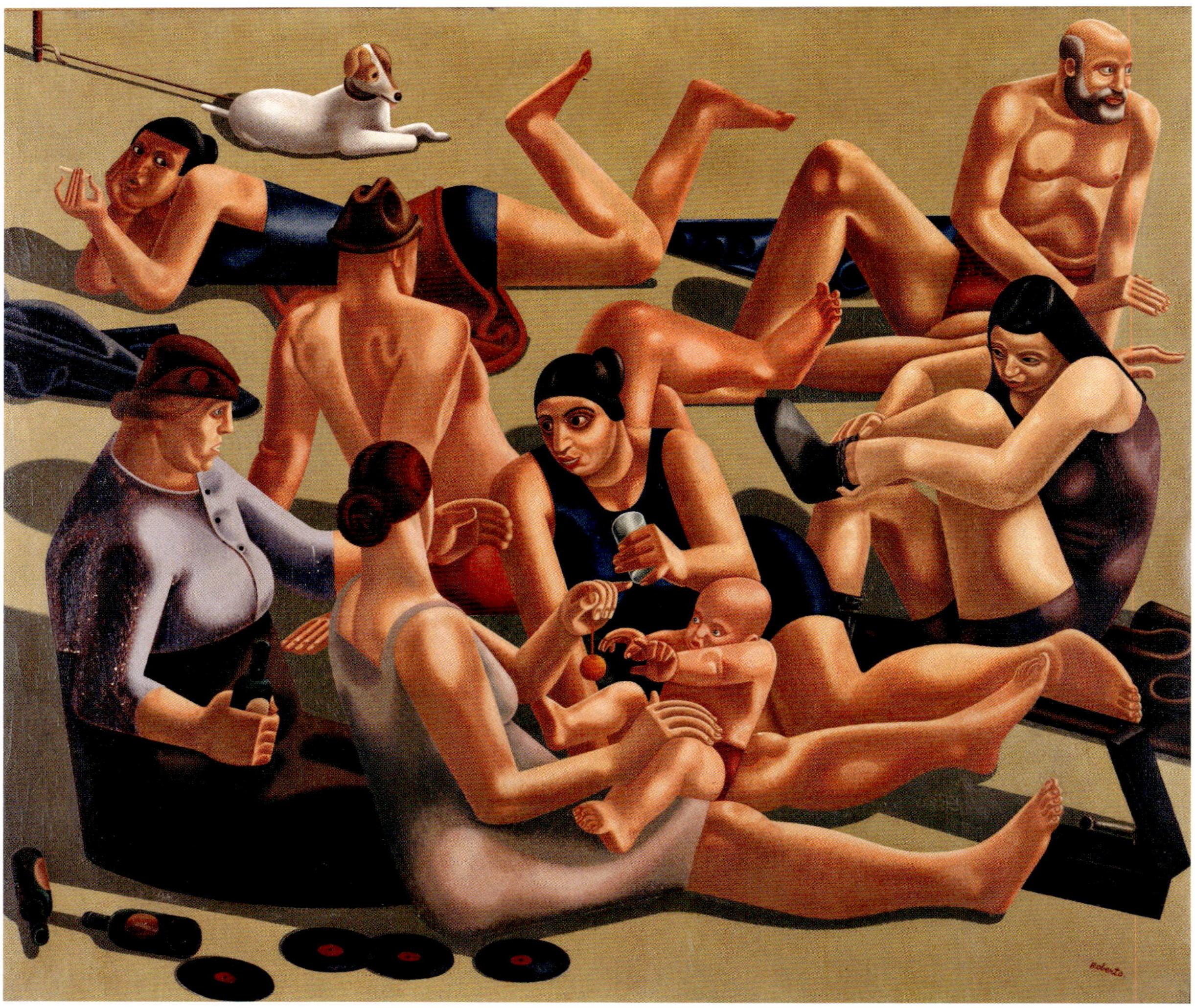

FIG 13

William Roberts

Sunbathing 1936 (cat. 31)

The painting is probably based on crowds observed in Regent's Park, near Roberts' home in Camden, north London. The enjoyment of sunny weather is, by his account, not something confined to the younger generation.

Gallery in 1937, it brought to this still dubious subject an almost old-masterly respectability.

In its early days, sunbathing implied nudity. Roberts' canvas of 1936 shows the wider acceptance of the practice, with a mixed group of sunbathers who remain partly clad. The scene was most probably observed in Regent's Park, near Roberts' home in Camden (fig. 13; cat. 31). The gramophone records, bottles and dog all contribute a sense of the everyday, deflating the high-minded rhetoric which only a few years before had gained sunbathing the exclusive status of a cult. In 1944, when Roberts had moved from London to Oxford, he portrayed the nude male bathers at Parson's Pleasure (fig. 14; cat. 32). These portly figures have a curious fascination, ancient and modern, a throwback to more carefree days, before the theories of body culture had been taken to previously unthinkable extremes.

FIG 14

William Roberts

Parson's Pleasure 1944 (cat. 32)

During the Second World War, Roberts left London for Oxford. This painting depicts the secluded bathing place on the Cherwell where university men preserved a long tradition of naked bathing.

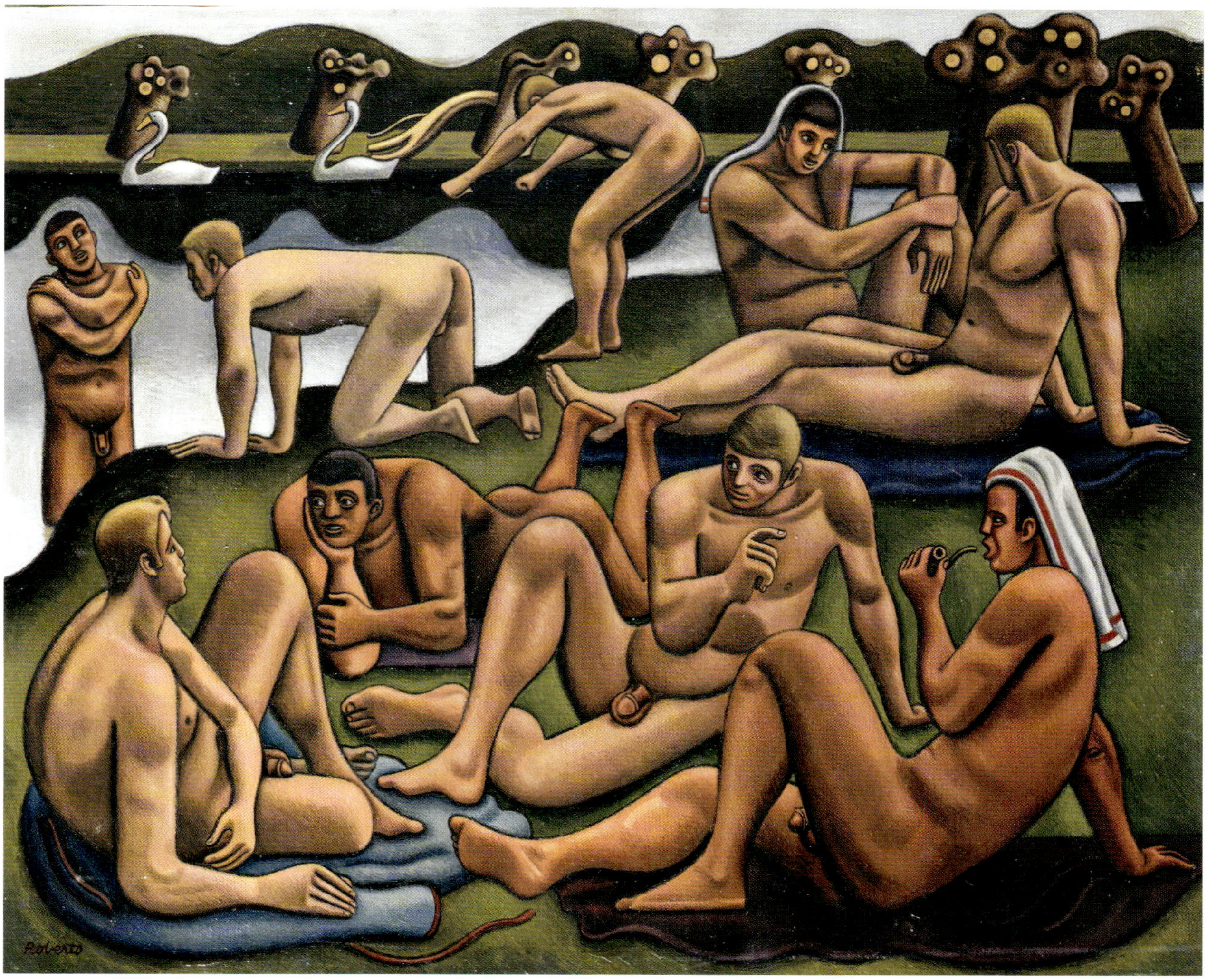

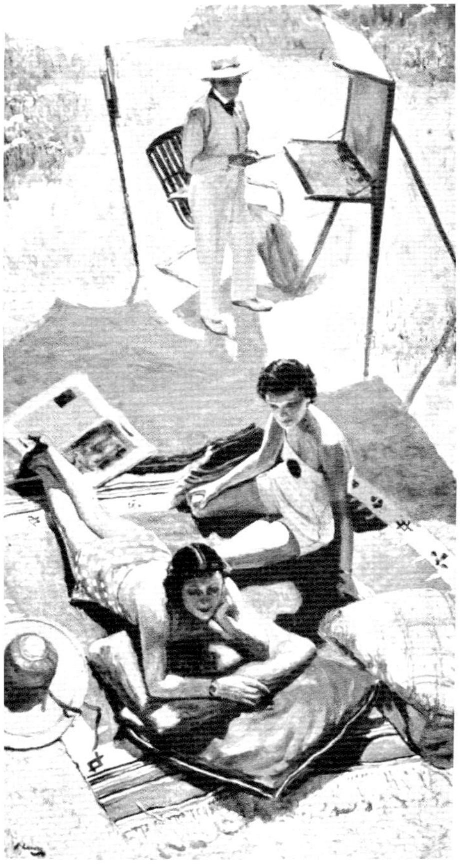

The maintenance of an all-year round tan remained a mark of wealth and a leisured existence. Sir John Lavery's painting has an air of Hollywood glamour (fig. 15). It was exhibited in 1937, the same year as a Daily Herald photograph of a sunbather in Honolulu which seems to take for granted the desirability of this form of relaxation, however unattainable for most (fig. 16; cat. 45).

FIG 15

John Lavery
Sun-Bathers
(exhibited Royal Academy 1937)
A favoured portrait painter of the leisured elite, Lavery painted many pictures of their chosen pastimes of golf, tennis and swimming. The models here are believed to be two friends of the artist, Diana Dickinson and Lilian Millar, pictured during Lavery's stay in California.

FIG 16

On the Sands of Waikiki Beach, Honolulu
14 August 1937 (cat. 45)
In the middle of an English summer, the Herald offered its readers this image of truly committed sun worshippers in Hawaii, an unattainable ideal most could only envy.

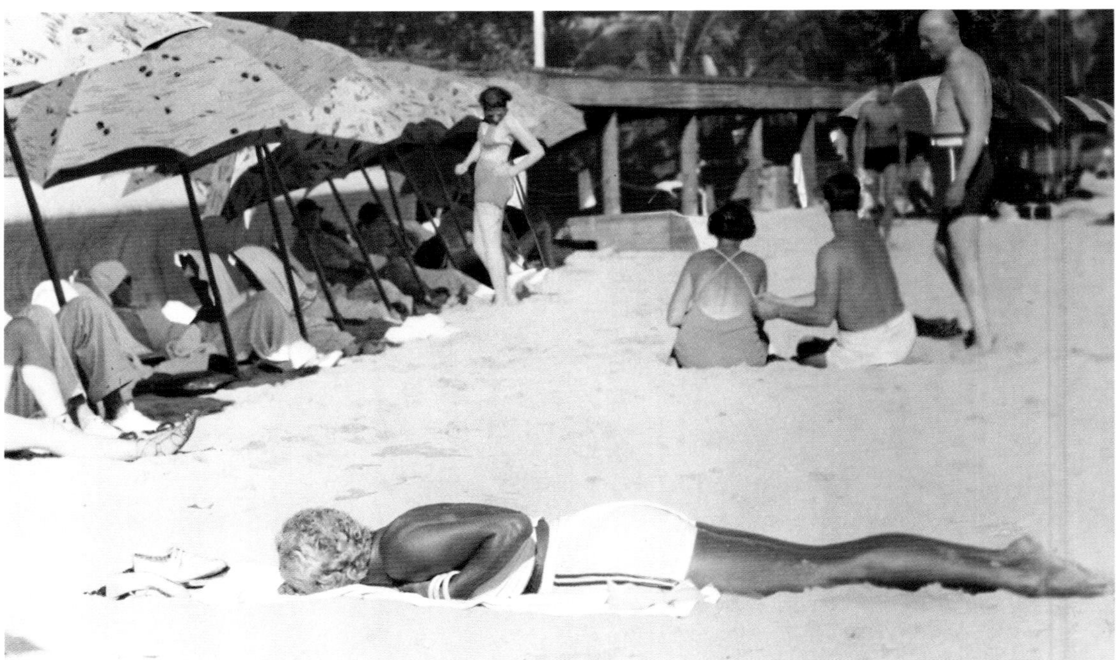

Swimming

By the middle of the decade, public facilities for sunbathers were appearing all over the country, as part of the government-backed building programme of outdoor swimming pools (fig. 17; cat. 50). They became known as Lansbury's Lidos, after George Lansbury, Minister of Works in the second Labour administration, elected in 1929.[10] There were over sixty such pools in Greater London alone; not all of them newly constructed, but jointly part of the greatest expansion in leisure provision ever seen in England. (fig. 18; cat. 54). Announcing a proposed extension to its building programme in January 1937, the London County Council proclaimed 'London will become a city of Lidos'.[11] Photographs of crowds of bathers at the Serpentine in Hyde Park

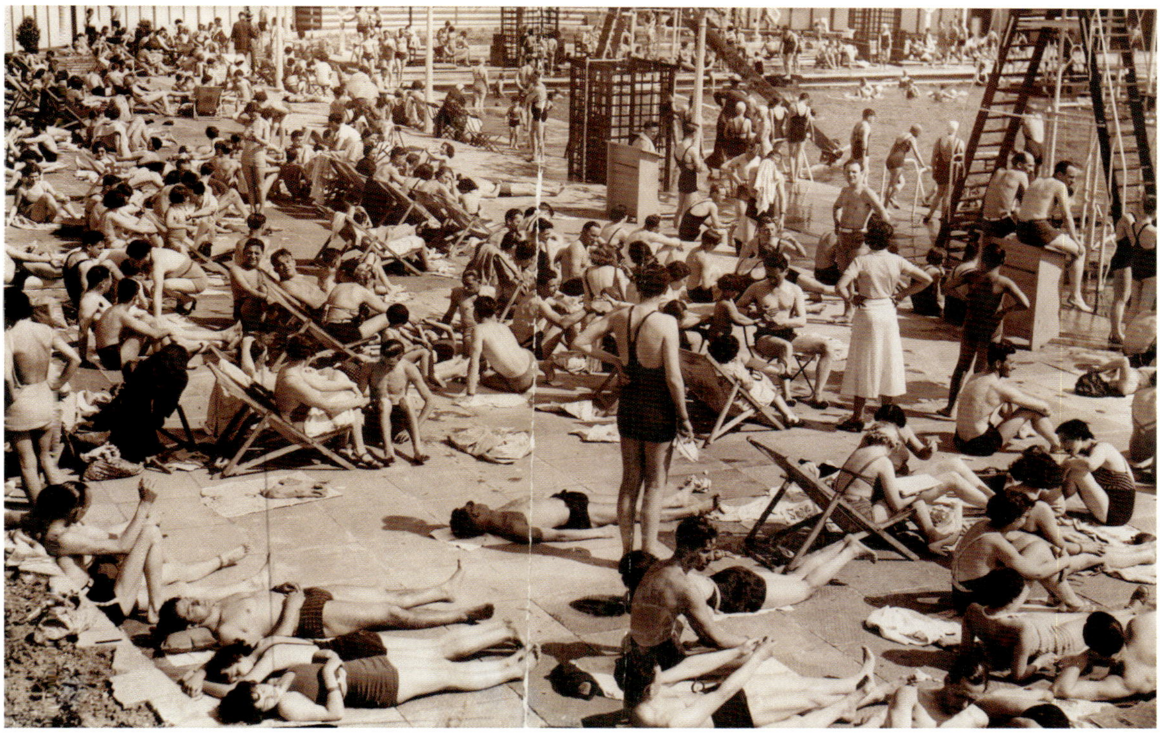

FIG 17

Sun seekers at Enfield 6 June 1937 (cat. 50)

The Enfield Lido opened in 1932 and had one of the longest pools in the capital. As the title published with the photo underlines, just drinking in the sun was as much of an attraction as swimming or diving.

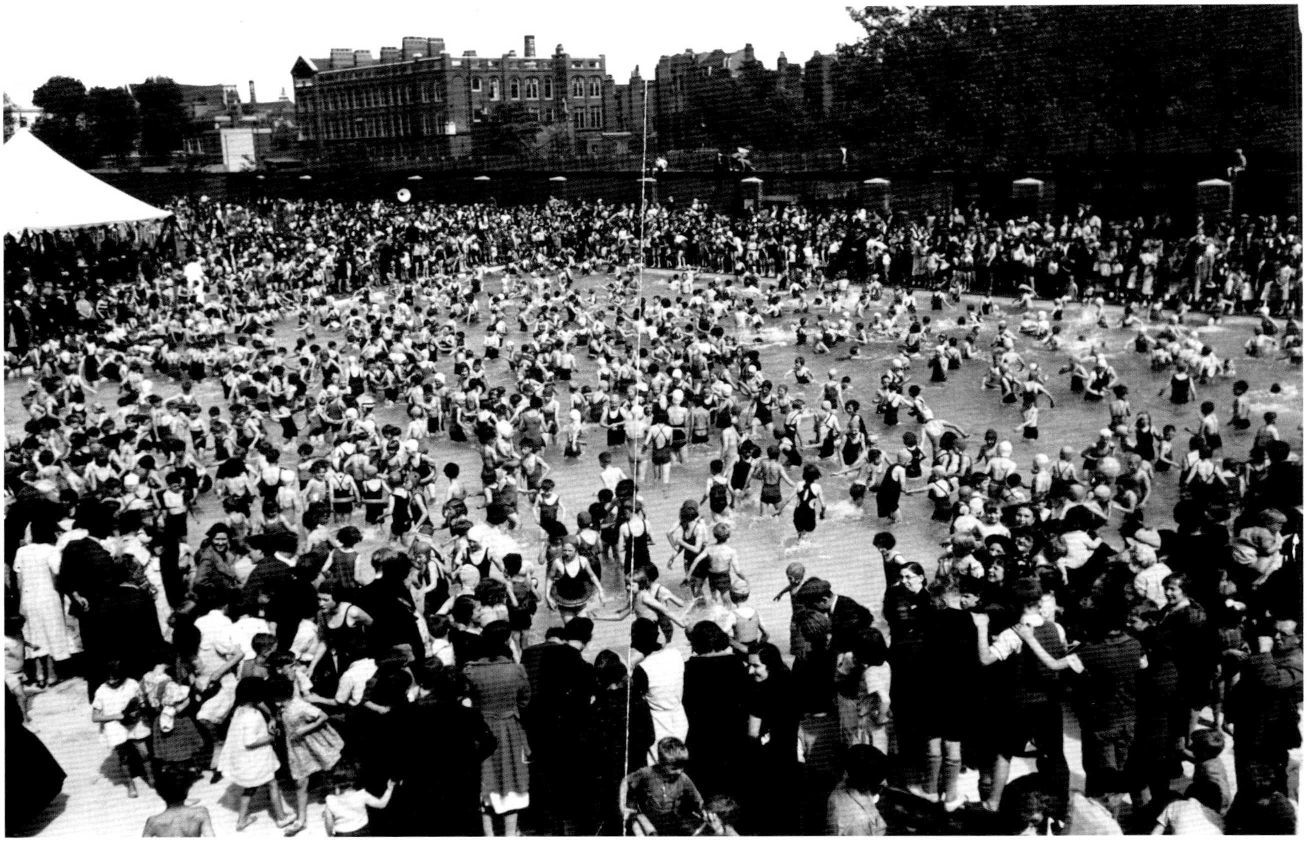

FIG 18

New swimming pool in Geraldine Mary Harmsworth Park, Lambeth Road, Southwark 6 August 1938 (cat. 54)

This shallow, learners' pool in an inner London park is far too full for anybody to swim in it; yet such is the enthusiasm of the local population for this new facility that on the first summer holiday after its opening, the whole area seems to have turned out to watch, or join in the fun.

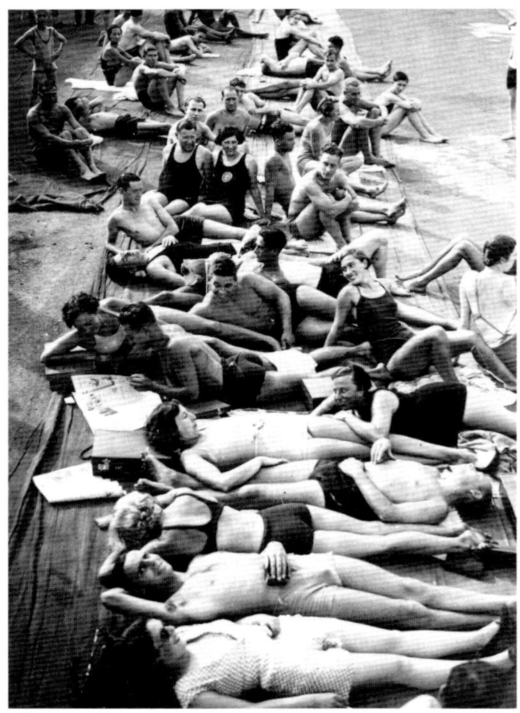

FIG 19

Sun bathers at the lido 14 September 1934 (cat. 63)

Swimmers have used the Serpentine pond for swimming since its creation in the eighteenth century. Its rebirth as the Serpentine Lido in 1931, and the institution of mixed bathing, made it a popular haunt for thousands of Londoners.

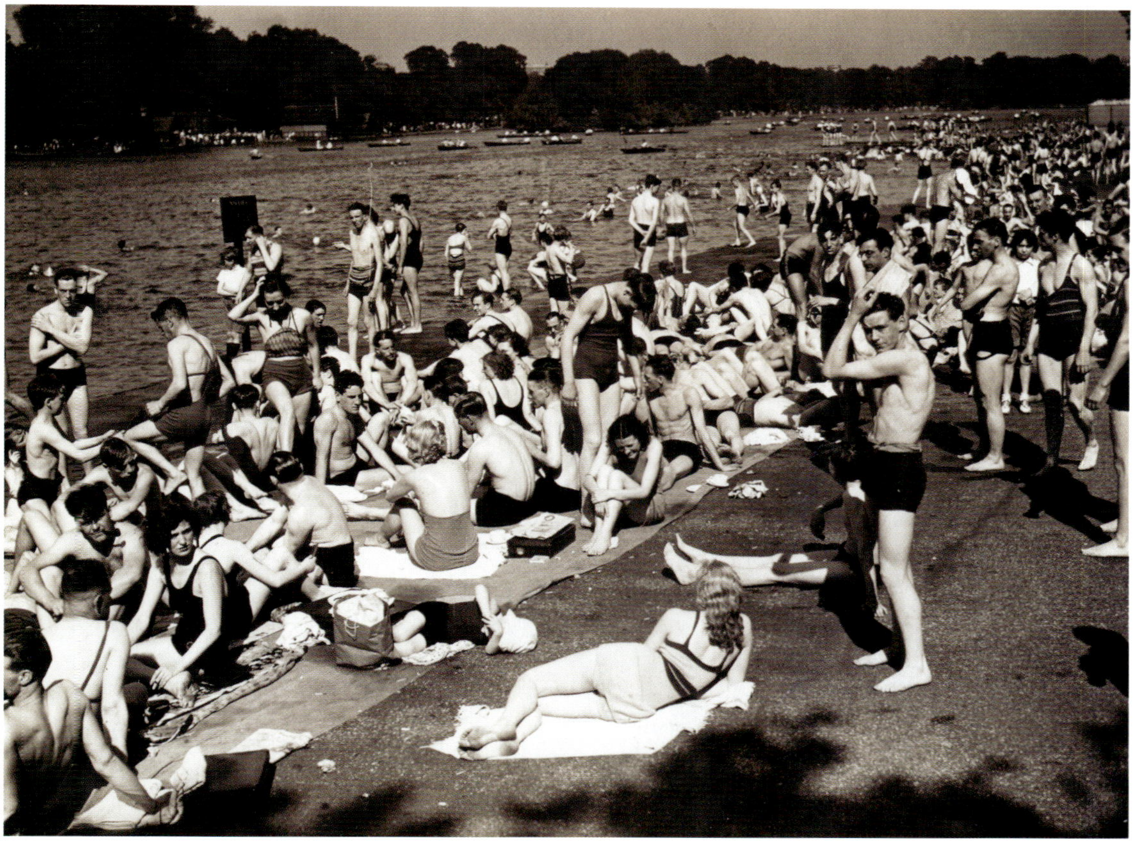

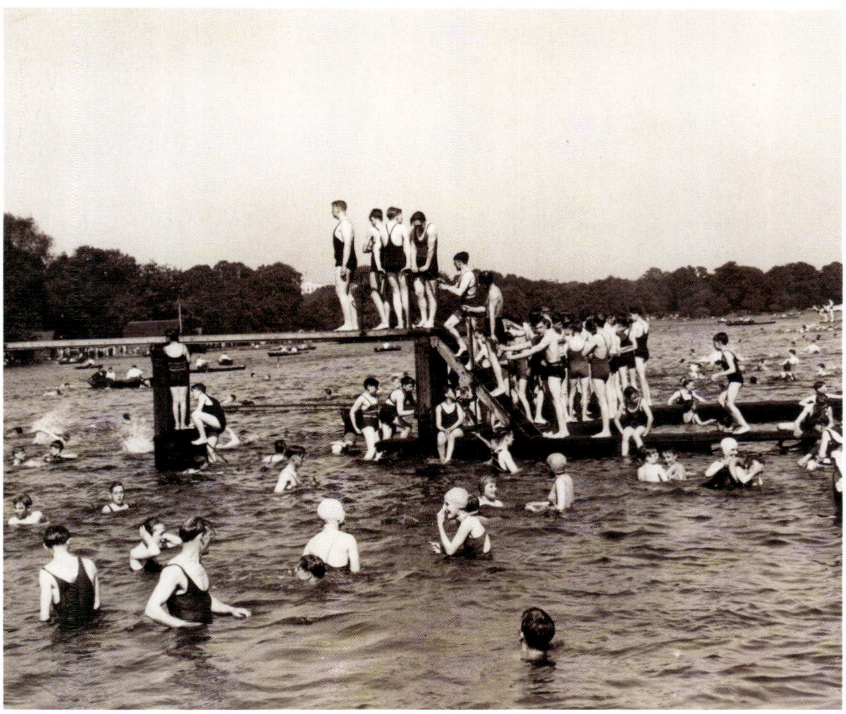

FIG 20

Scenes at the Serpentine Lido. Sunbathers
23 June 1935 (cat. 64)

'Lansbury's Lido', nicknamed after the Minister of Works in the Second Labour Government, became a massive popular success, drawing crowds from across the capital.

FIG 21

Scenes at the Serpentine Lido 23 *June* 1935 (cat. 60)

At the end of a spell of hot weather, the weekend crowds at the Serpentine were larger than ever; this photograph was probably taken on a Saturday afternoon and shows a predominance of young men soaking up the sun.

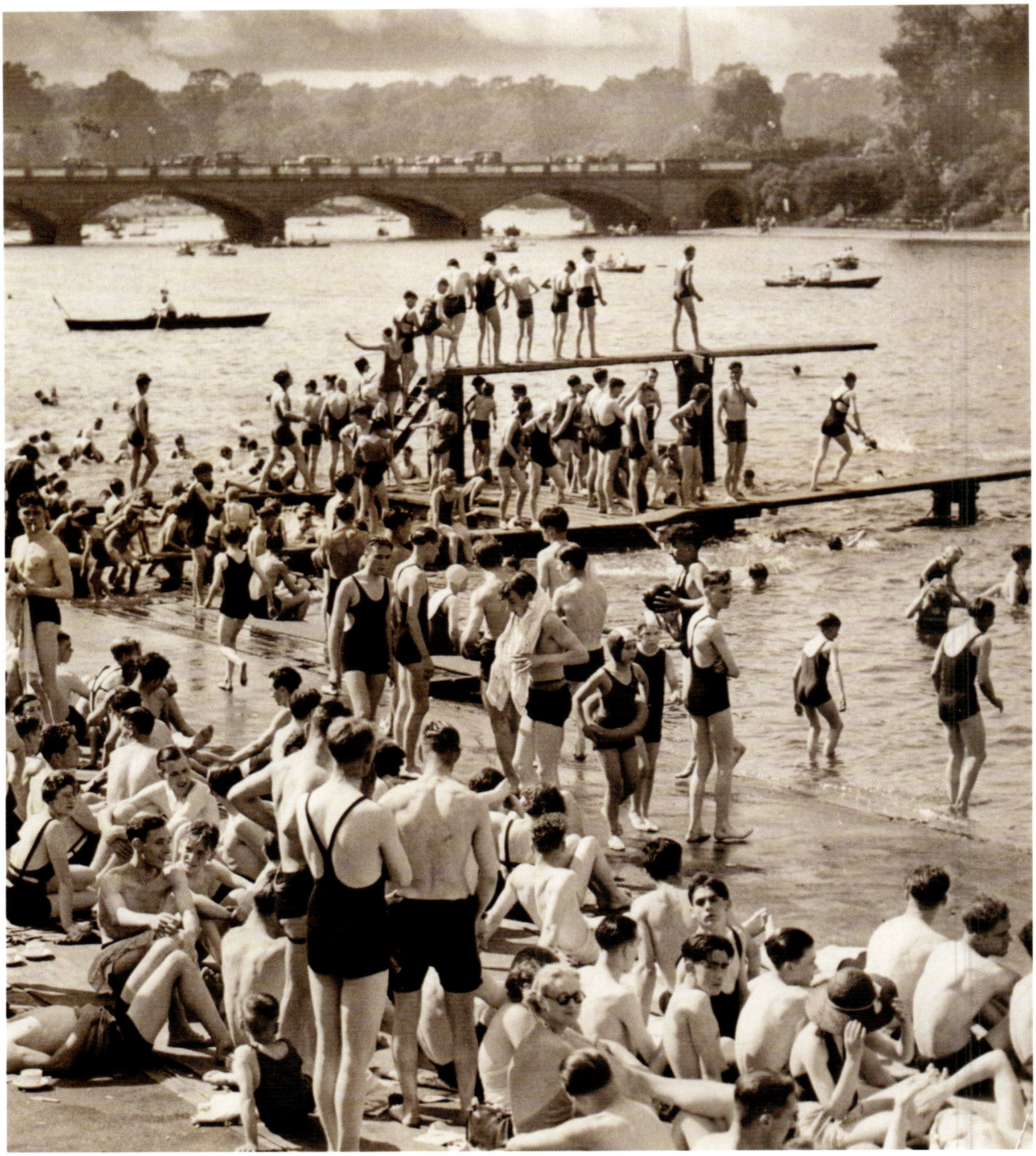

FIG 22

London's famous open spaces being fully appreciated by her citizens. A typical scene at the Serpentine Lido 21 June 1937 (cat. 58)

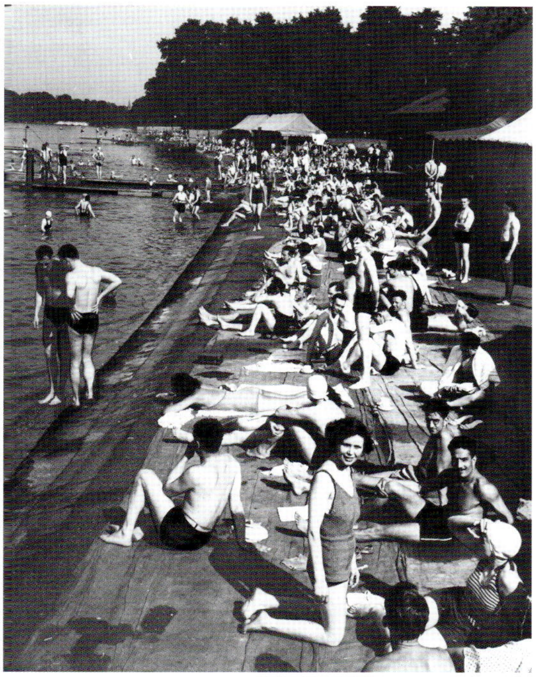

FIG 23

Heat wave scene at Hyde Park Lido
6 August 1937 (cat. 59)

FIG 24

Record crowd of the year at Serpentine Lido
20 August 1939 (cat. 56)

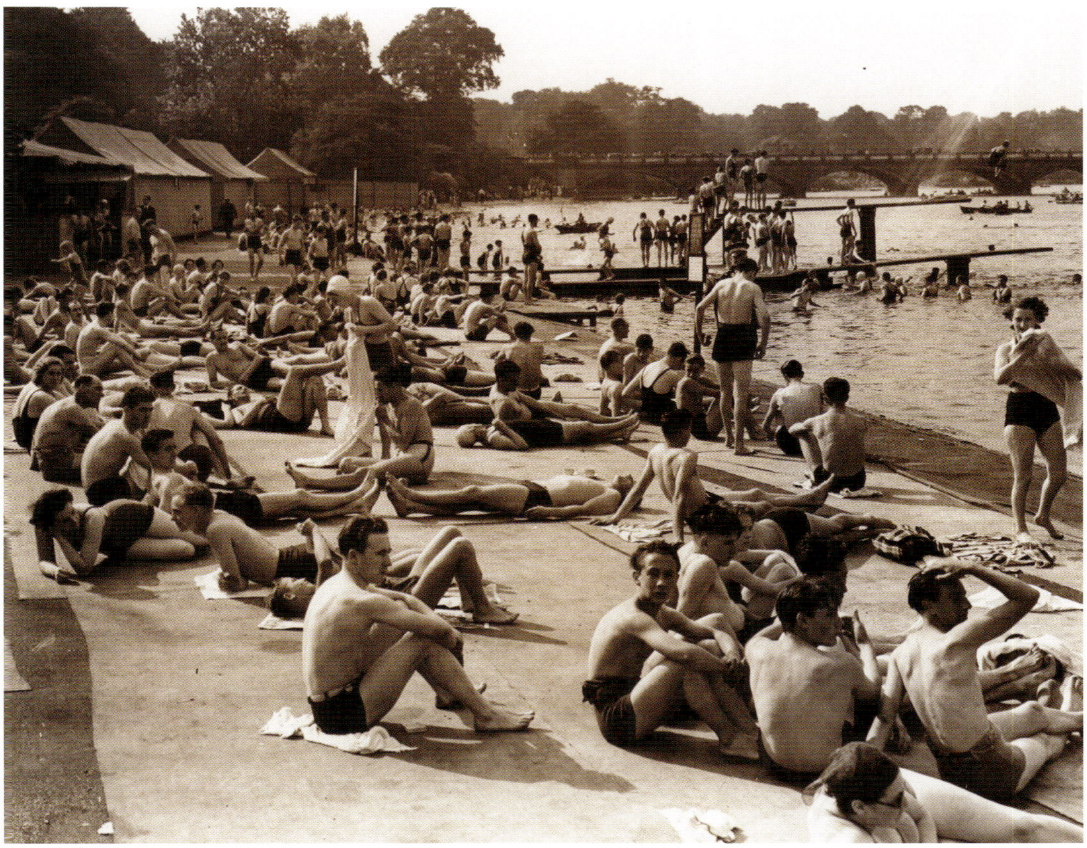

appeared almost every year in the Daily Herald (figs. 19–20; cats. 63–64; figs. 21–24; cats. 60, 58, 59, 56). Lansbury broke with 200 years of tradition when he opened it to mixed bathing in 1929, then had the facilities rebuilt and upgraded, to reopen as the Serpentine Lido in 1931. The new bathing pools were equally popular in seaside towns, the object of major investment from Blackpool and Scarborough to Penzance. The largest of them, such as the seawater pool at Tinside, below the Hoe in Plymouth, could accommodate thousands (fig. 25).[12]

The title of Miguel Mackinlay's 1933 painting of the open-air pool at Bushey is indicative of the extent to which the new swimming pools had become a part of life; *Summer* (fig. 26; cat. 23) is no longer represented as an annual pilgrimage to the seaside, but by clusters of young figures on the diving boards. The colouring and handling of paint on Mackinlay's large

FIG 25

Dermot Patrick Fitzgerald
Hoe Bathing Pool c. 1960
Tinside Lido, in a spectacular setting below the Hoe at Plymouth opened in 1935. It was a typical mixture of swimming facilities with sunbathing terraces, which on gala days offered a vantage point for hundreds of onlookers.

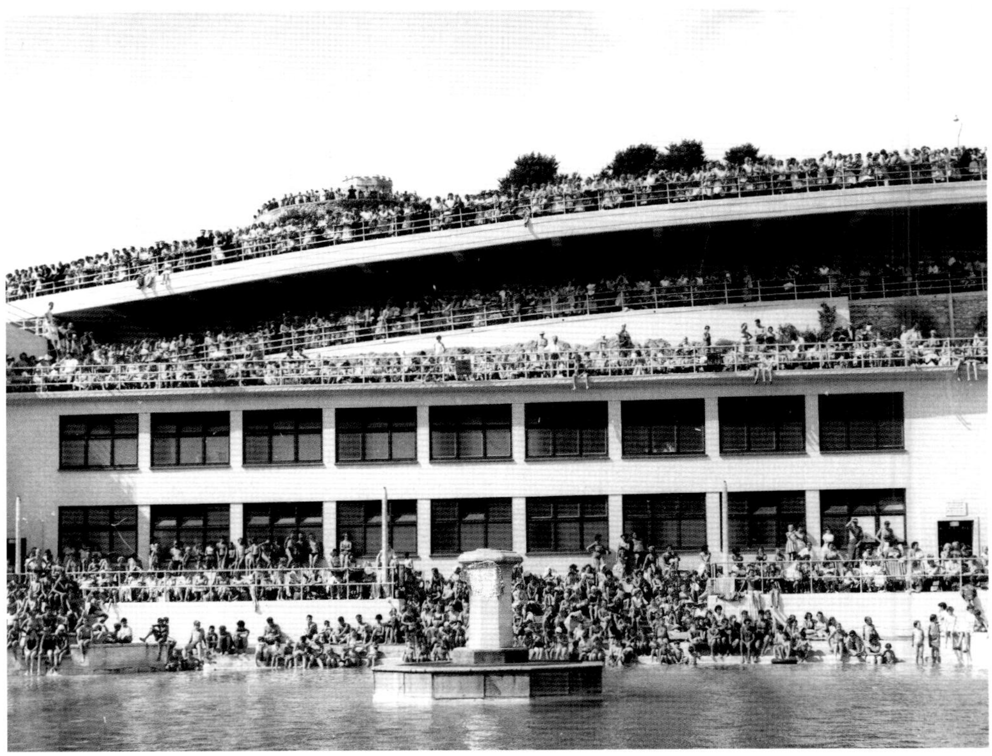

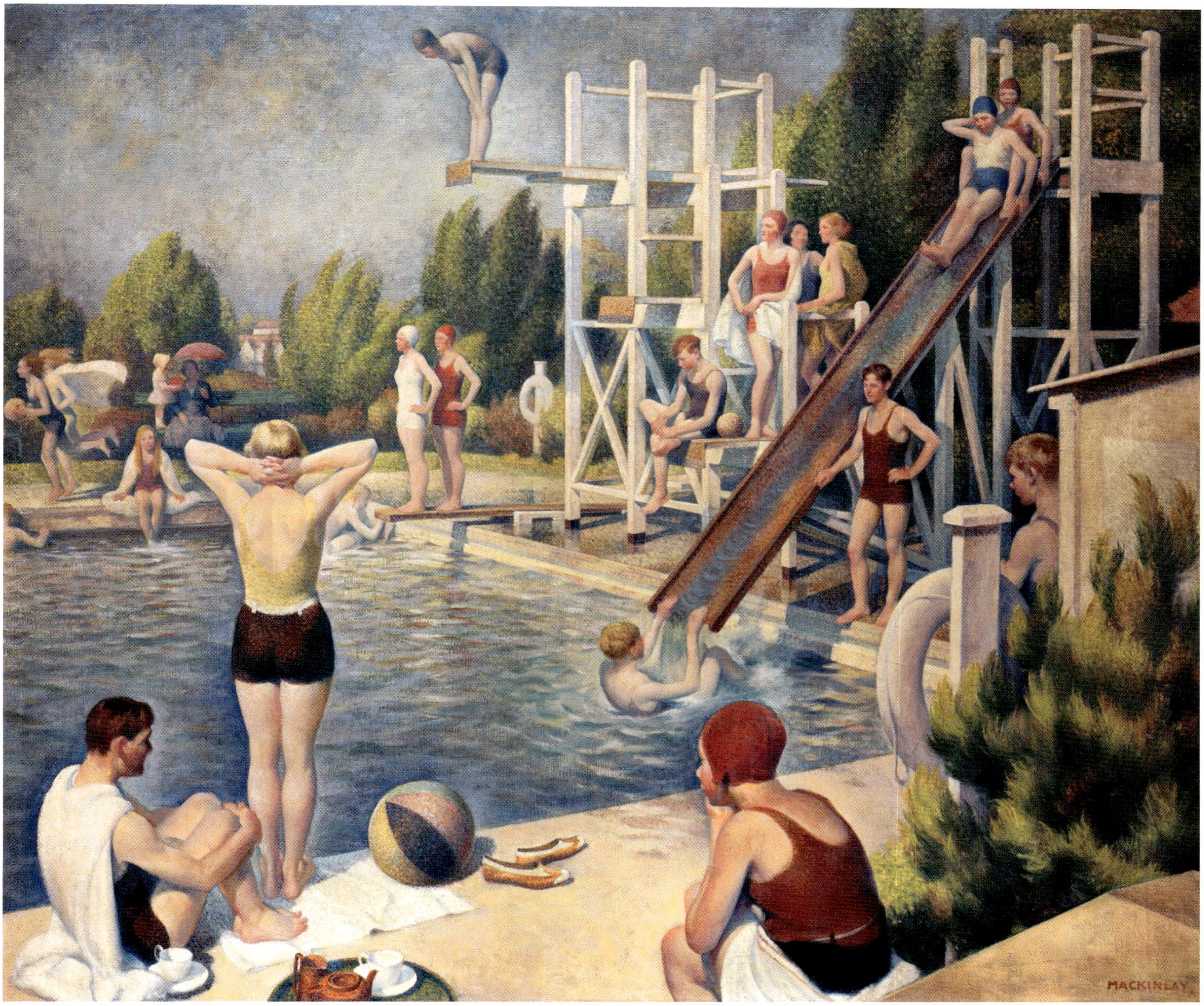

FIG 26

Miguel Mackinlay
Summer 1933 (cat. 23)

Set at the open-air pool at Bushey, where he lived, Mackinlay's large painting draws much of its authority from its subtle reworking of Seurat's monumental depiction of urban leisure, *Bathers at Asnières*, recently acquired by the National Gallery.

canvas are indebted to Seurat's *Bathers at Asnières*, acquired for the Tate Gallery as recently as 1924. The choice of this late nineteenth-century image of urban workers' recreation was a singularly appropriate and perceptive one, at a time when the Seurat was not nearly so universally accepted as it is now (fig. 26; cat. 23; see also fig. 27; cat. 57).

In the 1920s, swimming had been one of the few strenuous sports where women were admitted to Olympic Games and competed over the same distances as men. The American Gertrude Ederle gained international notoriety not only as the first woman to swim the English Channel, but to do it two hours faster than any previous male.[13] Swimming costumes revealed more of the female body than had ever been permissible before; the loose, baggy shape of the Edwardian era was dispensed with and replaced by the sleek, figure-hugging profile celebrated in the posters of

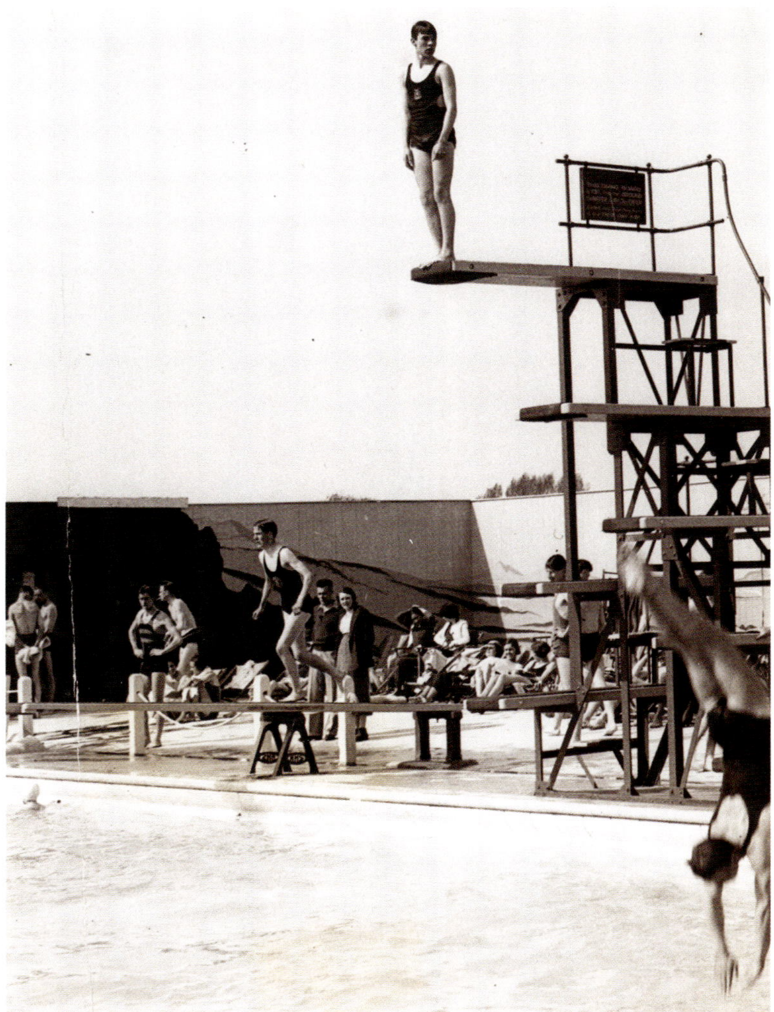

FIG 27

'The Blue Lagoon' 11 April 1935 (cat. 57)

New lidos were opening in London every year during the 1930s. This one, which from the background seems hardly finished, was supplied with the latest multi-level diving platform for swimmers to plunge into the pool dubbed the 'pièce de résistance' of the whole complex.

FIG 28

Andrew Johnson

The South Coast is the Sunny Coast 1933

(cat. 18)

An unabashed sun-worshipper, rendered with the purity of an uninterrupted flowing line.

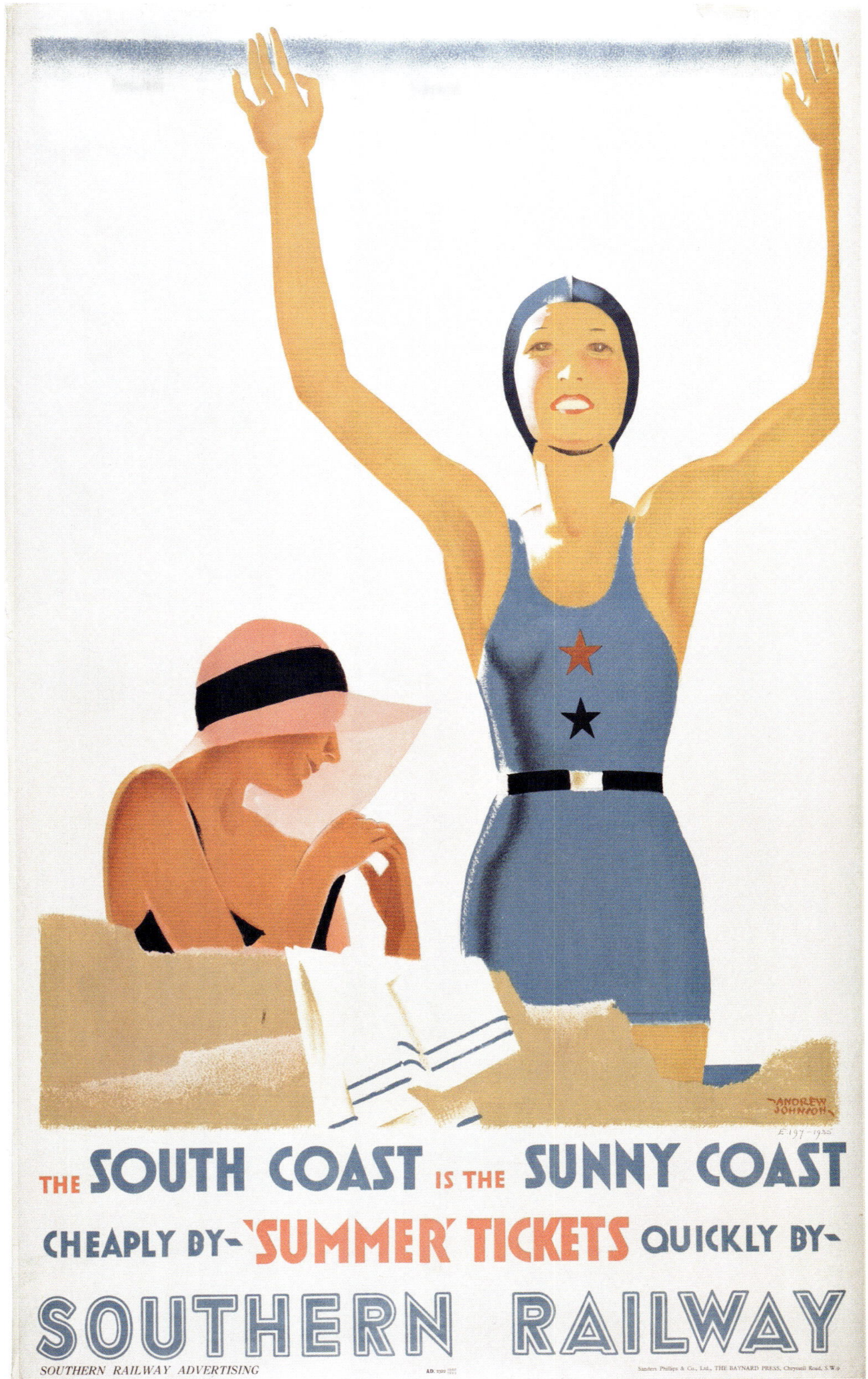

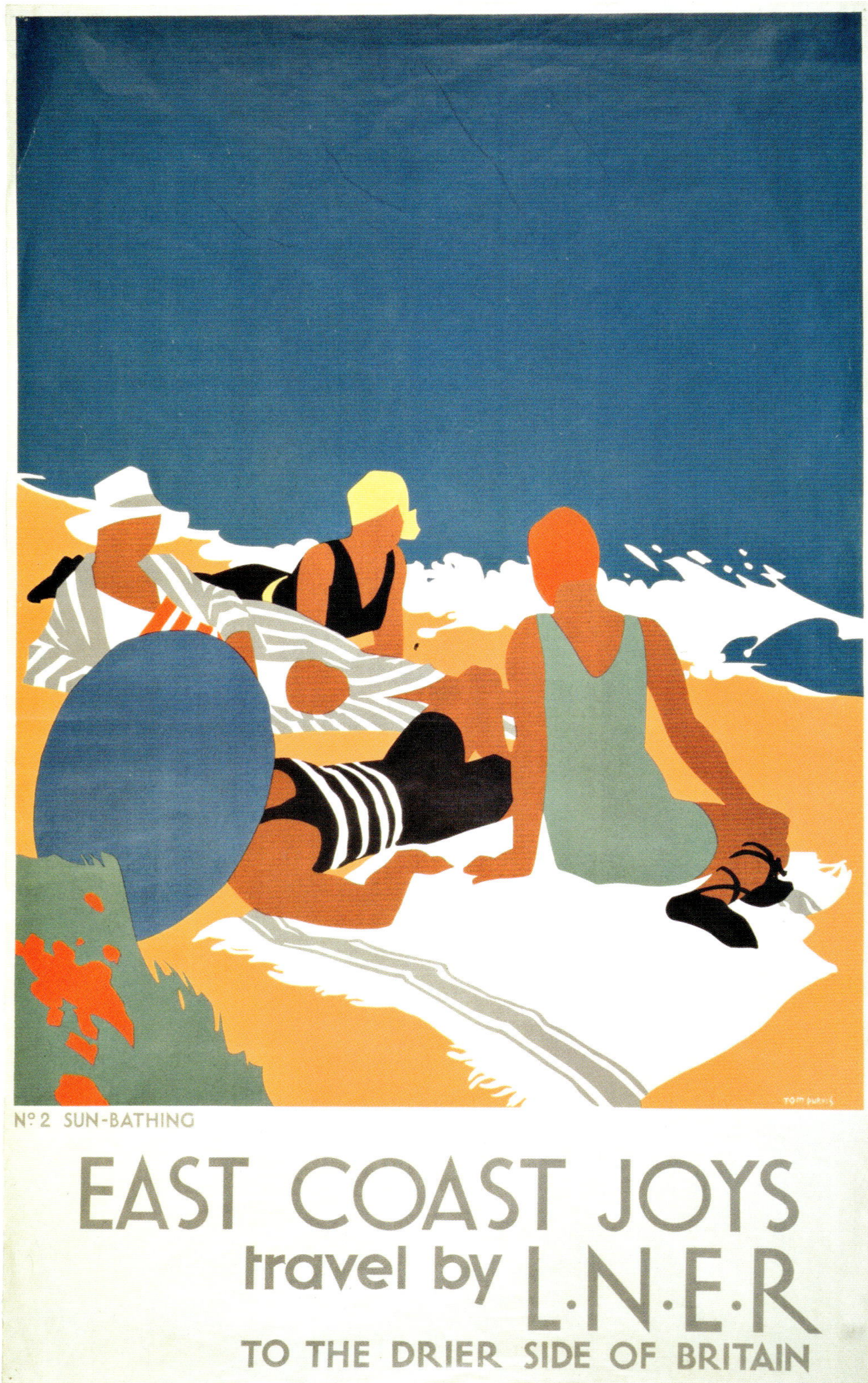

FIG 29

Tom Purvis

East Coast Joys: Sunbathing c. 1925 (cat. 28)

The solid colours and pared-down silhouettes of Tom Purvis' posters became in themselves signs of modernity. His work achieved the unusual recognition of being included in the 1928 Olympic Art exhibition in the Fine Art, rather than the Graphics section.

Andrew Johnson and Tom Purvis (figs. 28, 29; cats. 18, 28). With the 1936 Olympic Games in Berlin this body was further transformed through the photography and the cinematography of Leni Riefensthal, who was given unprecedented access to the sporting arena; the images she captured with cameras attached to the pole vaulter's pole, or from the top platform of the diving pool provided a new, intimate sense of participation in the elite events. Her unexpected camera angles heightened the drama through the unusual foreshortening and mid-air suspension of the figure.[14] Harold Williamson's *Spray*, exhibited in 1940 (fig. 30; cat. 42), owes its plunging viewpoint to such widely disseminated images. The animation of the body is one of the legacies of the decade, a stark contrast to the more passive, posed figures which had earlier been the norm. The floating bodies in William Roberts' *Water Wings* (fig. 31) may be those of learners, but they owe

FIG 30

Harold Williamson
Spray 1940 (cat. 42)
Williamson's dramatic perspective is undoubtedly due to advances in recent sports photography. The plunging viewpoint creates a real sense of dynamism and mobility, aspects of modernity reinforced by the revealing swimsuit and the woman's distinctly muscular back.

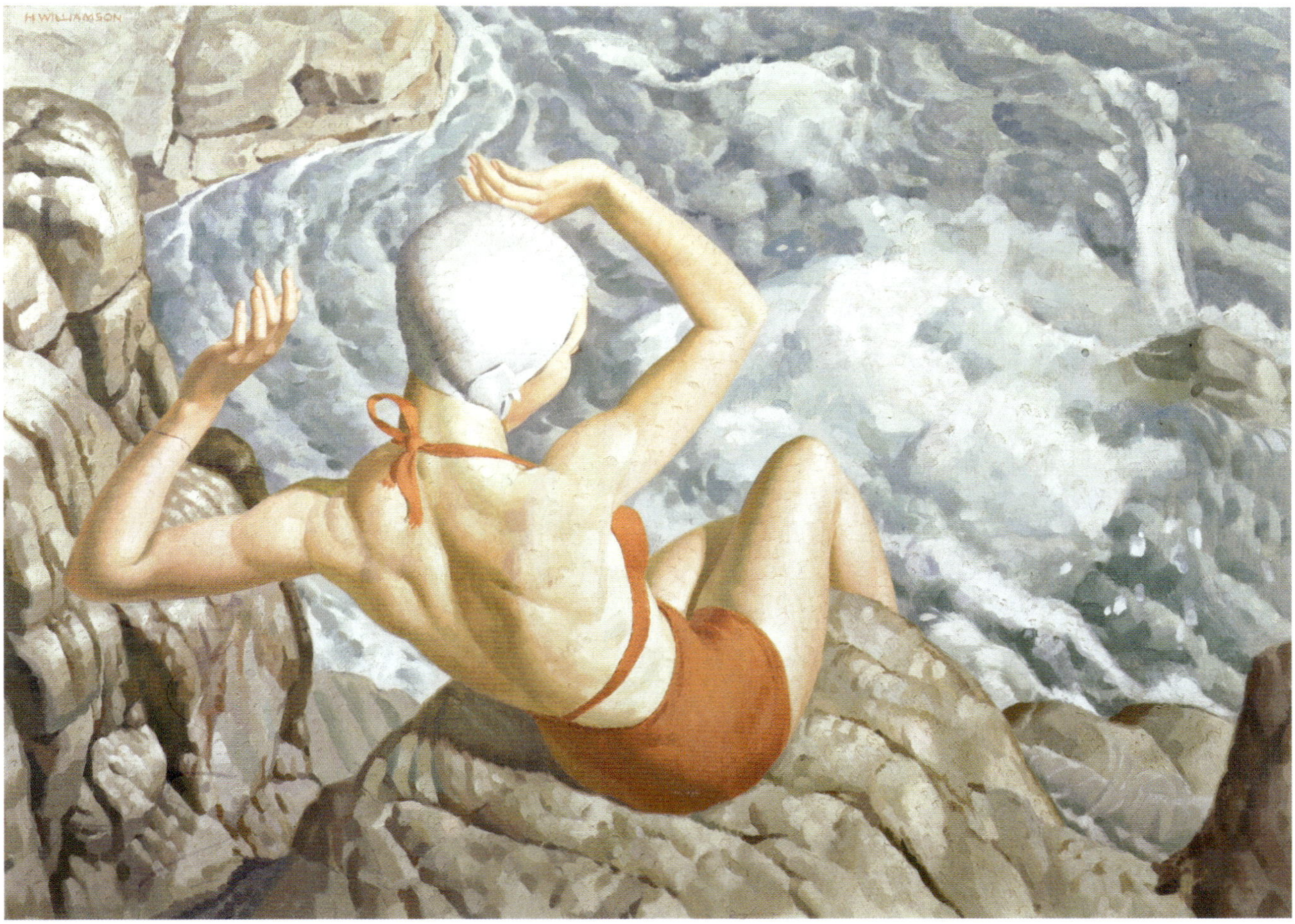

something to the Olympic ideal, even if only by way of contrast; the awkward shapes and flailing limbs express the beginners' want of control, something the geometric rigidity of the pool edge only accentuates. The cramped space the swimmers have to negotiate is perhaps not far from the truth, as photographs reveal. In *Going to Swim* (fig. 32; cat. 29) Roberts created an even more congested scene of ungainly male bodies. At the same time, he nods to the art of the quattrocento, and the topos of the male figure caught in the act of undressing which occurs as a background detail in countless paintings of the Baptism of Christ.

A similar perception led Stanley Spencer to paint a *Baptism* in 1936 set on the banks of the river Thames at Cookham, with men in bathing suits in the background.[15] *Girls returning from a Bathe* (fig. 33; cat. 38) is unequivocally contemporary, but was conceived as a sort of side panel in a polyptych

FIG 31

William Roberts
Water Wings 1938

Before the First World War, only a small proportion of working-class males learned to swim. Roberts' painting highlights the expansion of a popular movement, while also relishing the visual opportunities it offers for unexpected contortions of the human body.

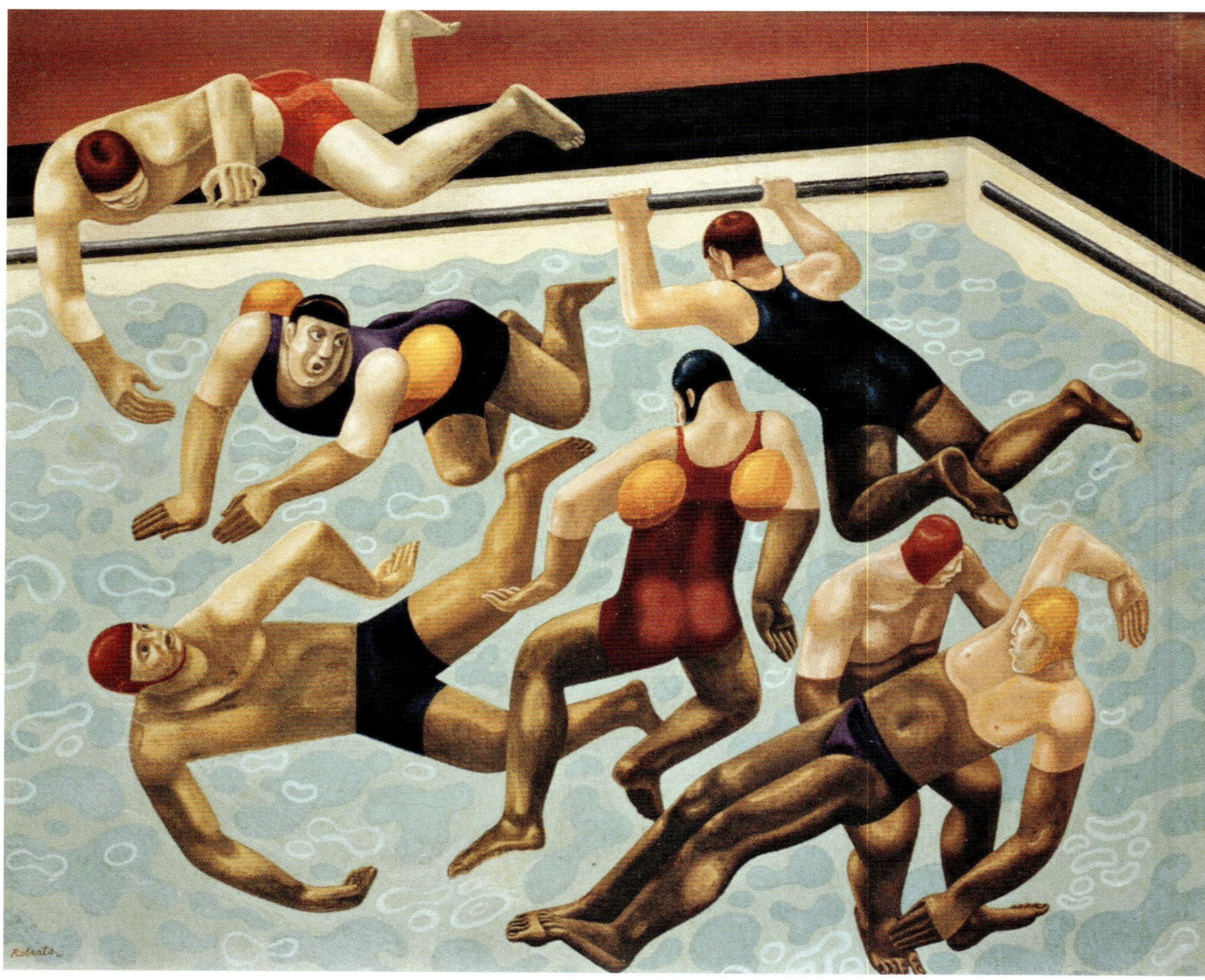

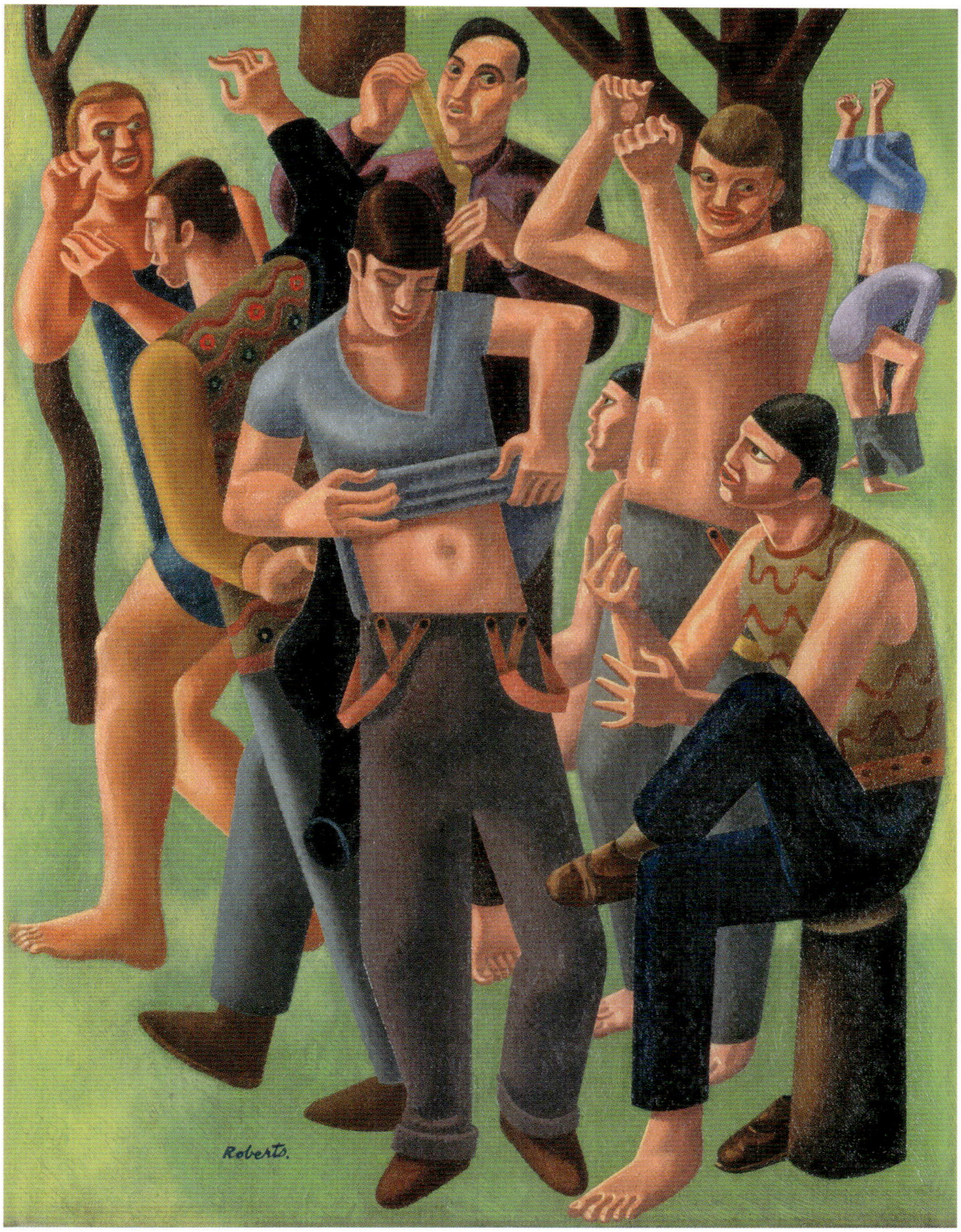

FIG 32

William Roberts

Going to Swim 1930 (cat. 29)

Many of Roberts' paintings of the 1930s dwell on the democratisation of leisure. Here, a group of ungainly working men pull off jackets, shirts and ties in ways that suggest pent-up energy and the liberating effects of the exercise that awaits them.

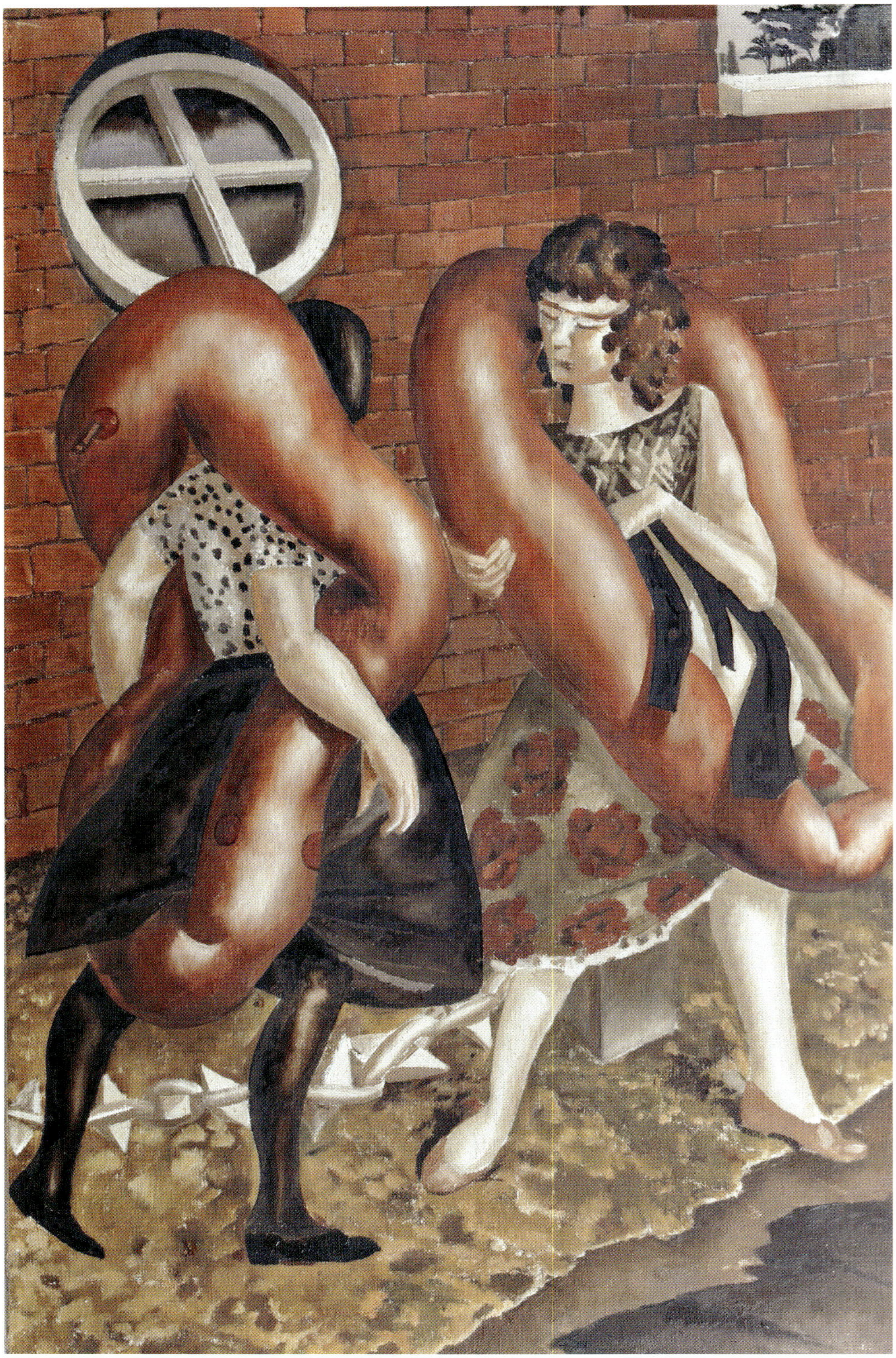

FIG 33

Stanley Spencer

Girls returning from a Bathe 1936 (cat. 38)

Spencer seems to have delighted in the disjuncture between the ancient ritual of baptism and the modern rage for bathing. These girls with their inflated inner-tubes were originally planned as part of a polyptych centring on a painting of Christ being baptised in the Thames.

centred around the *Baptism*. A slightly earlier canvas, painted as this subject was maturing in Spencer's mind, *Sunbathers at Odney* (fig. 34; cat. 37), is also inspired by the same bathing place on the Thames near Cookham. The mass of naked men may be a memory of bathers from Spencer's childhood rather than a recent incident; his rendition of the figures seems to conjure up a deliberate ambiguity between Renaissance prototypes (such as the foreground figure) and ones that are gracelessly modern.

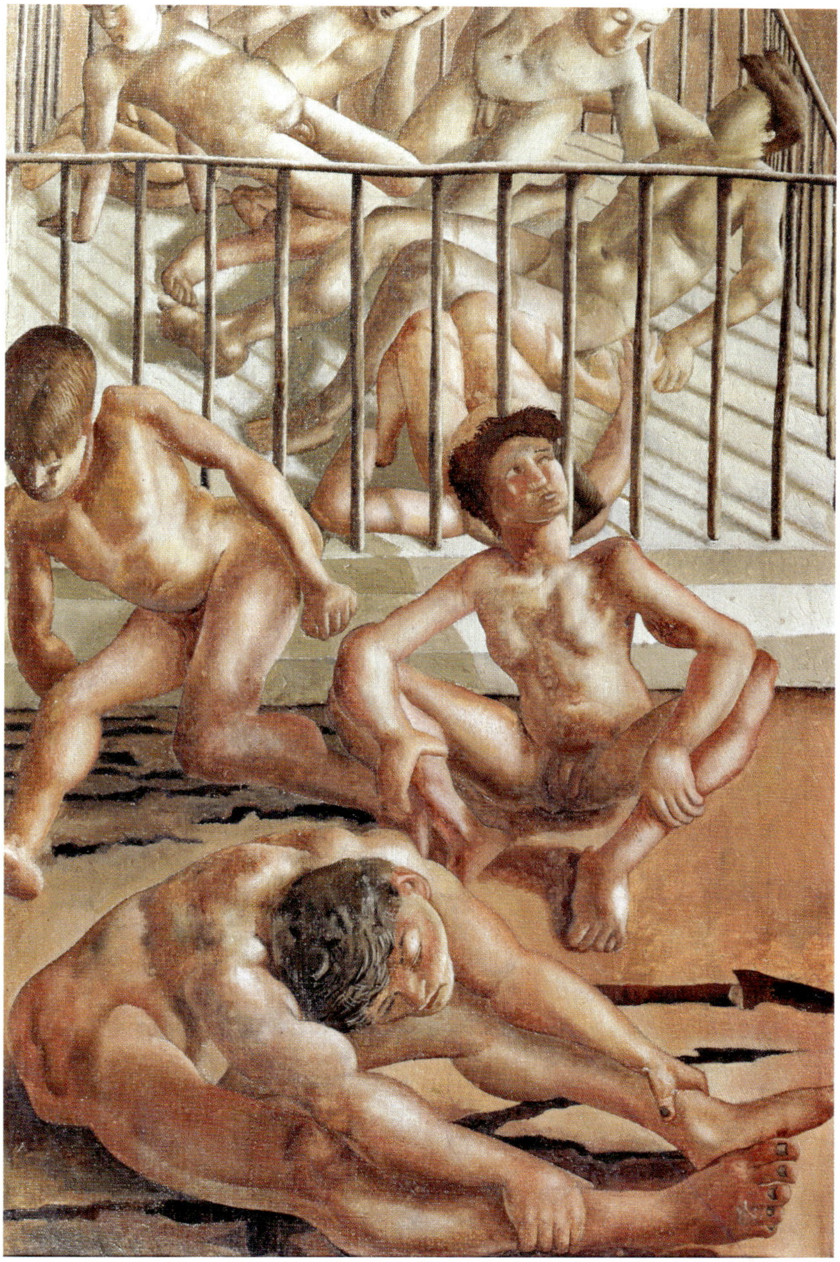

FIG 34

Stanley Spencer
Sunbathers at Odney 1935 (cat. 37)
The bathing place on the Thames at Odney, just along the river from his birthplace at Cookham, must have been known to Spencer since childhood. Here, he views the bathers through the lens of Renaissance paintings by Signorelli, Giulio Romano and others.

Sport

In Roberts' paintings of swimmers, there is no doubt that he is depicting a mass movement. Other forms of physical exercise gradually gained approval during the 1930s, sometimes with the support of government, but often independently. The most famous must be the Women's League of Health and Beauty, founded in 1929, which by 1937 had 120,000 members (fig. 35; cat. 53). Most of the Physical Training instructors in boys' schools still came from a background in the forces, and in the population at large there was some resistance to adult physical training for its militaristic associations. The WLHB sought to dispel such suggestions by its overtly pacifist agenda; its mass demonstration in the Albert Hall in 1933 included a mime depicting

FIG 35

Catching the sun in the open air baths at Blackpool 1930s (cat. 53)

Blackpool's massive Open Air Baths opened in 1923 and were proclaimed by the local authority to incorporate 'the finest pool in the whole world'. A wide variety of popular events was held there, including the occasional spontaneous display of synchronised exercise, captured here.

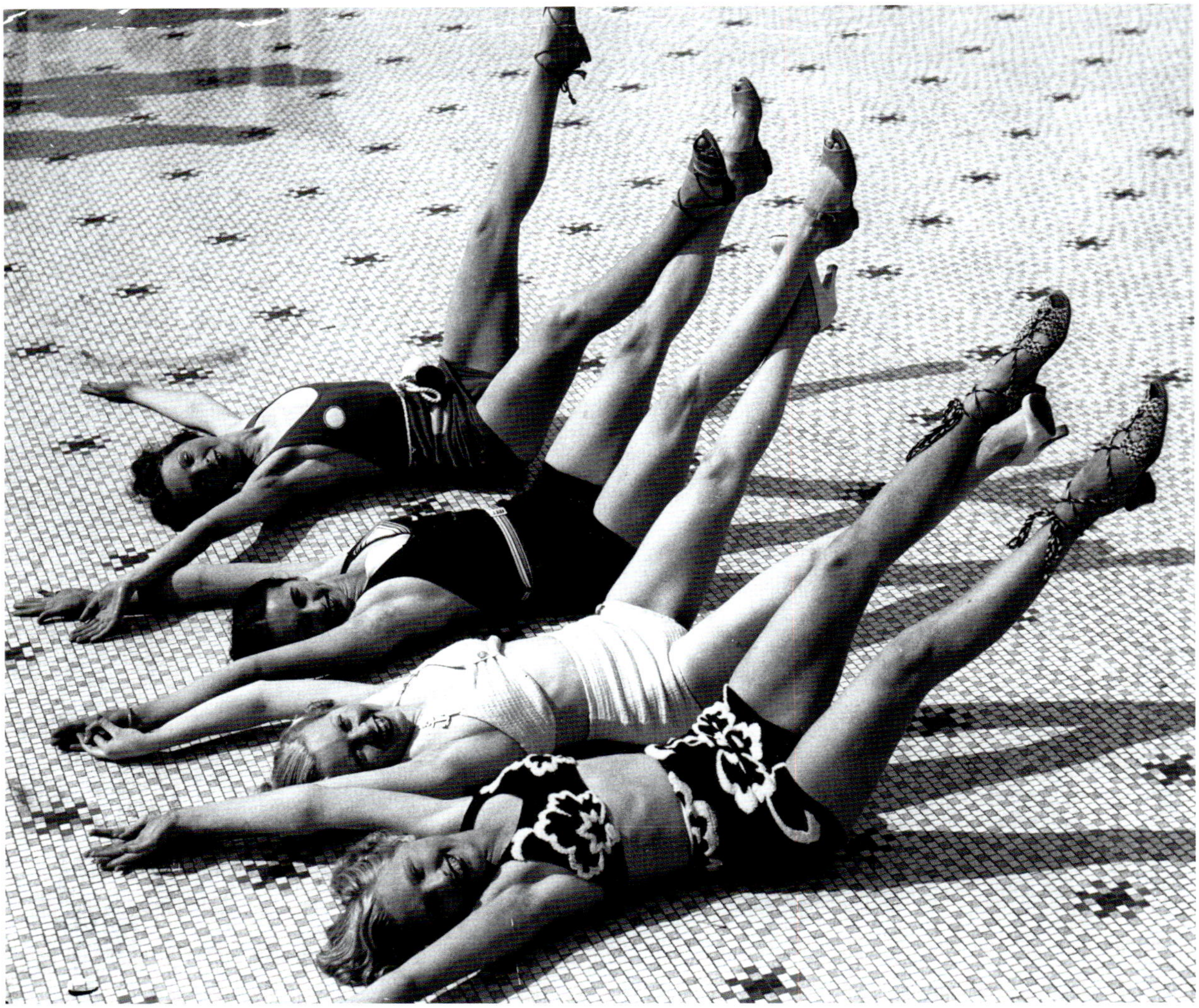

the reconciliation of Capital and Labour.[16] The British Film Institute set up a Physical Education Committee in 1933, which sponsored a series of films promoting sport and physical training to the huge cinema audience (fig. 36; cat. 62). In 1935, the Central Council of Recreative Physical Training saw the government beginning to intervene more directly in the nation's state of health. A Board of Education circular issued in January 1936 implicitly compared Britain with the superior facilities and methods of organisation in Germany and Italy; physical fitness could not escape being linked with readiness for combat. Percy Shakespeare's self-portrait *Morning Exercise* (fig. 37; cat. 34), completed in 1934, conveys something of the diffidence large sections of the male population felt for regular physical training. Alone in his room, the figure he eyes in the mirror may present himself with a flourish, but looks a woefully inadequate physical specimen. As Britain sought to drag

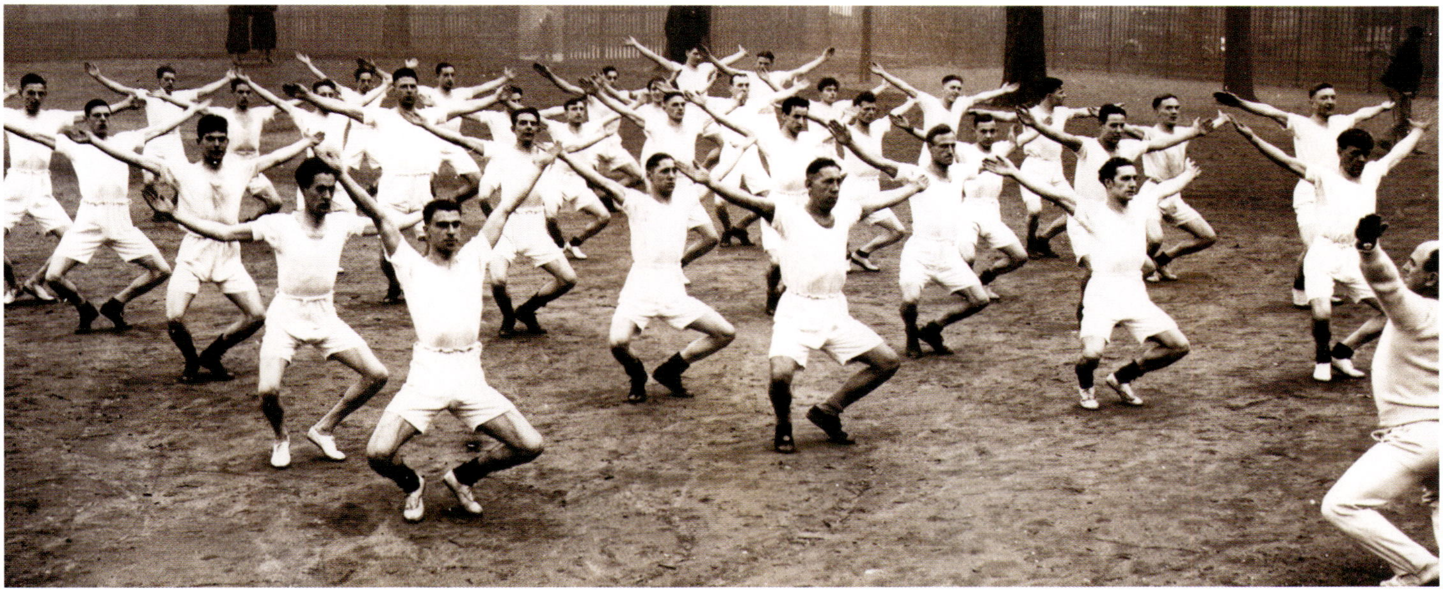

FIG 36

P.T. classes for workless. Unemployed men under instruction at Nottingham 19 December 1934 (cat. 62)

The mining communities of the Midlands, the north-east and south Wales were especially hard hit by the Depression. Despite attempts to occupy the unemployed profitably, the initiatives that were sustained in the long term were not imposed from outside, but came from the men themselves.

itself out of the Depression, when malnourishment among the unemployed was not uncommon, Shakespeare's ironic self-image shows honesty and determination. The painting was accepted by the Royal Academy in 1934, but not hung, and the following year the artist succeeded in exhibiting it at the Paris Salon.

Shakespeare's eccentric assertion of his masculinity may have been influenced by one of the most celebrated sporting paintings of the decade, Lancelot Glasson's thoroughly feminine *The Young Rower* (fig. 38; cat. 14). Nominated Picture of the Year at the Royal Academy in 1932, this painting made Glasson's name; it was widely reproduced and the artist was able to capitalise on its success by posing with his wholesome model, Freda Walker, at work on a follow-up, *The Four*, shown in 1933 (fig. 3). The *Tatler* informed its readers that 'Captain Glasson is himself a rowing man';

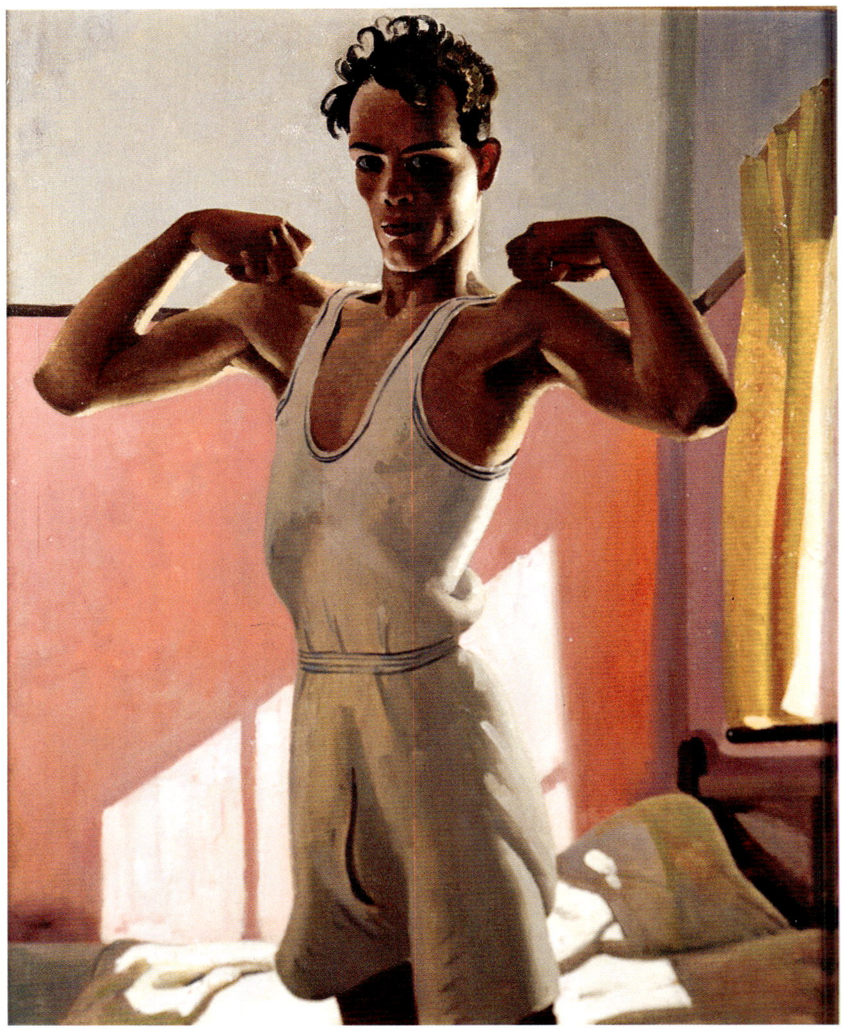

FIG 37

Percy Shakespeare
Morning Exercise 1934 (cat. 34)

Many of Shakespeare's paintings have contemporary sporting themes, but here he turns the spotlight on himself in an ironic self-portrait suggesting desire and potential rather than the actual achievement of an athletic body.

FIG 38 (OPPOSITE PAGE)

Lancelot Glasson
The Young Rower 1932 (cat. 14)

In *The Young Rower* Glasson created a more positive and purposeful image of the nude (or semi-clad) figure than that of the indolent sunbather. Hailed Picture of the Year, the work would have been bought by Blackpool Art Gallery, had not another purchaser stepped in first.

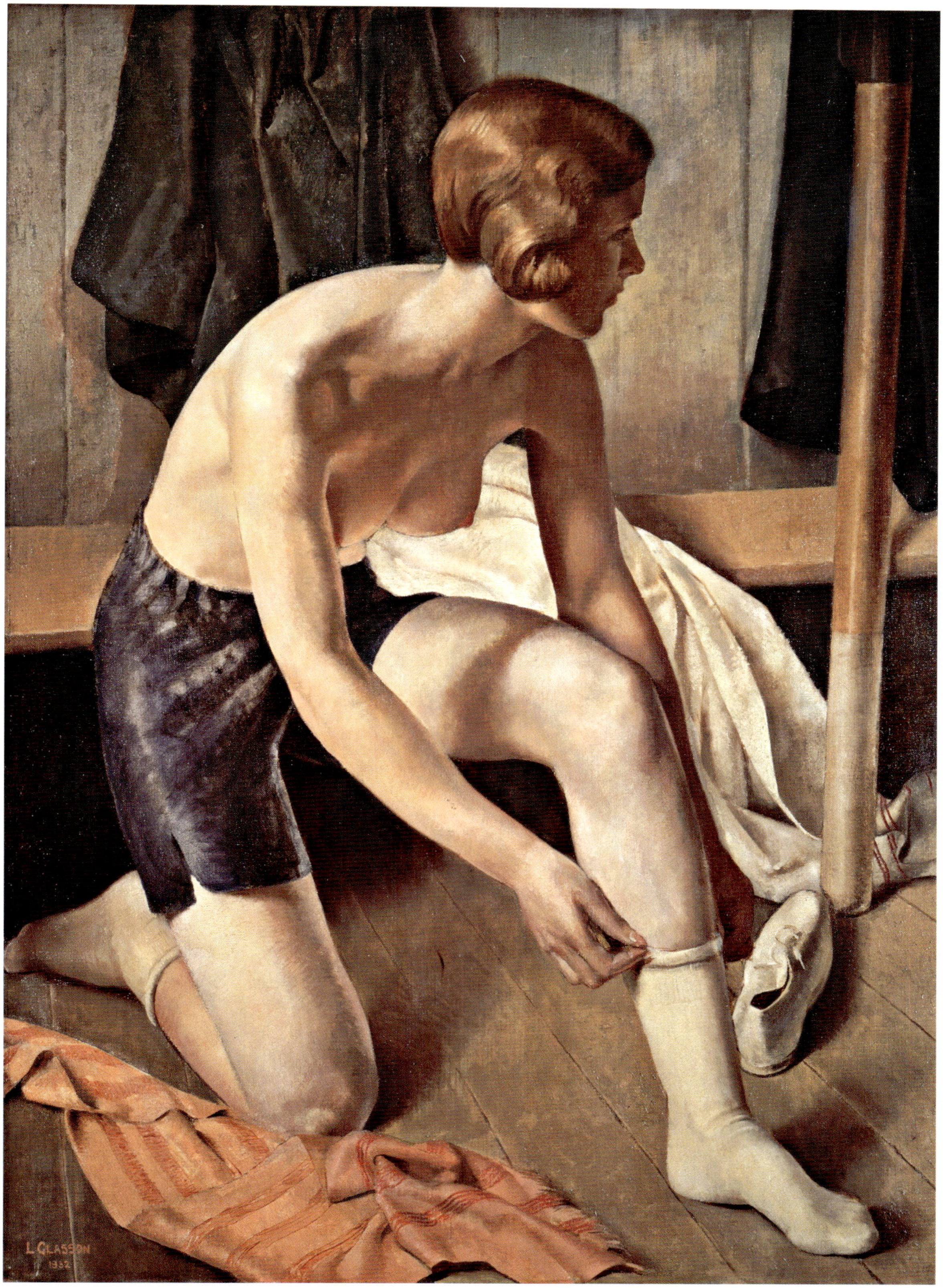
L. GLASSON
1932

accounting for the work's strong appeal, Glasson suggested 'the athletic river girl has not been done before'.[18] A female columnist for the *Yorkshire Herald* was apparently not ready fully to accept the modern sportswoman, commenting, 'Though lacking the muscular development that would justify the word 'athlete' used by some critics, Mr Glasson's young woman stands for sexless outdoor femininity'. The rise of the woman athlete was still more foreign to Cyril Strugnell, a correspondent in Guildford, who thought the work depicted, 'the clean and sportsmanlike mind of a thorough English gentleman'.[19]

Rowing was one of the most conservative sports in England, with the amateur-professional divide rigidly enforced. Women's rowing, advocated by Lucille Eaton Hill in her 1903 manual, *Athletics and Outdoor Sports for Women*, became increasingly popular after the war, leading to the foundation

FIG 39

Lancelot Glasson with Freda Walker
Reproduced with kind permission of William Glasson

Glasson at work on his follow-up to the hugely successful *The Young Rower*. The finished painting, seen in fig. 3, does not include this pose, staged for the press photographer, to make the most of Glasson's recent celebrity.

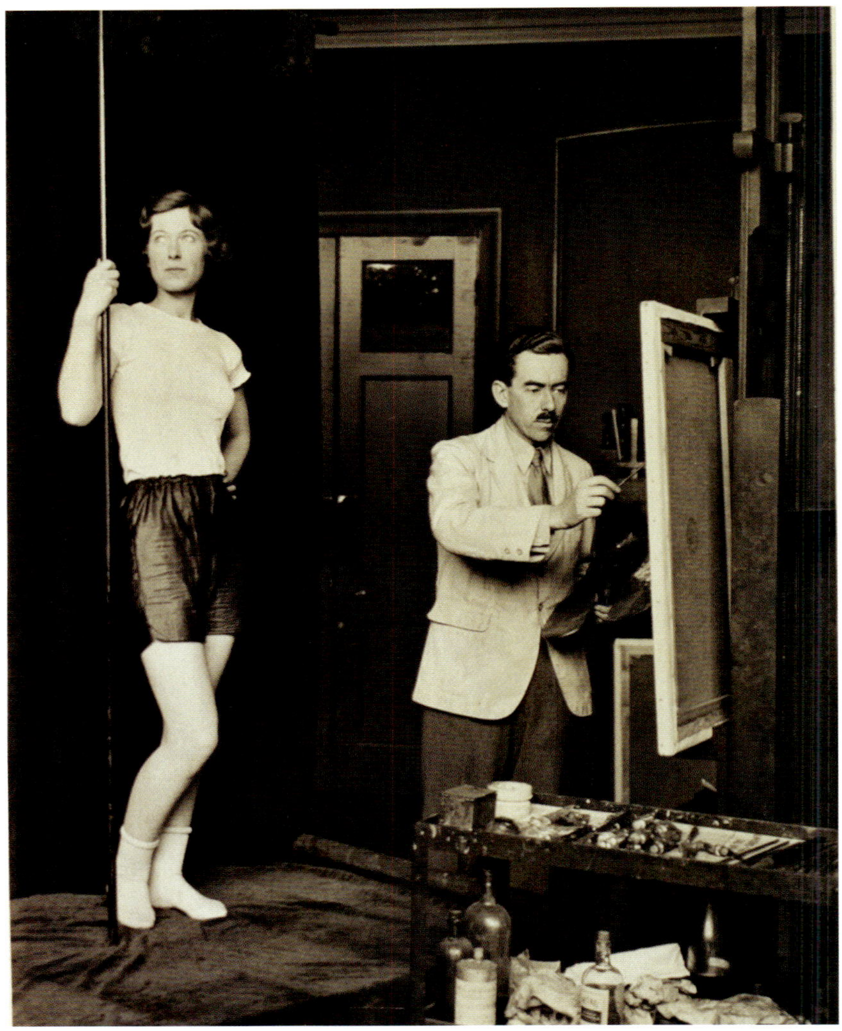

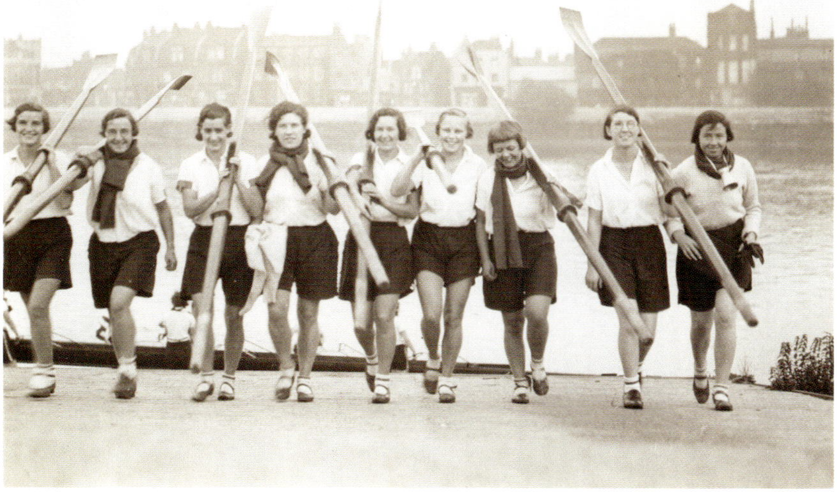

FIG 40

Civil service girls. Rowing girls at Barnes
30 September 1932 (cat. 69)

For many women, sport may not have continued through into marriage and family life, but it nonetheless provided a valuable expression of female solidarity for the younger office workers in the capital.

FIG 41

Jean Dupas
'Where is this bower beside the silver Thames?'
1930 (cat. 9)

Dupas was one of the undisputed masters of the Art Deco style in France and brings a highly individual sense of modern indulgence to this complex blend of old and new.

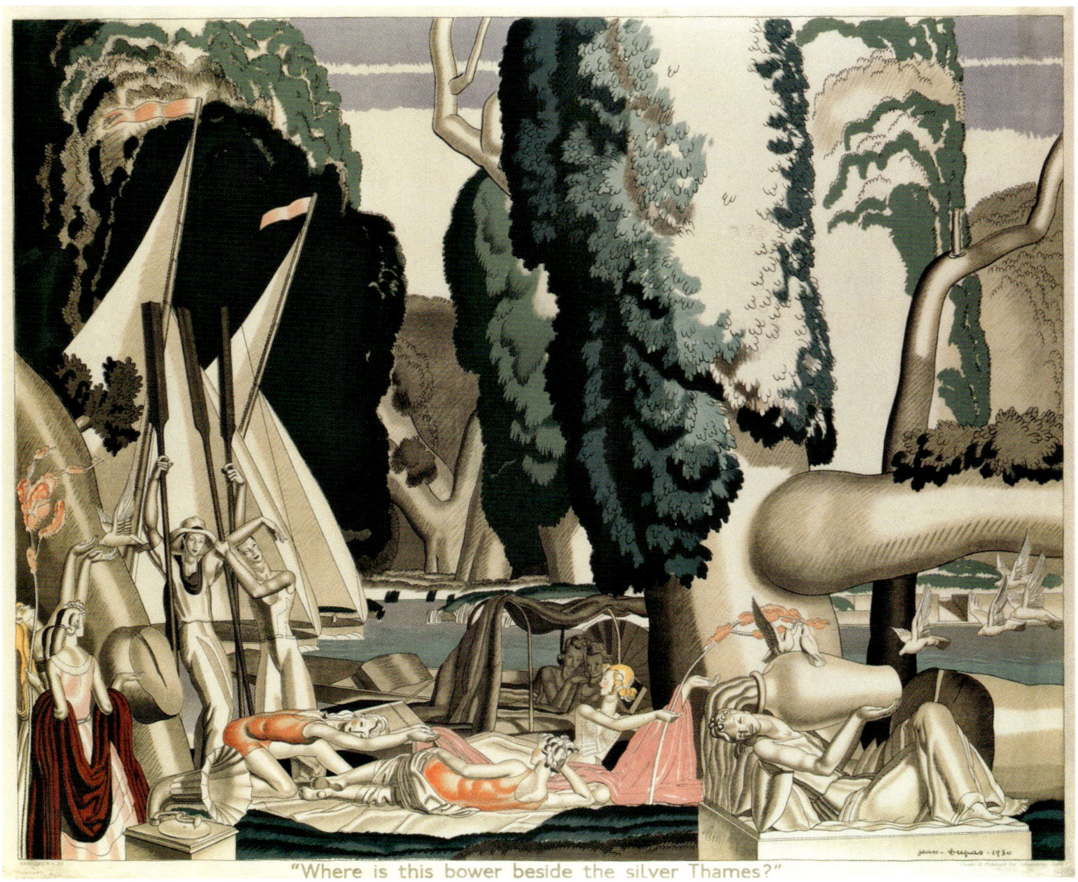

in 1926 of the Women's Amateur Rowing Federation (when neither of the existing male organisations would admit women) and the first Oxford and Cambridge race in 1927 (in fours, not eights) (fig. 40; cat. 69).[20] Its appeal as an elegant recreation, rather than as a sport, is apparent in the Thames-side idyll drawn for London Transport by Jean Dupas in 1930 (fig. 41; cat. 9). The rowing crew may embody a new type of female solidarity, but, for Glasson, for Dupas, and for Harry Morley in a boating scene of 1937 (fig. 42), its image was kept quite distinct from the muscularity which characterised the male version of the sport.

Tennis was another sport which was shedding its elite, middle-class image during the inter-war years. With swimming, it was also the sport in which a new type of female athleticism impressed itself on the public at large. Immediately after the war it was Suzanne Lenglen who achieved star

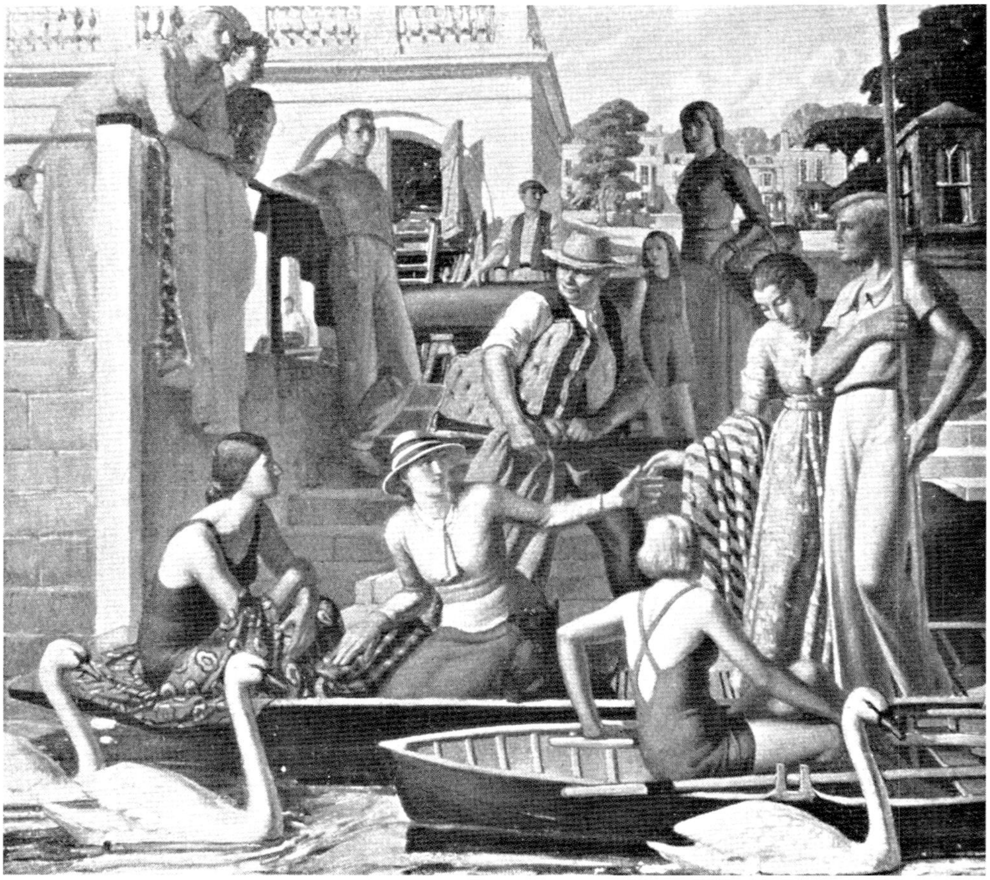

FIG 42

Harry Morley
Riverside
(exhibited Royal Academy 1937)

Morley celebrates the very boat trips on the Thames which were the subject of London Transport's advertising campaigns. Despite the emphasis on geometry and the formality of the painting's structure, the women in their swimsuits suggest a very relaxed atmosphere to this boating expedition.

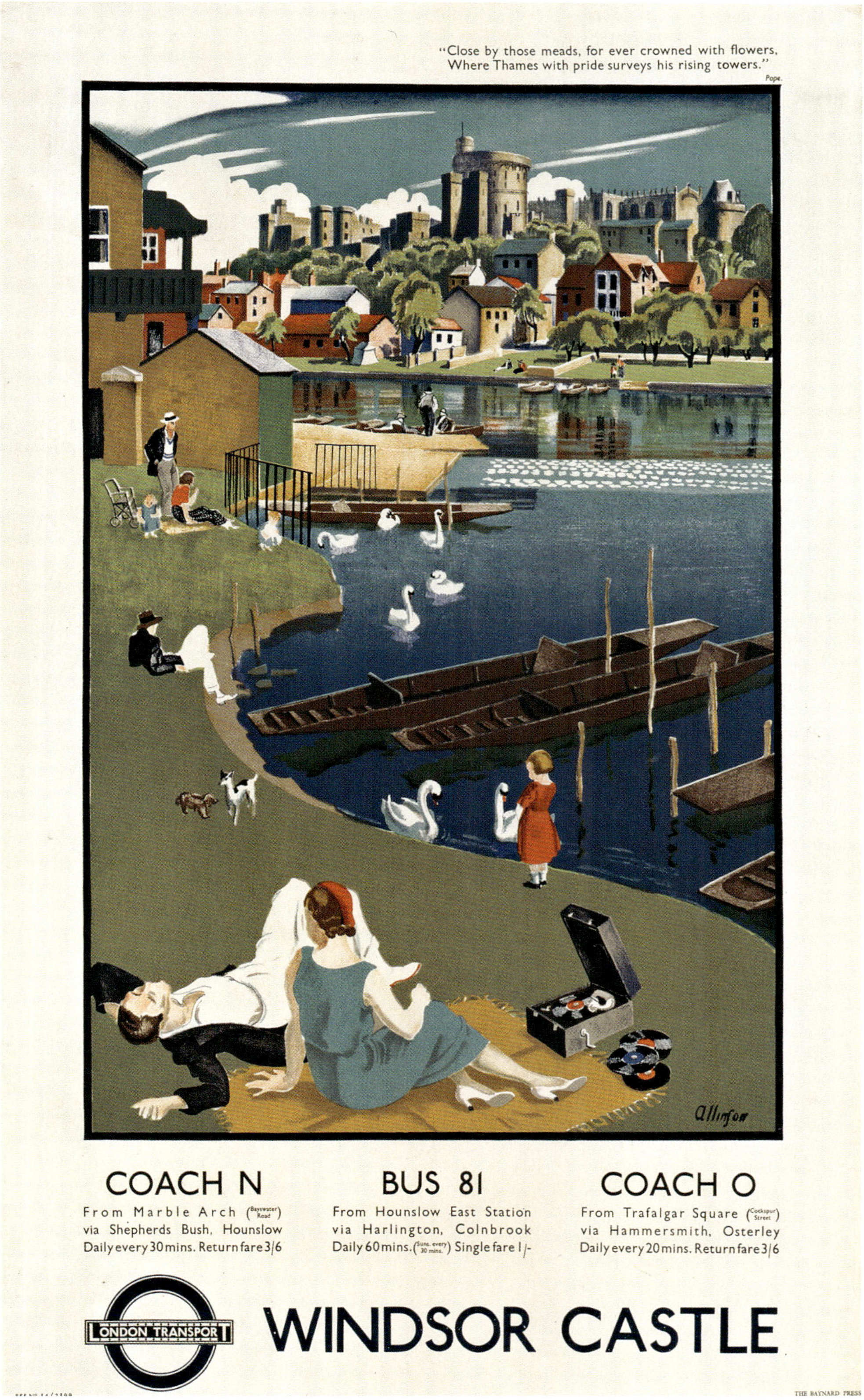

FIG 43

Adrian Allinson

Windsor Castle 1934 (cat. 4)

In the traditional society that Britain in the thirties in many respects remained, the modernity of the portable gramophone is in no way incongruous against the backdrop of Windsor Castle.

status with her freedom of movement and almost balletic swooping strokes. She was supplanted by Helen Wills, who gained the first of seven US singles titles in 1923 and then won Wimbledon eight times, beginning in 1927.[21] While the number of tennis clubs in Britain almost doubled between 1925 and 1935 (rising to 3,220 in 1938), there was in fact almost no increase in the courts built in public parks, at least in London (fig. 44; cat. 70).[22] The game's widening appeal, despite the exclusivity of the majority of the clubs, is demonstrated by the 'Workers' Wimbledon' tournaments held from 1933 at Reading LTC.[23] Mackinlay's *Tête à Tête*, showing two girls sprawled in the shade, apparently after having played tennis, touches on a new type of physicality in women, where the end of the match is followed by relaxation, rather than the formalities of tea in the clubhouse (fig. 45; cat. 22).

The game of tennis Eric Ravilious painted in 1933 for the music room of

FIG 44

Tennis and lunch in the open at Lincolns Inn Fields 3 July 1934 (cat. 70)

The sight of sport and al fresco dining in the heart of thte legal establishment, surely the most staid of all the professions, seems to suggest that the passion for the open air really is somehow touching all parts of British society.

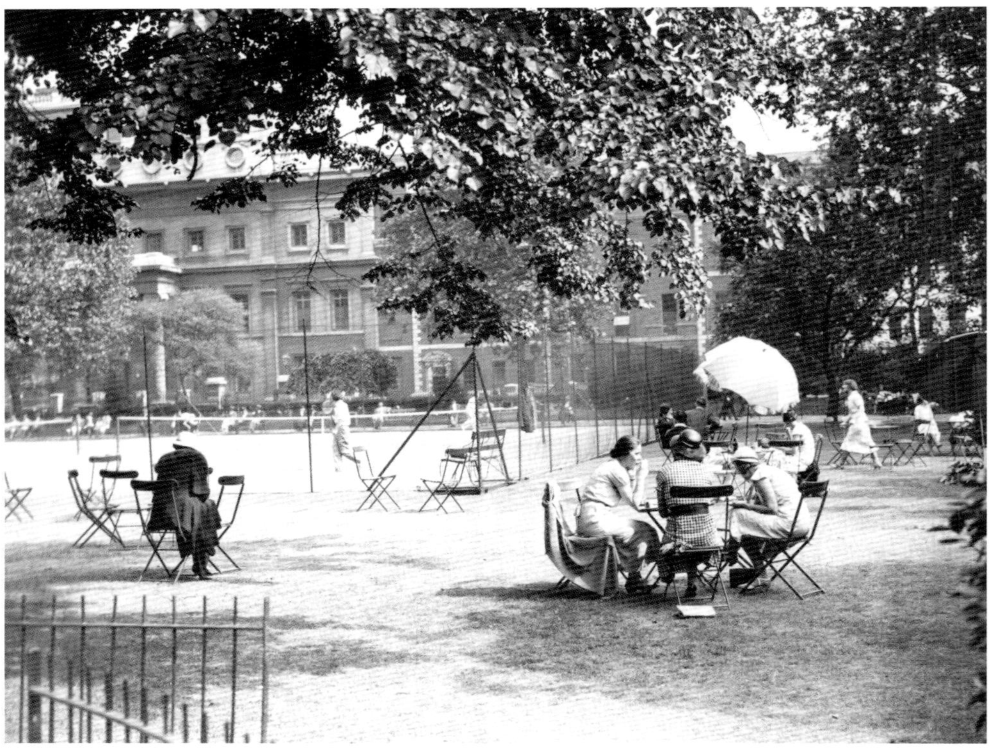

Sir Geoffrey Fry, private secretary to former Prime Minister Stanley Baldwin, is set in Manor Gardens, a park in Eastbourne (fig. 46). The women are far more active than the men, for whom cricket was generally viewed as a more manly and sociable summer recreation; their bare arms and stockingless legs, an assault on convention just a few years before, now pass unnoticed in the heart of the establishment.

In the levels of society where such paintings were consumed, it was the recreative, rather than the competitive aspect of sport which was celebrated. Indeed, one of their functions as art may have been to assert the more traditional values of simple participation and bonding, rather than the preoccupation with records and outstanding performance, which was one aspect of modern sport many in Britain found distasteful. Not only in Britain; the Czech historian, Jan Huizinga, in his *Homo Ludens; A Study of the*

FIG 45

Miguel Mackinlay

Tête à Tête 1930 (cat. 22)

It is no coincidence that these independent, self-sufficient women are also sporting women, perfectly comfortable relaxing in public after the exertions of a game of tennis.

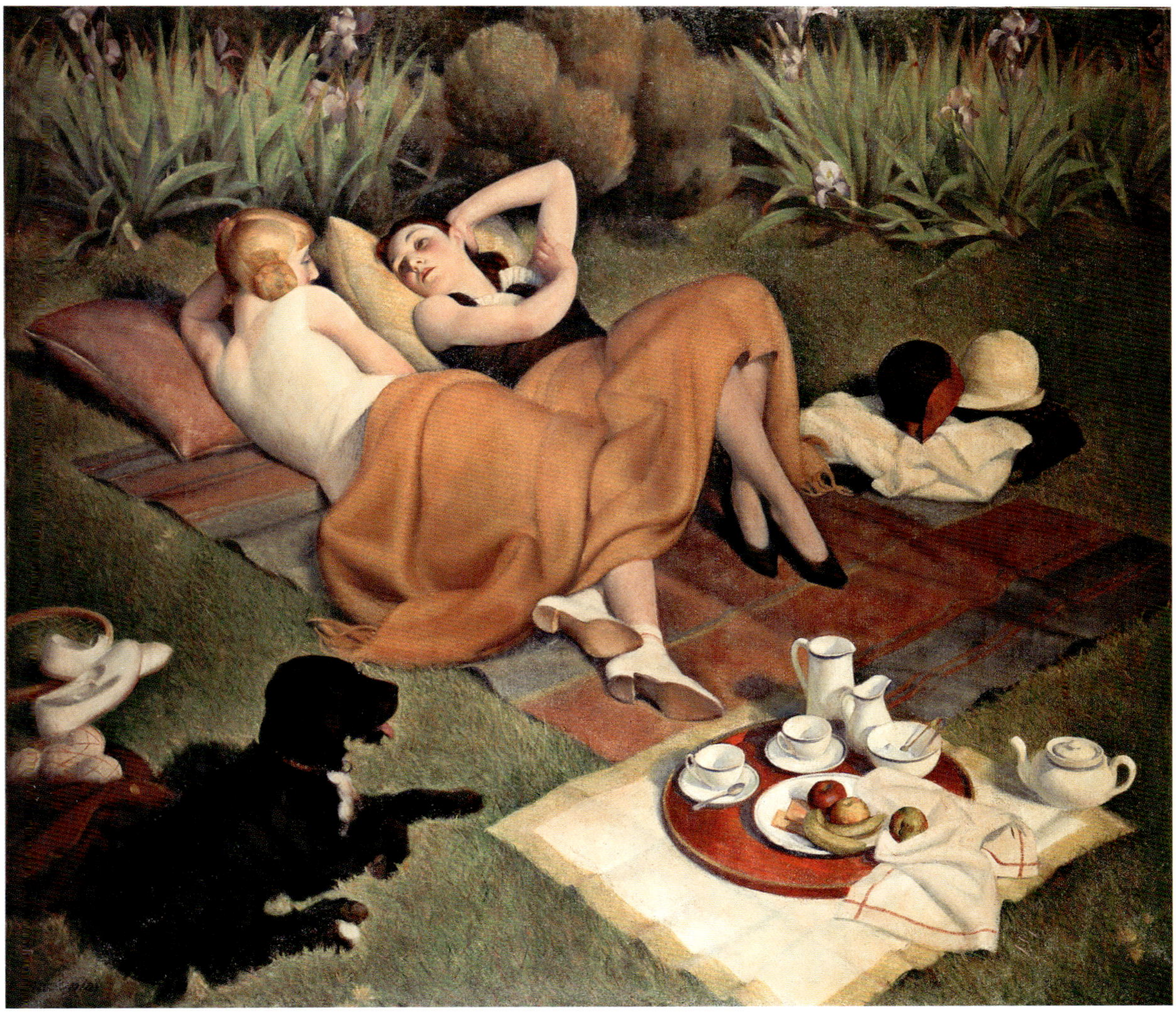

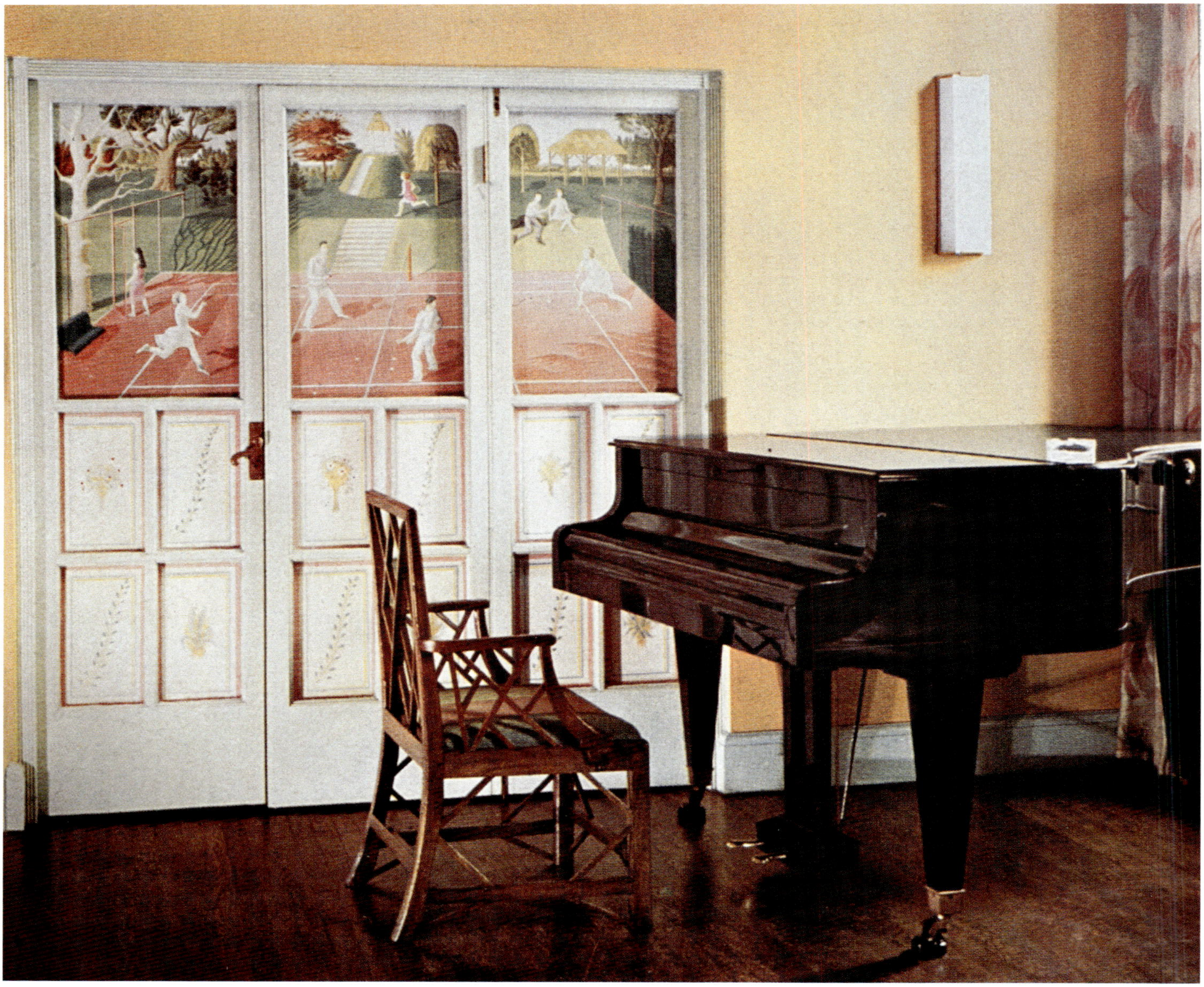

FIG 46

Eric Ravilious
Tennis 1932–33

There is almost a hint of an eighteenth-century rococo revival in Ravilious' choice of a tennis match in a park as the theme to decorate this high-class London apartment.

Play-Element in Culture, completed in 1938, viewed modern sport as sterile and degrading. Writing in the aftermath of the Berlin Olympics, he maintained that the 'fatal shift towards over-seriousness', though 'counter to the popular feeling of today' deprived sport of any cultural value.[24] From 1912 to 1948, one aspect of the Olympics which aspired to realise the broad ambitions of De Coubertin, the founder of the modern games, was the international, competitive exhibition of sporting art, at which medals were awarded to different nations, in the same way as they were at the sporting events. At the 1928 exhibition in Amsterdam, Laura Knight won silver in the painting category. Britain's exhibits at Los Angeles in 1932 included many pictures of horse racing, shooting and fishing; hardly representative of the Olympic ideal, but certainly a reflection of what was still meant by sport to the majority of the buyers of paintings (fig. 47).[25]

FIG 47

James Stroudley
The Games c. 1930
Stroudley's mural reasserts all the idealism of the Olympic movement, which in the modern world was increasingly mired in politics, national interest and differing interpretations of what constituted sportsmanlike conduct. Athletics, rarely a subject for artists, becomes of interest when its classical roots can be brought to the fore.

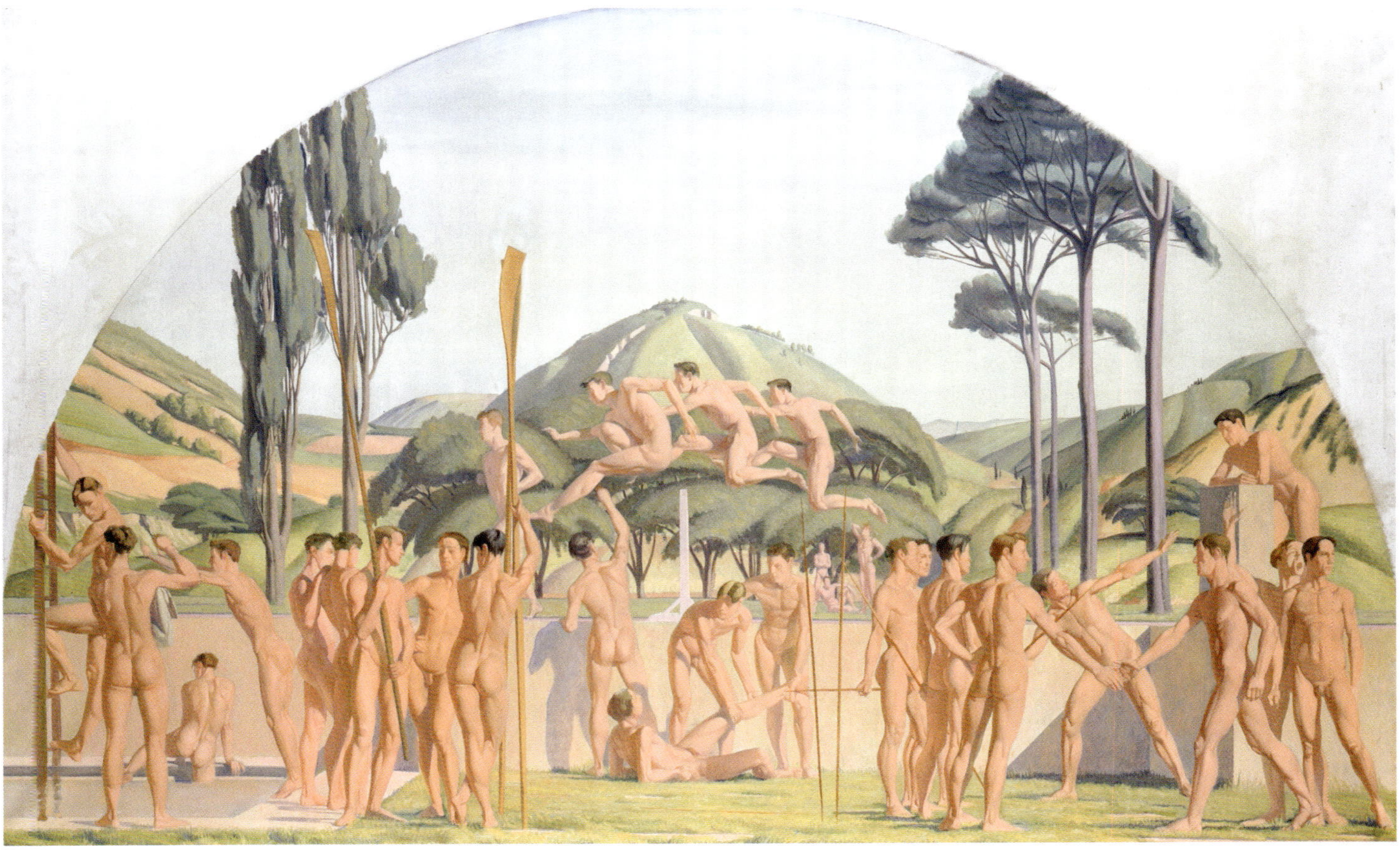

The Countryside

The more truly democratic expansion in leisure activity was happening elsewhere, with the hordes of ramblers, hikers and cyclists swarming into the British countryside (figs. 48, 49; cats. 67, 72). The value of exercise, the escape from the humdrum life of the office or the factory, and a growing appreciation of the landscape as itself under threat from the encroachments of modernity all gave impetus to the movement. The Clarion Clubs and other groups had organised country rambles since the 1880s, but after the war participation became much more widespread.[26] Public transport companies, supported by imaginative publicity, played a large part not only in making the countryside more accessible, but in crystallising the image of its

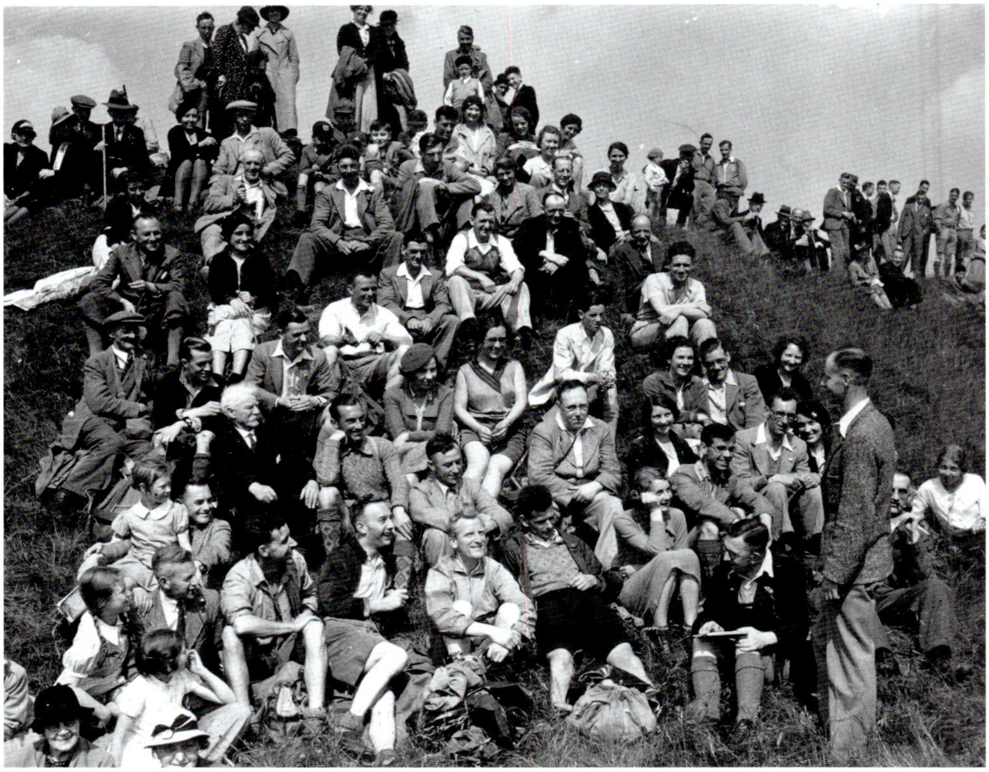

FIG 48

Ramblers Association West of England Rally at the White Horse, Westbury. Professor R J Brocklehurst, Vice President of the Federation addressing the rally 20 June 1937 (cat. 67)

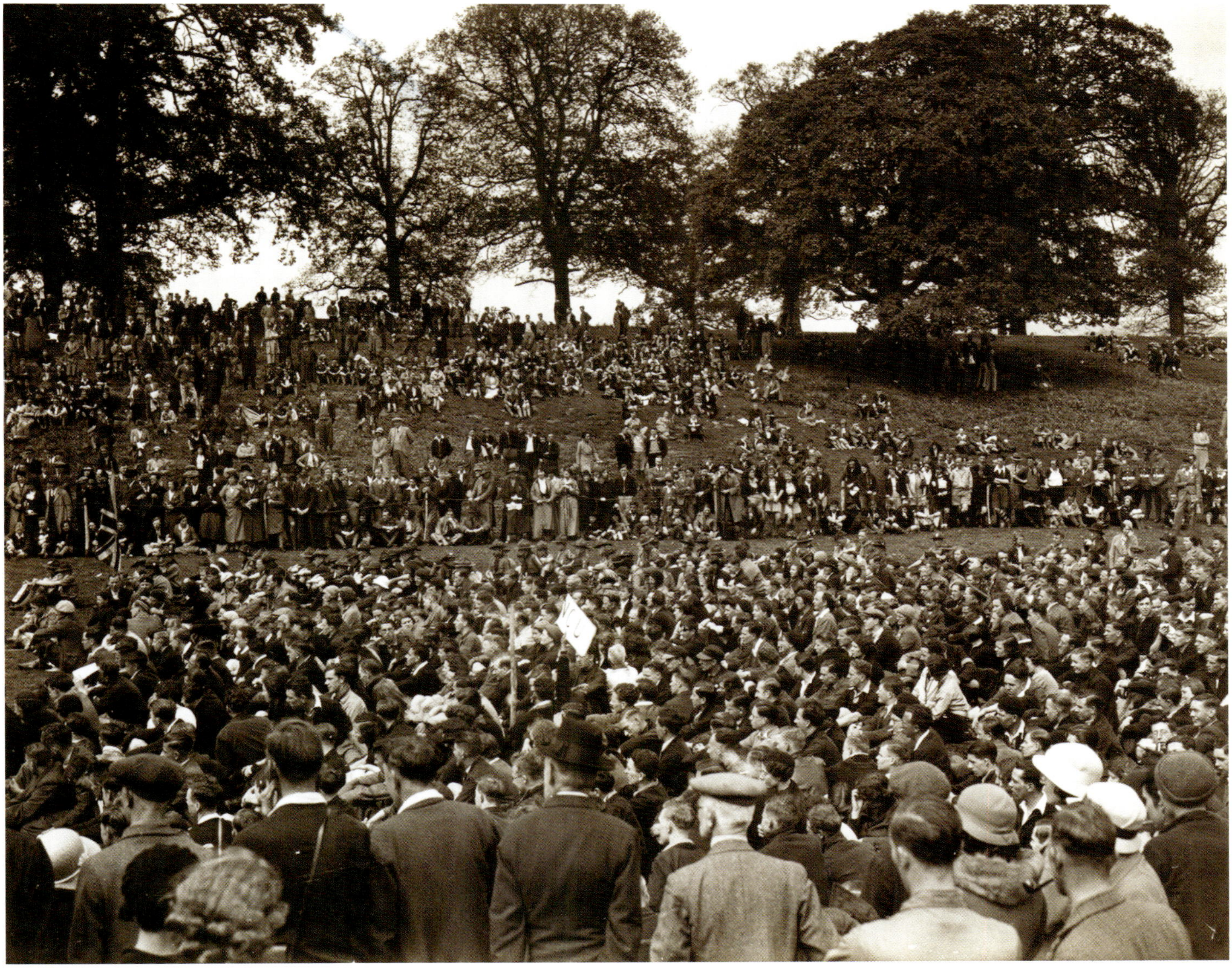

FIG 49

The Kent Rally of Out Door Folk at Mote Park, Maidstone. The crowd listening to the Health Minister Sir Hilton Young 26 May 1935 (cat. 72)

The British outdoor movement arose from the grass roots, with little government intervention; the contrast with the similar, state-supported developments in Italy and Germany was often made at the time. However, as the decade progressed, ministers did seek to harness popular enthusiasm in a more organised programme to improve the nation's health.

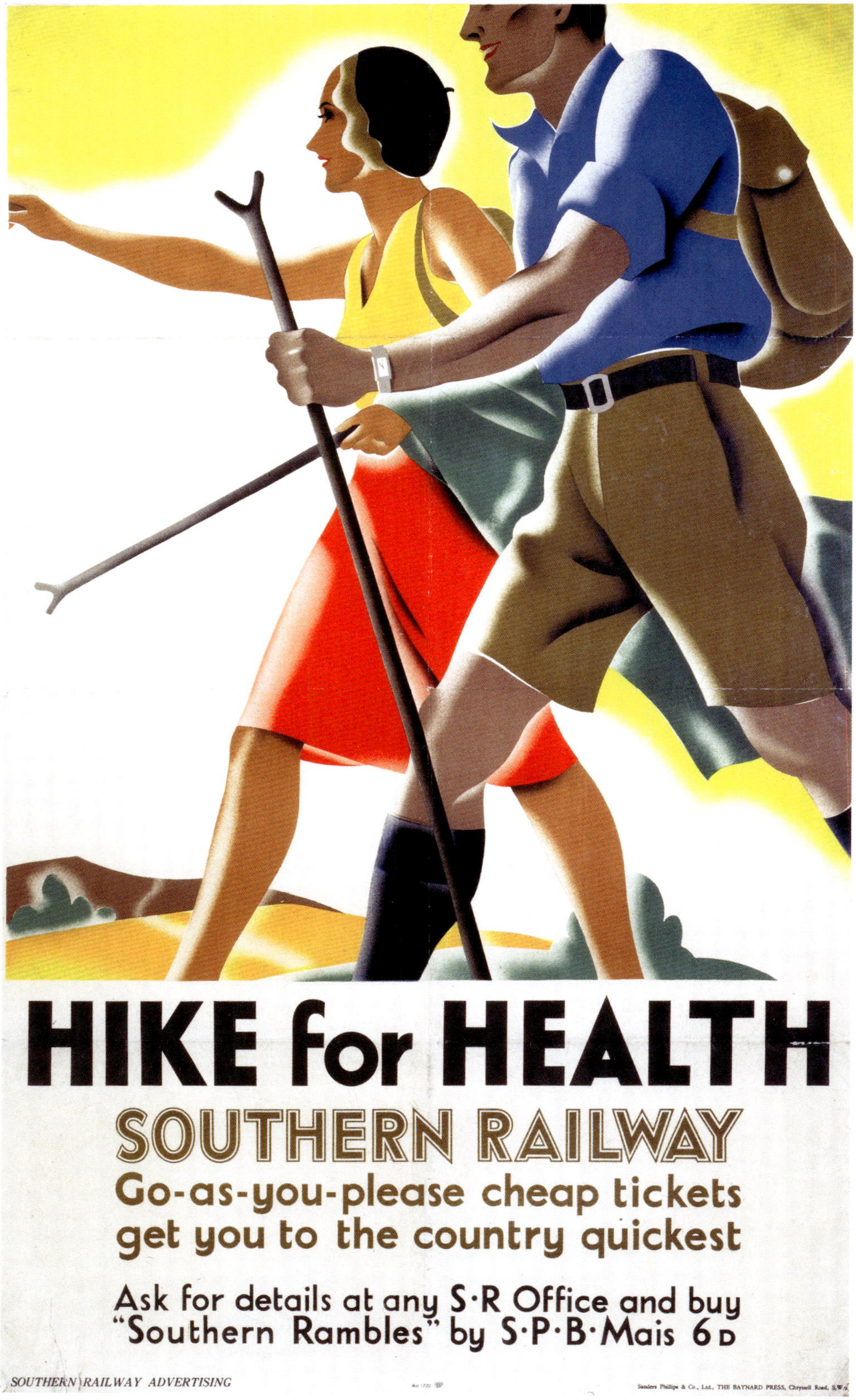

FIG 50

Anonymous
Hike for Health 1931
Southern Railway poster

The tight focus of the image and towering stature of the figures all add to the sense of power and energy unleashed through a country walk.

attractions.[27] 'Hike for Health' proclaimed one railway poster of 1931 (fig. 50). The word itself was new: first recorded as an American import around 1920, 'hiking' remained in inverted commas in the columns of *The Times* throughout the 1920s. It conveyed a purposefulness that made rambling seem almost effete; but this was also part of rambling's essential Englishness, why the over-earnest 'hikers' were never fully naturalised (fig. 51; cat. 66). Percy Shakespeare understood this in portraying his Amazonian hiker in the Rhineland; she is familiar, yet foreign (fig. 52; cat. 35). Not only was the open-air movement Germanic in inspiration, the Youth Hostel Association, which provided the cheap accommodation which made the longer walks possible, had been founded in 1930 on a model already well established in the Weimar Republic.[28] By the time Shakespeare visited Germany in 1934 or early 1935, the political situation had changed again; the swastika flutters on the black

FIG 51

Hikers at Box Hill 20 March 1932 (cat. 66)

In what has the look of a carefully composed tableau, the magnificent spreading boughs of the leafless tree seem to encapsulate all the ancient, time-honoured virtues of the English countryside. Walkers were not just indulging in a recent craze, but connecting to an English past.

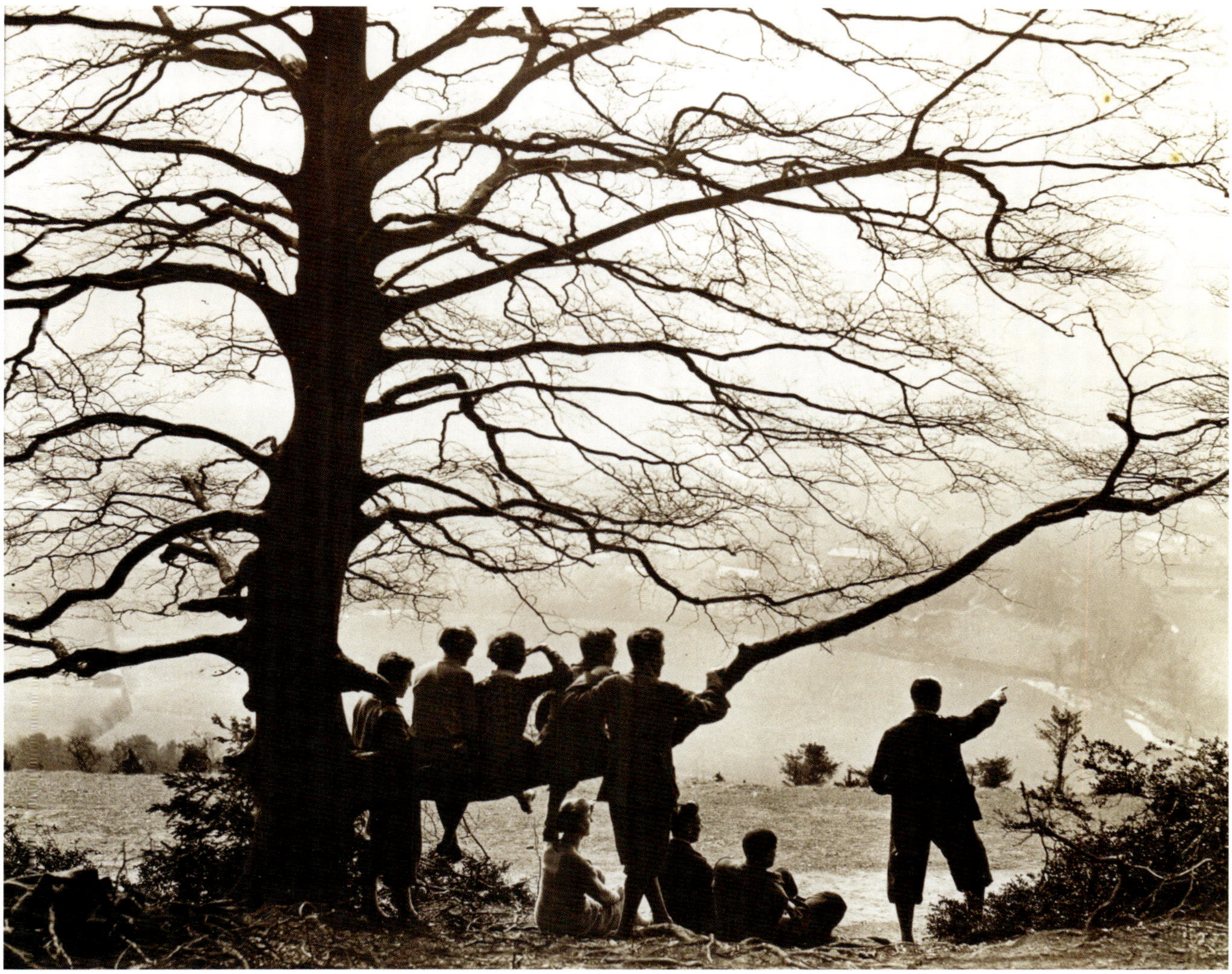

and red banners, ominously anticipating Hitler's annexation of the Rhineland in 1936.

In the 1920s, walking was promoted as a cheap and wholesome alternative to the cinema that couples could enjoy together. The painters that chose to give prominence to women ramblers, as Allen, Tucker and Henry all do, may well have wished to celebrate an aspect of modern life while removing any of its threat to the social order (figs. 53–56; cats. 3, 40, 65, 16). The organised trespass on Kinder Scout in the Peak District on 24 April 1932 remained a cause célèbre not only for its overt challenge to land ownership, but as a rare moment when the political dimension of mass leisure, always present, but generally carefully concealed, came, literally, out into the open. Commentators at the time and more recent scholars are in agreement that the open-air movement was a conspicuous and distinctive

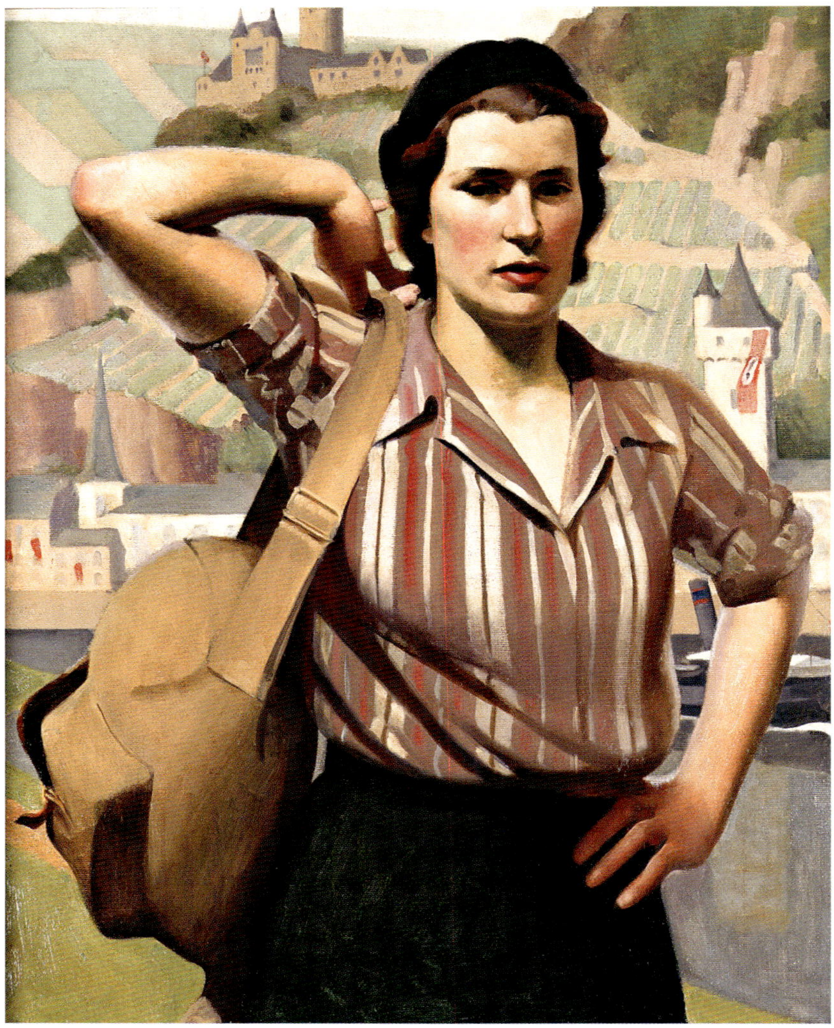

FIG 52

Percy Shakespeare

On the Rhine 1935 (cat. 35)

This Amazonian hiker, with her almost threatening bulk, may be intended to be read as German, and thus a product of the state-supported fitness culture, something rejected in a more liberal-minded Britain. Shakespeare visited Germany before Hitler's annexation of the Rhineland, yet the swastika banners sound an ominous note of imminent developments.

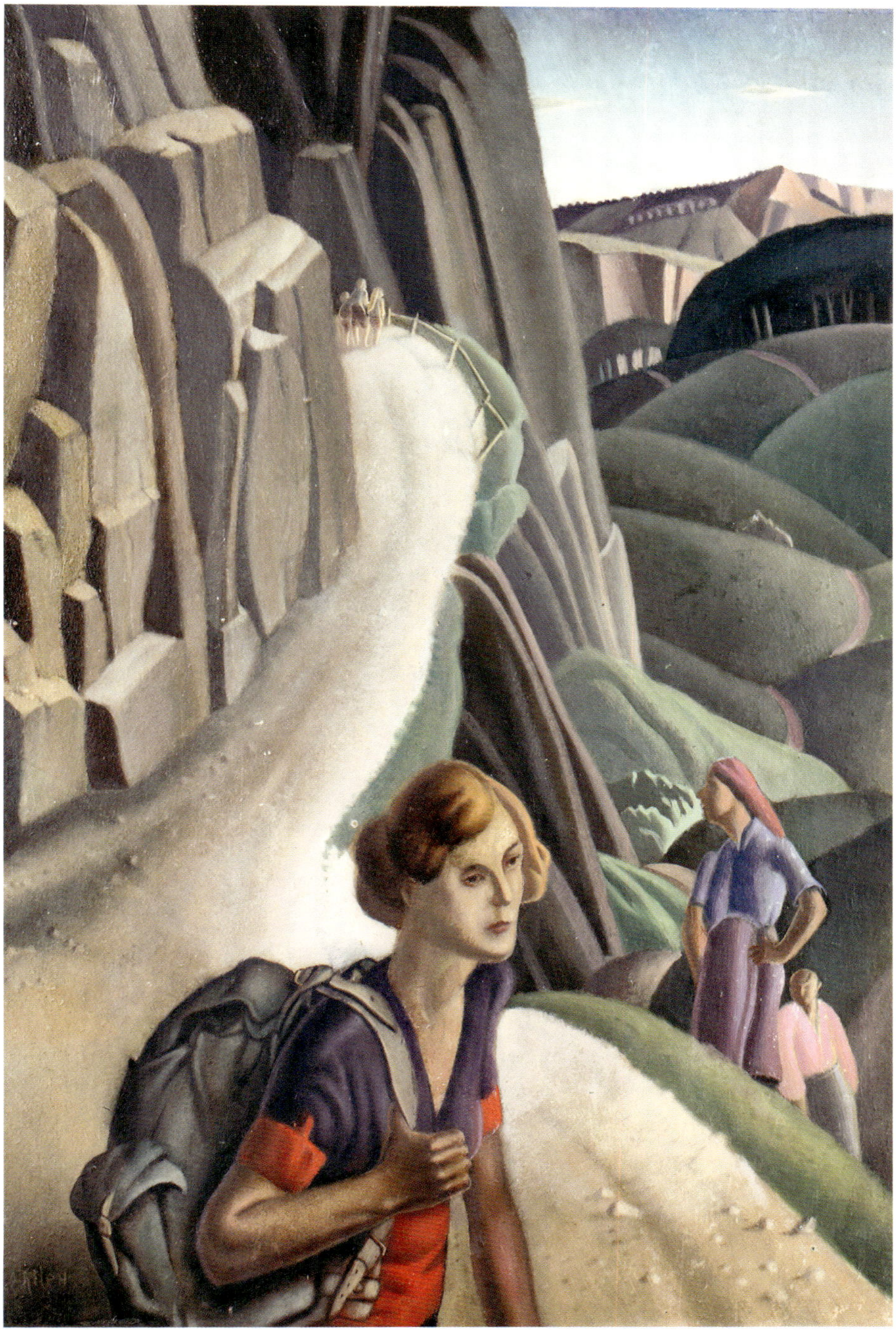

FIG 53

Harry Epworth Allen
The Hikers (cat. 3)

Allen was always concerned to bring out a sense of the physical structure of the land through his painting. Here its hard, rugged appearance seems to reflect on the character of the walkers.

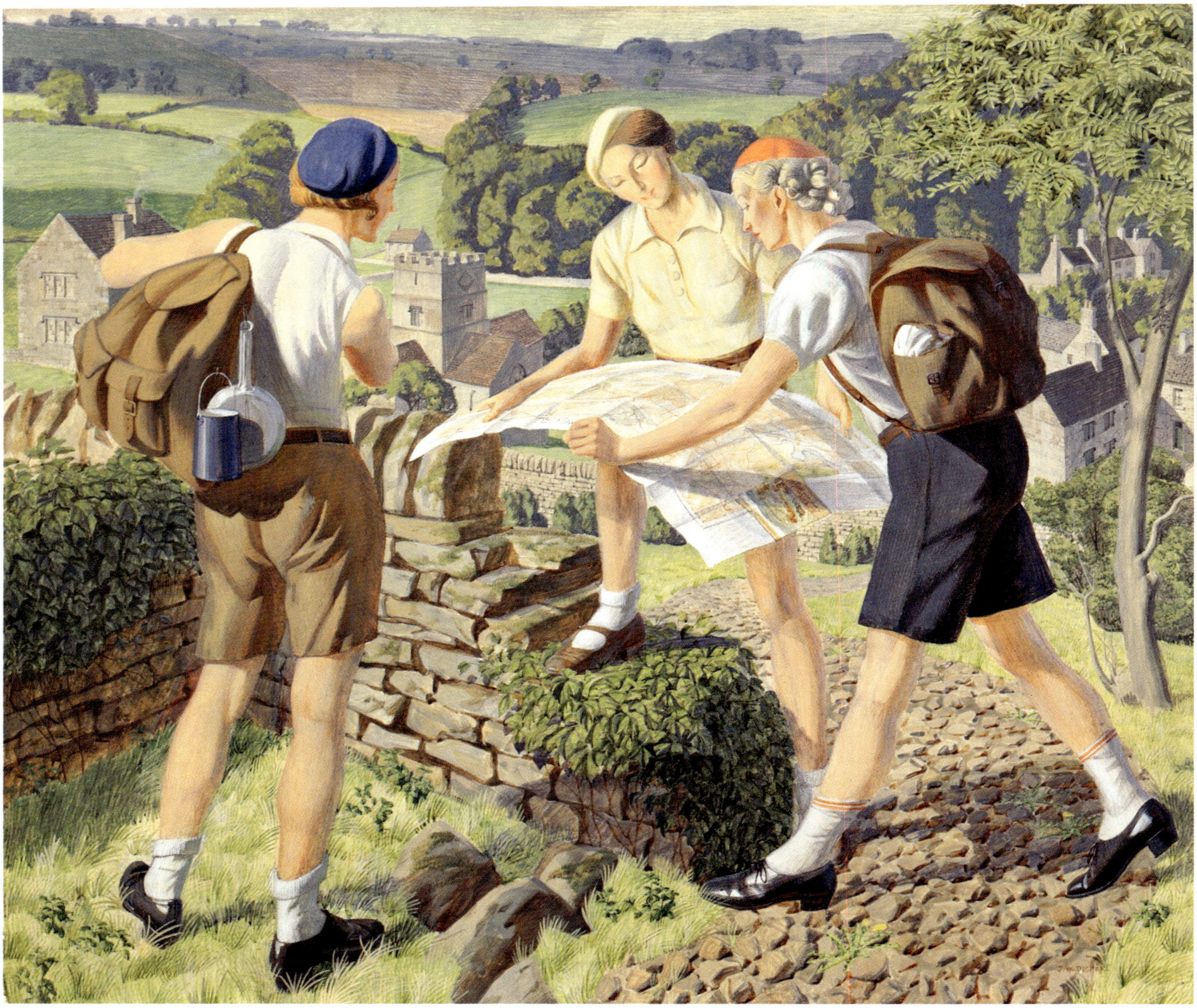

FIG 54

James Walker Tucker
Hiking 1936 (cat. 40)

Tucker spent his entire professional life in Gloucester, and this scene is probably set in the Cotswolds. It presents a strong image of female independence and solidarity, showing how important outdoor pursuits were to the burgeoning feminist movement.

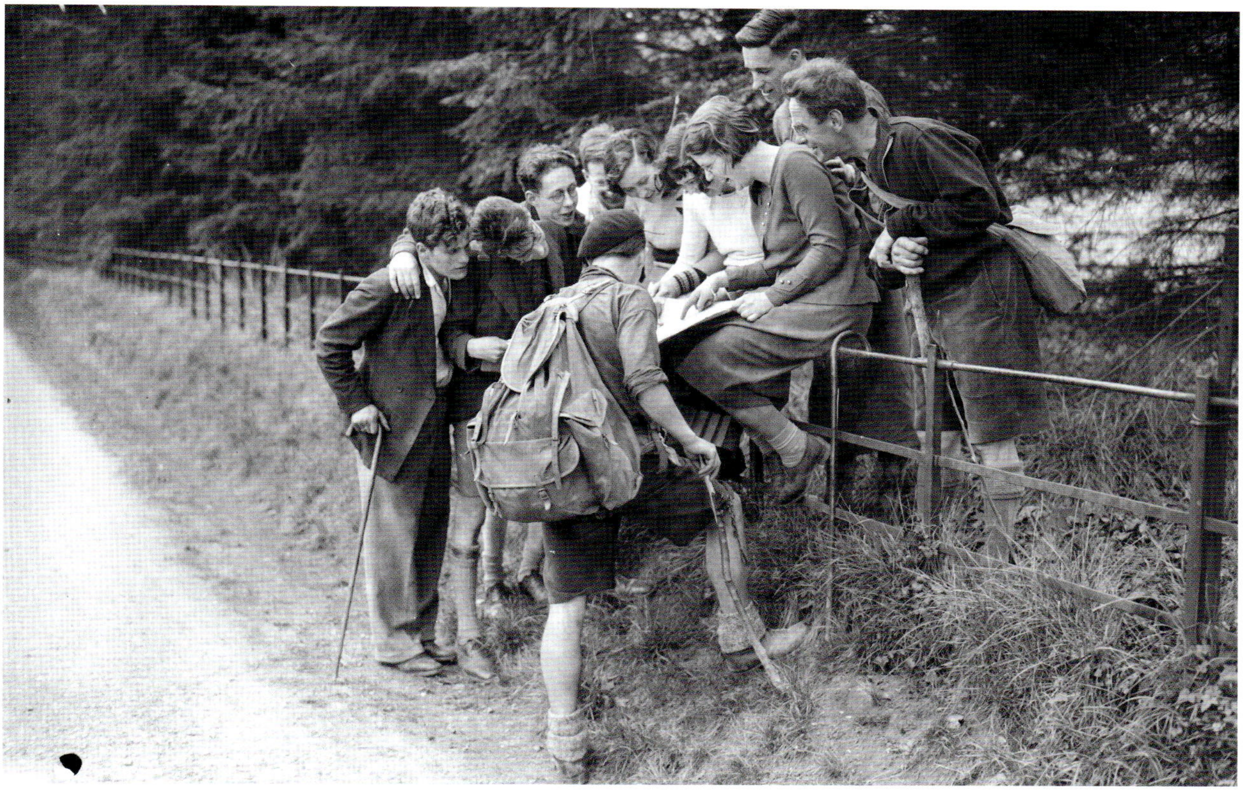

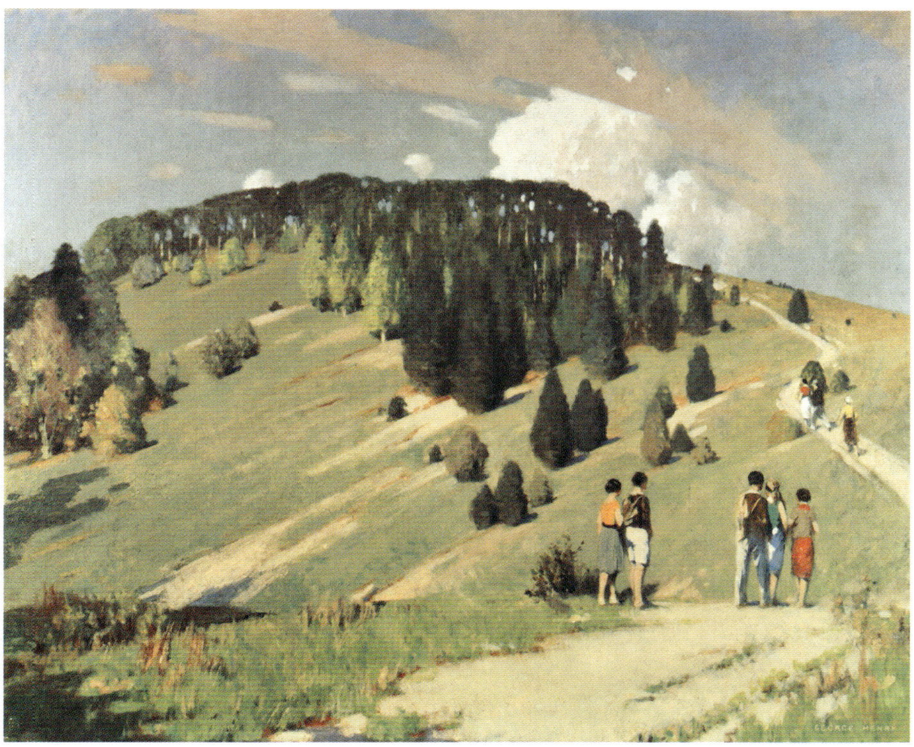

FIG 55

Hikers enjoying the sunshine at Box Hill
9 April 1935 (cat. 65)

The lanes and tucked-away villages of Surrey were popular destinations for day-trippers from London, and the sight of groups of walkers gathered at the roadside became commonplace.

FIG 56

George Henry
Hikers at Goodwood 1937 (cat. 16)

During the 1930s, Henry exhibited at least one painting of walkers on the South Downs every year, making him one of the most consistent promoters of this type of subject matter. These spacious views, enlivened with touches of sharp colour, appealed to a southern idea of a mild, easily accessible outdoors.

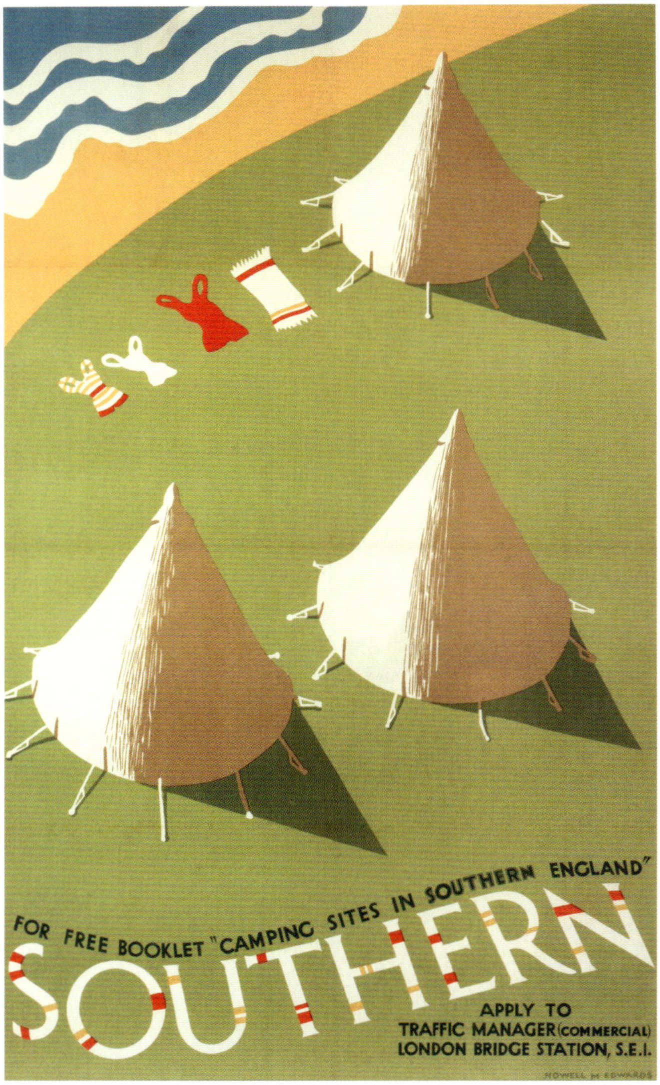

FIG 57

Nowell Edwards
Camping Sites in Southern England 1935
Southern Railway poster

The simplicity and clean lines of the image evoke a healthy and moral type of recreation; especially if the two smaller swimming costumes represent two women whose tents are kept at a safe remove from the single man, whose larger costume lies alongside.

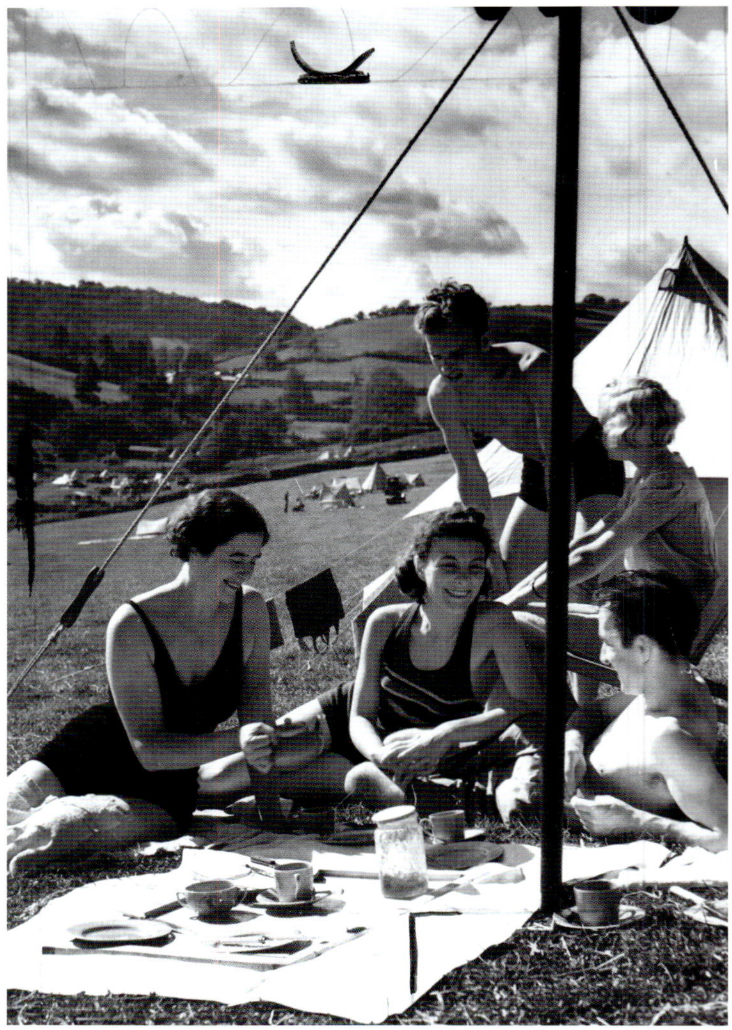

FIG 58

Under canvas – after a swim, a cup of tea, for holidaymakers in camp at Branscombe, South Devon 1 August 1938 (cat. 61)

Camping was no longer simply a low-cost option for the under-privileged. Photos like this extolled life under canvas as one of the great pleasures of the open-air movement.

aspect of inter-war culture in Britain. Yet it was not the creation of this age. Walking, cycling and camping all had long histories, both as group activities and for individuals. What was different, however, was the rapid growth in participation and the breadth and depth of coverage. As promoted by the Boy Scouts, an experience of camping might appear a worthwhile but rudimentary skill to be acquired; presented by a stylish, but anonymous designer for Southern Railways, its delights appear almost irresistible (figs. 57, 58; cat. 61).

Alongside walking, cycling too acquired all the trappings of a sub-culture, with its own clubs, mass rallies and excursions (fig. 59; cat. 71). A bicycle might cost around five guineas, yet most working-class buyers would pay for one in instalments. William Roberts' *Les Routiers* (fig. 60; cat. 30), painted in 1931, with its muscular riders and sporting machines, seems to evoke the

FIG 59

Girl cyclists rally, starting from Green Street Green 10 June 1934 (cat. 71)

Throughout the summer months, the pages of the *Daily Herald* were crammed with similar images, celebrating the simple pleasures of communal sorties into the countryside, here on the fringes of south-east London.

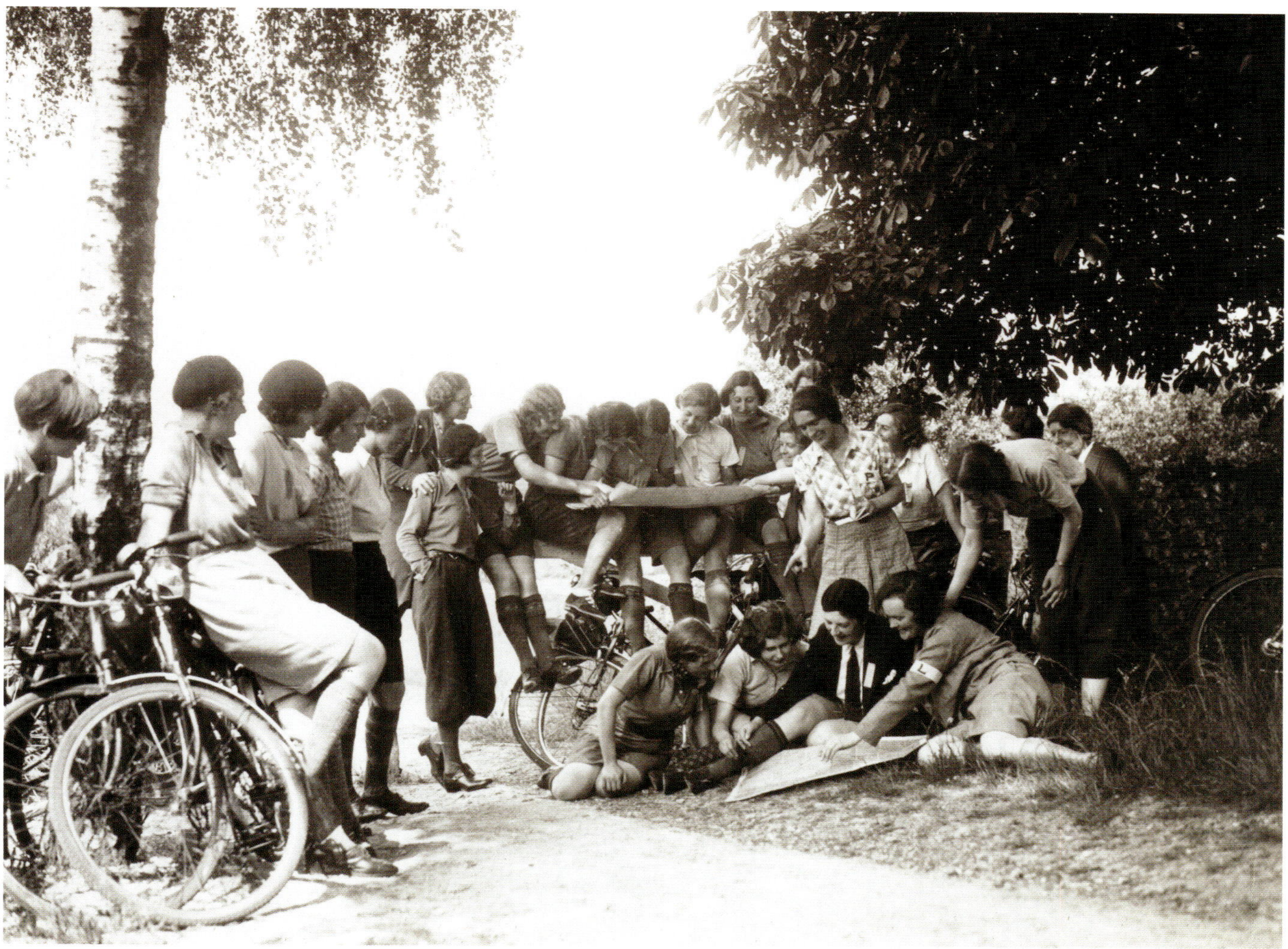

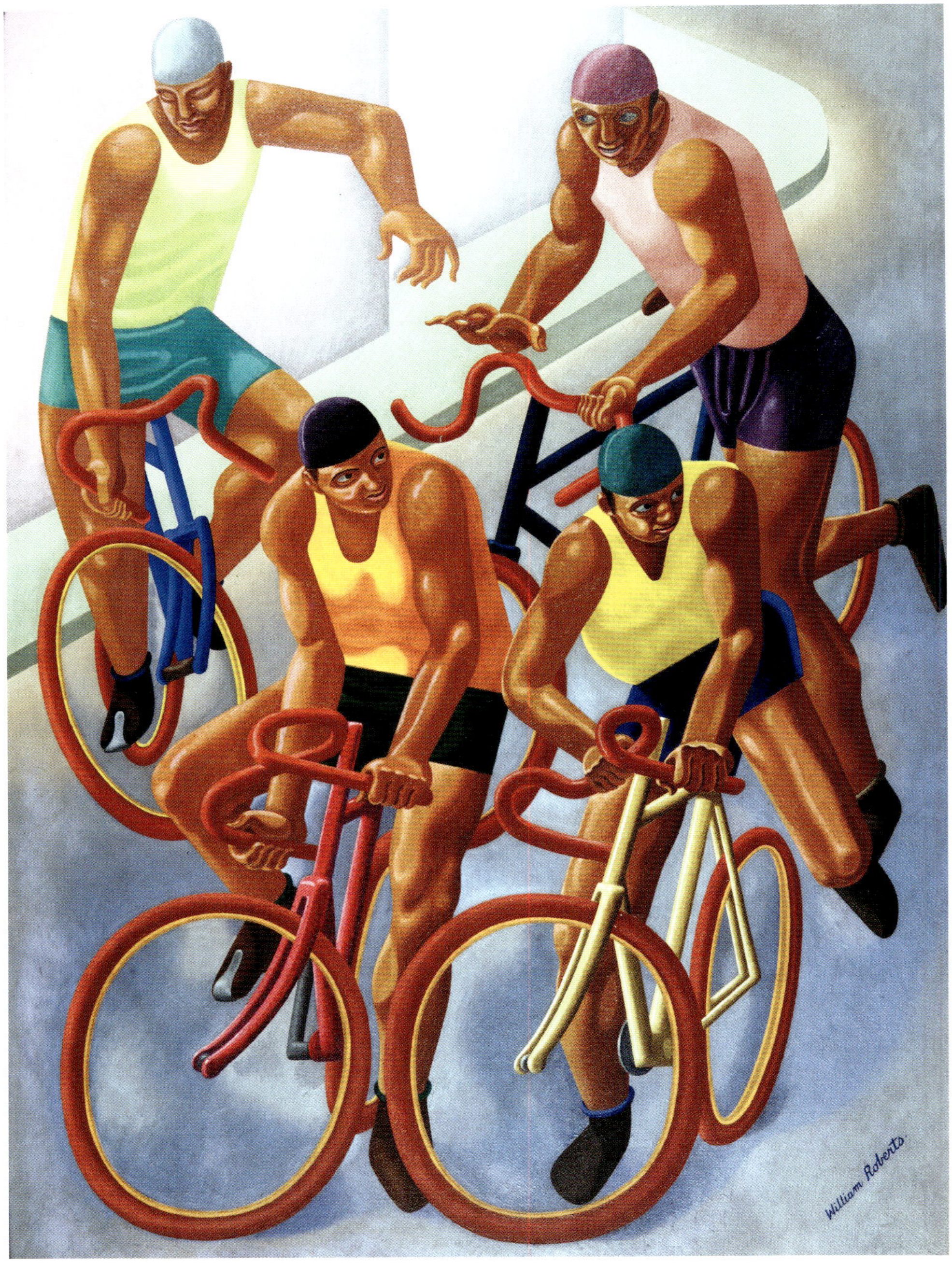

FIG 60

William Roberts

Les Routiers 1931 (cat. 30)

There were legal restrictions on road racing in Britain, which may be why Roberts gave this painting of cyclists a French title. For all the popularity of cycling as a mass leisure pursuit in Britain, the sleek, muscular body of the racing cyclist was something more associated with continental Europe.

Tour de France, then as now an event which was capable of gripping the entire nation. The French title may also be a reflection of the restrictions placed on road racing in England. This was among the first of Roberts' paintings of outdoor leisure; he may well have learnt something from the French artist Fernand Léger in his tubular simplification of the figure, but Roberts was well ahead of him in seizing on the potential of swimmers and cyclists as symbols of a more proletarian involvement in modern life.

Huge groups of walkers and cyclists were able to enjoy themselves all the more on country roads where a passing car was still a rarity (fig. 61; cat. 73). Motor cycles, priced at around £50–£100, were especially popular during the 1920s. Numbers peaked in 1930, owing partly to the increase in car ownership, from around 100,000 in 1919 to two million by 1939 (fig. 62; cat. 68; and fig. 63; cat. 48).[29] Allen's *The Caravan* (fig. 64; cat. 2), depicting a

FIG 61

Cyclists studying maps before proceeding from Box Hill 15 April 1938 (cat. 73)

The growth of practical skills like map-reading was one of the positive off-shoots of the outdoor movement. In a photo such as this, the activity also appears as a metaphor for freedom and self-determination.

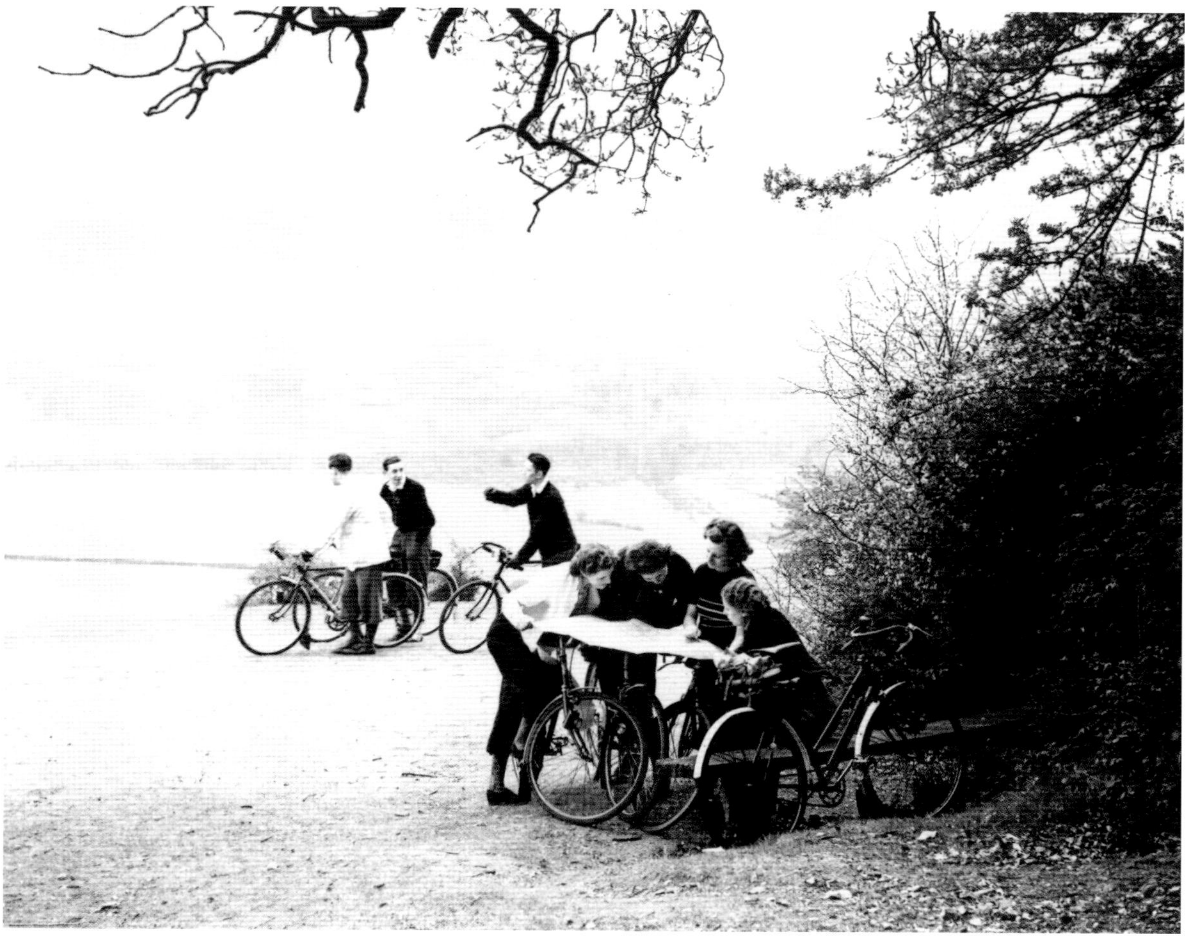

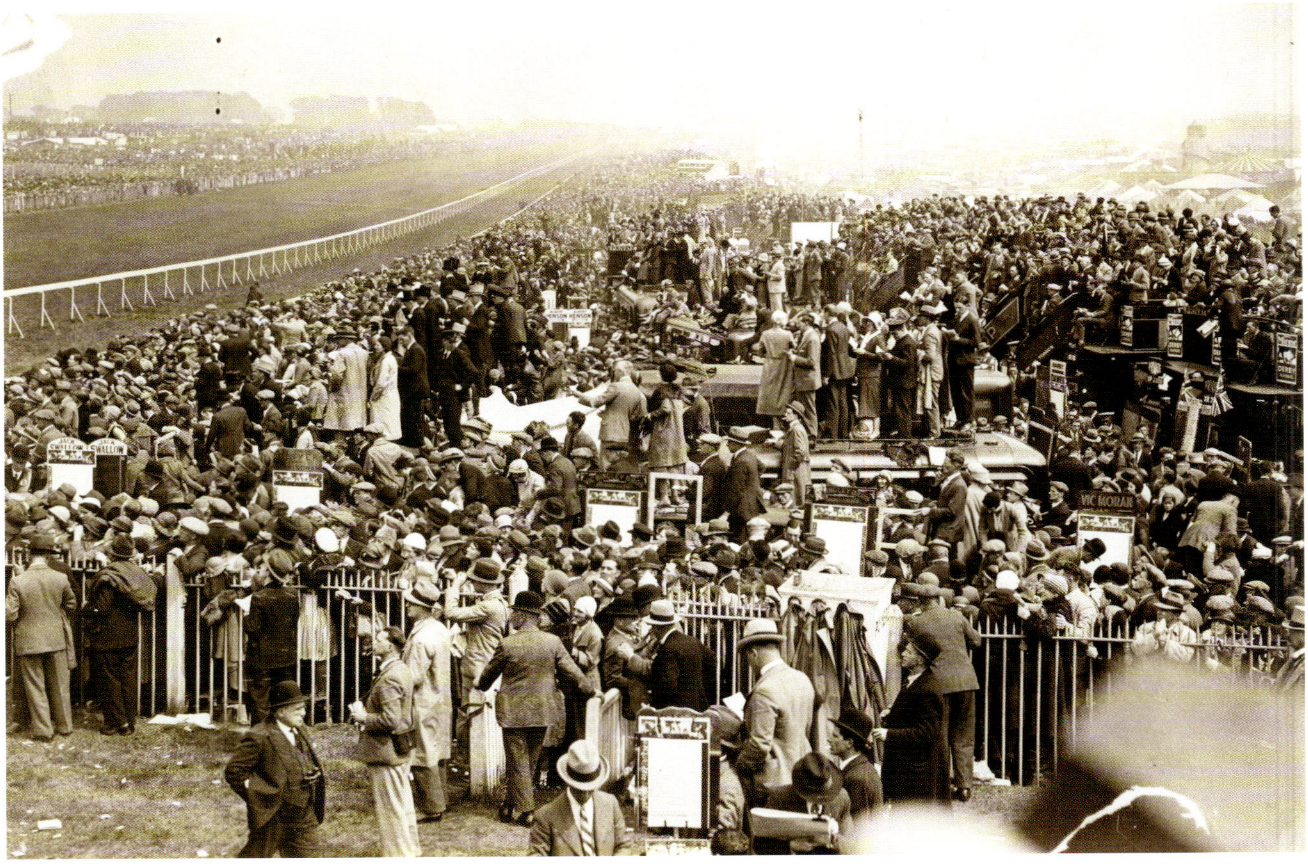

FIG 62

Epsom Racecourse. Derby Day. Finish of the course 2 June 1932 (cat. 68)

Derby Day continued to be one of the great summer outings for Londoners. As the thirties advanced, punters arrived increasingly by car, as well as by the myriad of special buses and trains.

FIG 63

Caravan by water 23 June 1934 (cat. 48)

The car enabled the lucky few to get away from it all and bring their music and their china with them. Membership of the Caravan Club mushroomed during the early 1930s.

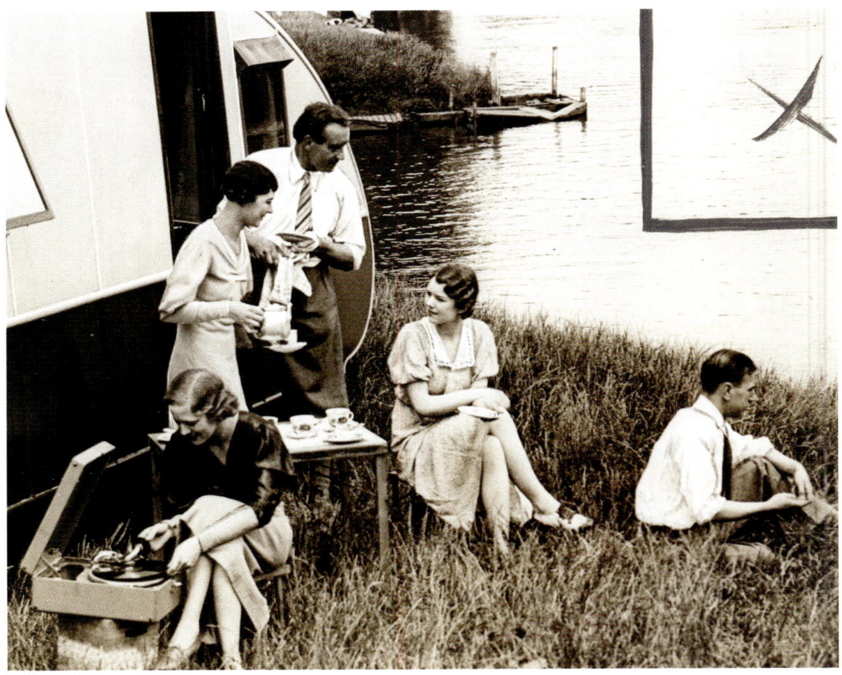

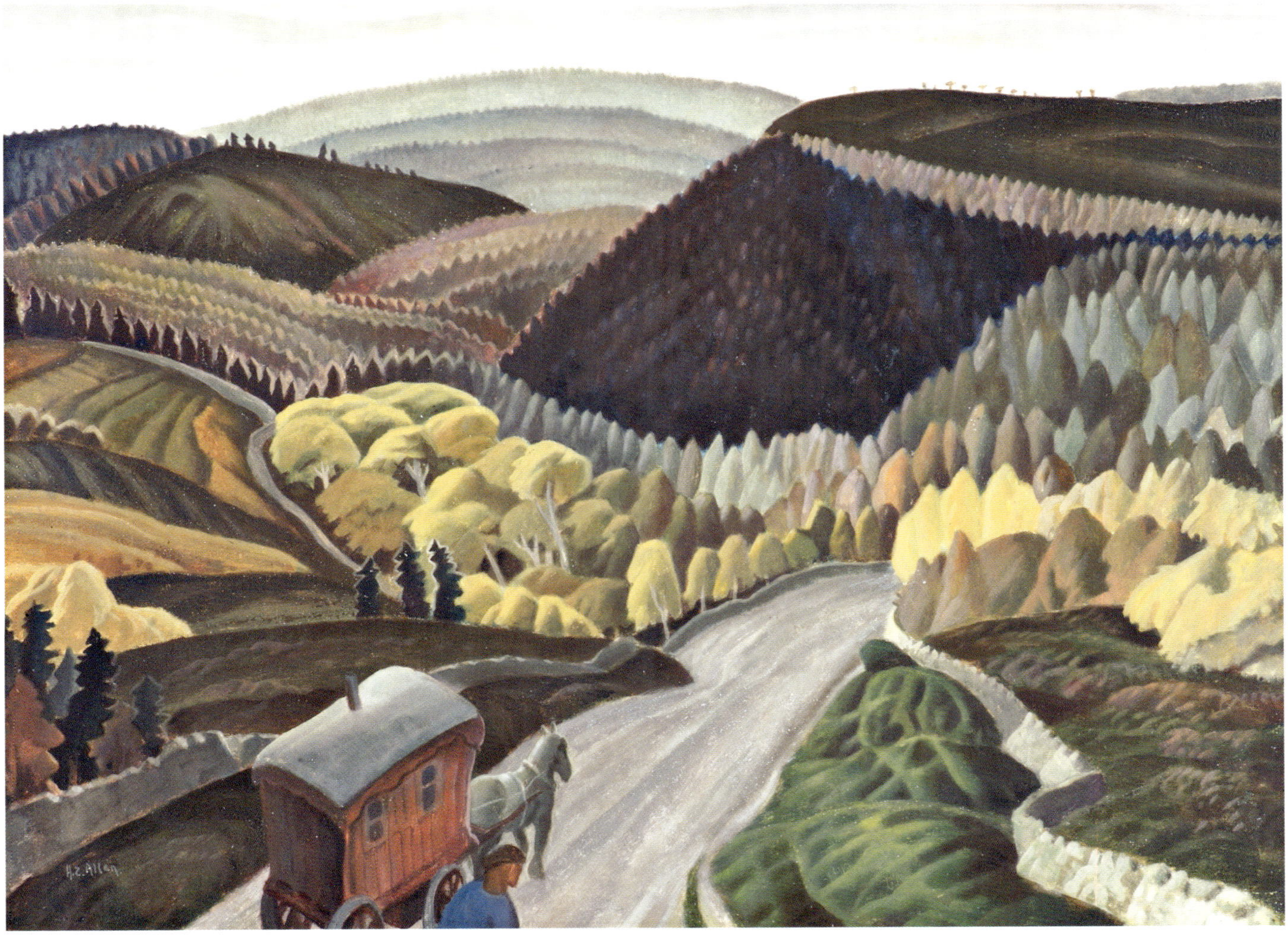

FIG 64

Harry Epworth Allen

The Caravan 1935 (cat. 2)

To Allen the beauties of what he described as 'the Derbyshire hill country' are timeless and can still be enjoyed in an old-fashioned way. For others, the land of the Peak District, sandwiched between the great population centres of Manchester and Sheffield, was one where access to the countryside had become highly contentious.

wooden horse-drawn vehicle, is a work full of nostalgia for a slower, simpler style of travel. Such things came to be appreciated all the more when motorised forms of transport were signalling their disappearance. Instead of the caravan's long, meandering route through the landscape, the motor car offered a compressed experience of time and space.

The picnic is the image par excellence of middle-class conquest of the countryside. All possible comforts are transported from home to the chosen location, effectively to minimise the sense of dislocation; clothes are often those of an elegant suburban garden party, rather than the hikers' khaki shorts (figs. 65, 66; cat. 24). Though London Transport' s advertising might encourage passengers to travel by rail or tube, it was becoming more and more likely that a car would be the prerequisite for the realisation of these fresh-air feasts (fig. 67; cat. 47). The picnic box which features

FIG 65

E. Dean

Little Orme Picnic 1935

Little Orme, on the north Wales coast at Llandudno, was a favourite holiday resort for the suburban middle classes from Liverpool, Manchester and the Wirral. Here, all the finer points of etiquette have been transported to the clifftop location, from the crisp collar and tie, to the flourish accompanying the offer of the sandwich plate.

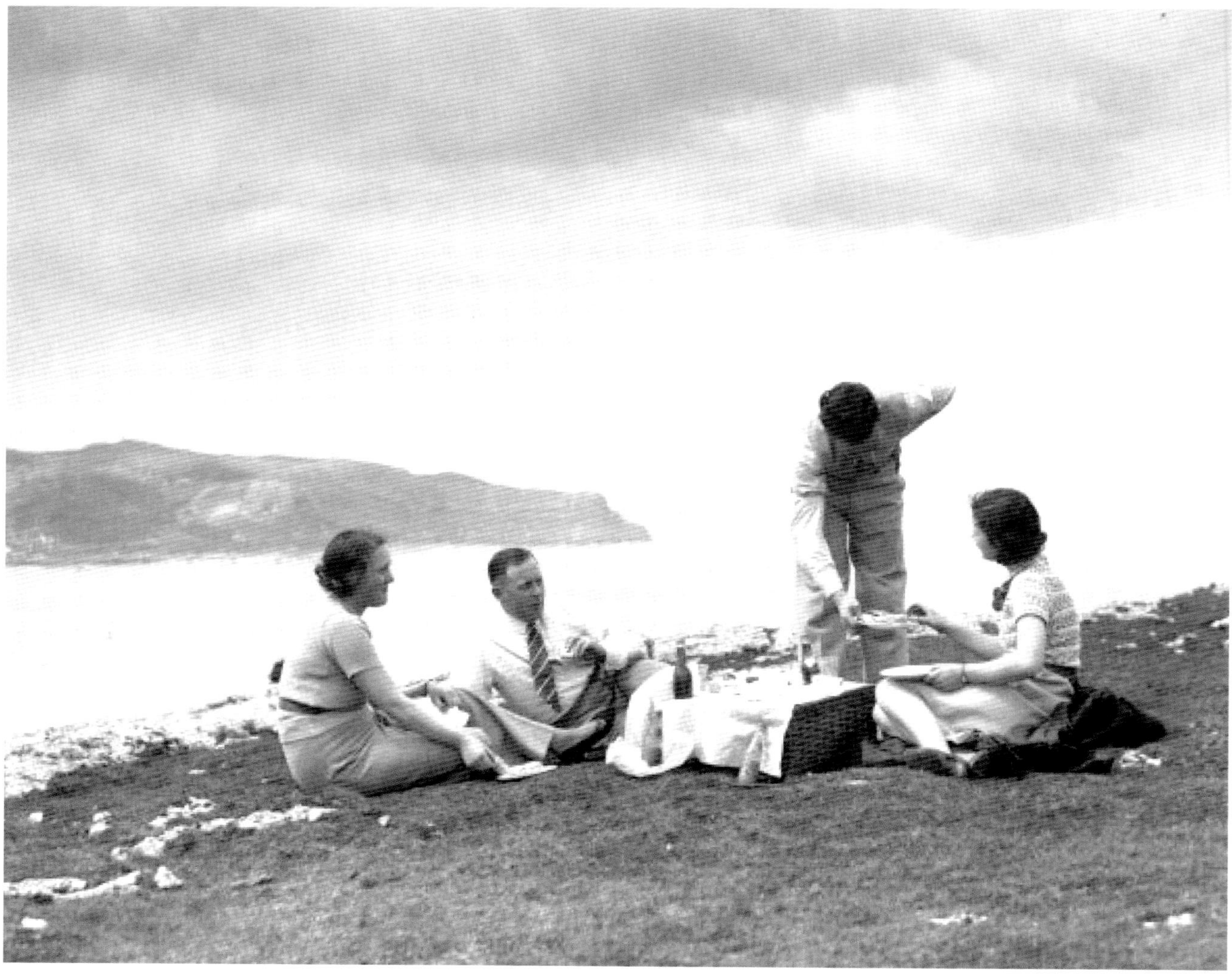

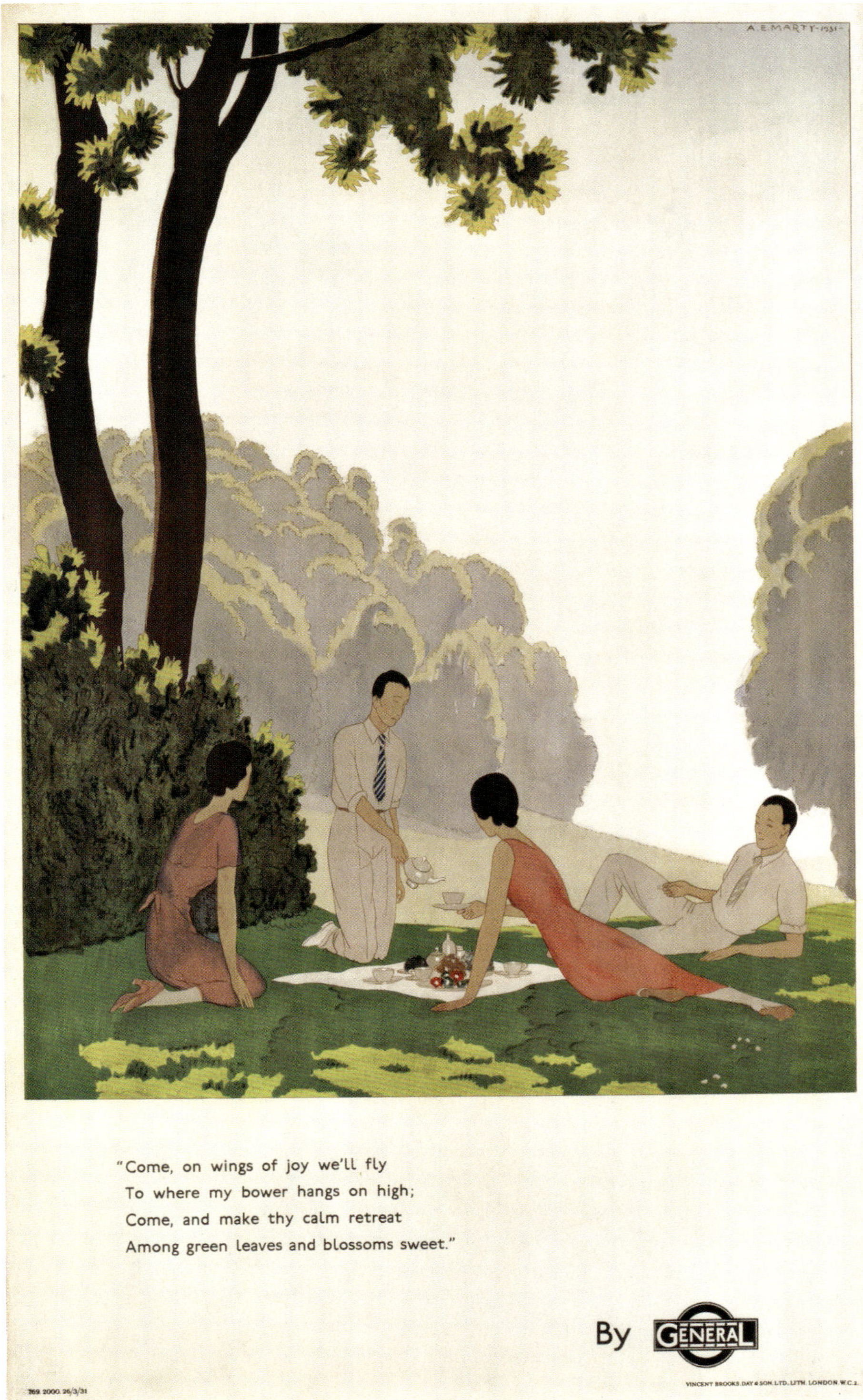

FIG 66

André-Edouard Marty
Picnic: 'Come on wings of joy we'll fly' 1931
(cat. 24)

The French illustrator Marty gives an air of refinement and elegance to a simple picnic. The experiment of using continental designers was, in the event, short-lived and these exquisite fantasies replaced by something more robust.

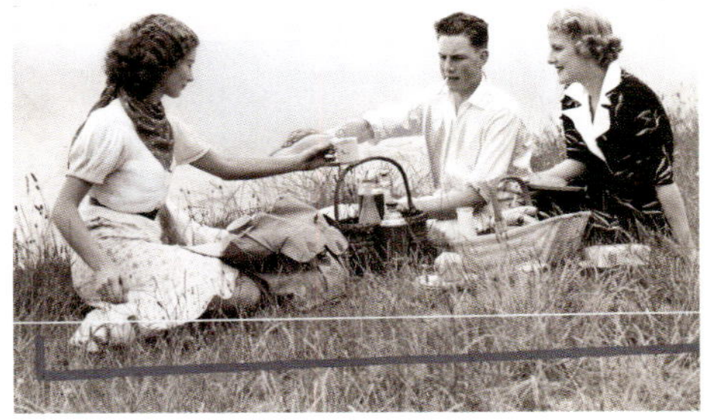

FIG 67

Young man with two women on a picnic
September 1939 (cat. 47)

An intriguing triangle, in which the young man, accompanied perhaps by his mother and his sister (or maybe his intended) takes charge of the serving of tea; is he asserting his masculinity by this, or is the usual assignation of gender roles suspended in the open-air setting?

prominently in Harold Williamson's 1938 painting is itself a recent innovation, making use of the new unbreakable plastics (fig. 68; cat. 41). In design and technology, it is emblematic of the commodification overtaking even the most simple pleasures. The small cheap basket holding fruit in Fleetwood-Walker's *Amity* (fig. 69; cat. 11) only superficially maintains the veneer of innocence Williamson so decorously preserves; the ripe apples appear to signal a drama of sexual tension, but one which, with a diffident youth and a self-possessed girl, will come to nothing. Fleetwood-Walker's main exhibit at the Royal Academy the previous year was *The Family*, in effect a self-portrait with his wife and two young sons (fig. 70; cat. 10). Until the First World War, images of family holidays or days out almost invariably meant the seaside. Here a younger generation are not simply passing the time, but being introduced to the pleasures – and the benefits – of days spent in the open air.

FIG 68

Harold Williamson
Picnic 1938 (cat. 41)

Against a background of stylised foliage, the modern drama of a picnic unfolds, each player making a distinctive contribution. The smart modern picnic set, like the impeccably parted hair, shows how, even for such an impromptu meal, decorum is rigidly maintained.

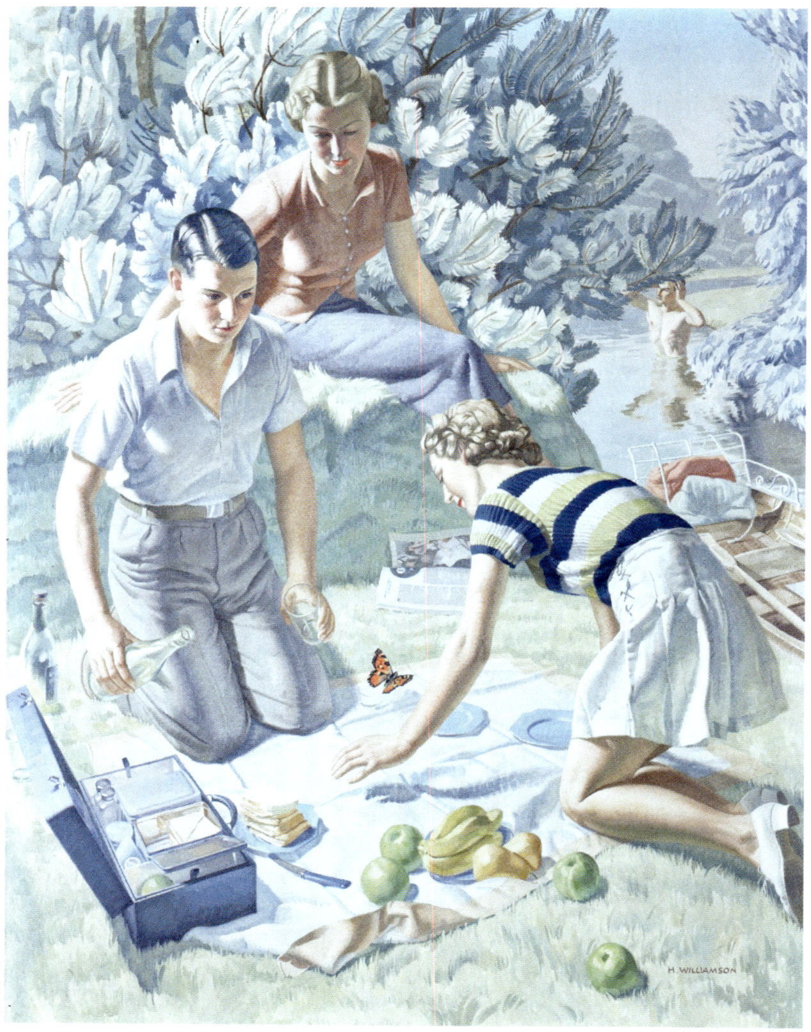

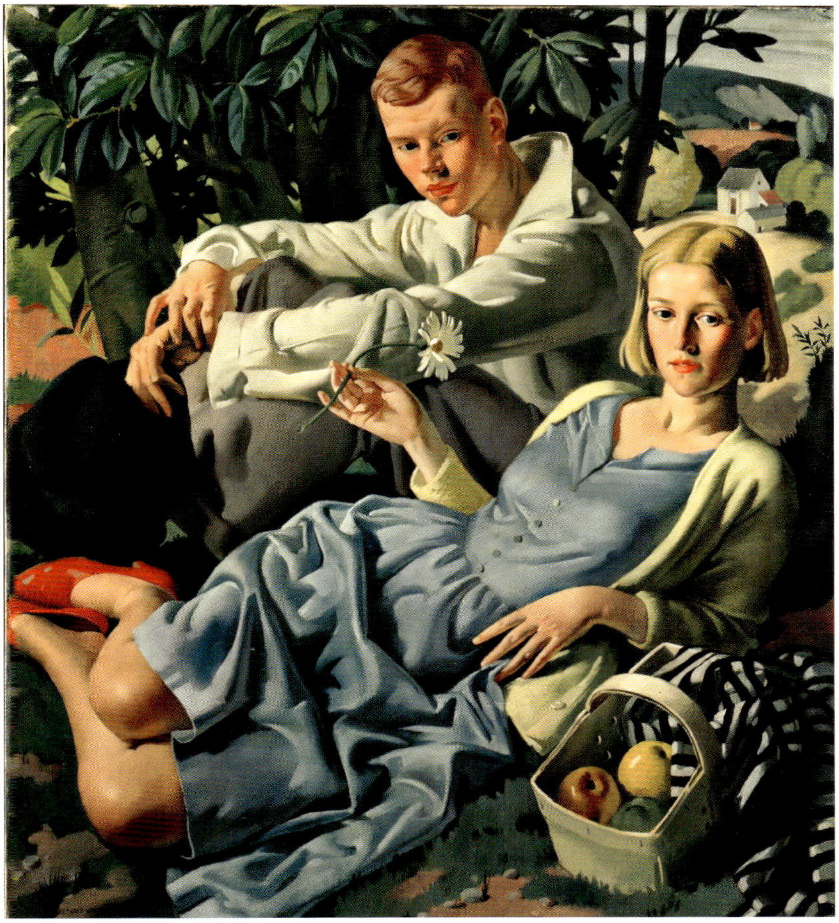

FIG 69

Bernard Fleetwood-Walker

Amity 1933 (cat. 11)

The image of the happy courting couple receives an unexpected twist in this painting, as the girl, provocatively toying with a daisy, seems to make herself available to anyone but the boy she is with.

FIG 70

Bernard Fleetwood-Walker

The Family 1932 (cat. 10)

Fleetwood-Walker depicts his own family in this group portrait, part of whose intriguing effect lies in the blend of the informality of the setting and the highly stylised rendition of the figures.

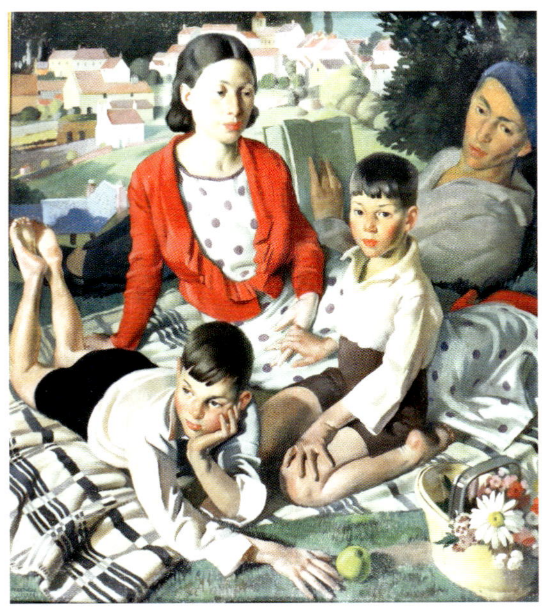

In 1936 Fleetwood-Walker completed another chapter in what almost had the makings of an autobiography in paint, *The Family at Polperro* (fig. 71; cat. 12). If he intended to advertise his talents as a portrait painter, then his campaign of self-publicity was already reaping rewards, since in 1935 he had been able to exhibit *Mr and Mrs Robert Butler and their Daughters*, a large group posed in a woodland glade.[30] Although working in the highly traditional field of portraiture, Fleetwood-Walker seems consistently to have used outdoor settings to add an air of informality and contemporaneity to his work, to differentiate it from the cavernous drawing rooms so often favoured by Sargeant and his Edwardian followers.

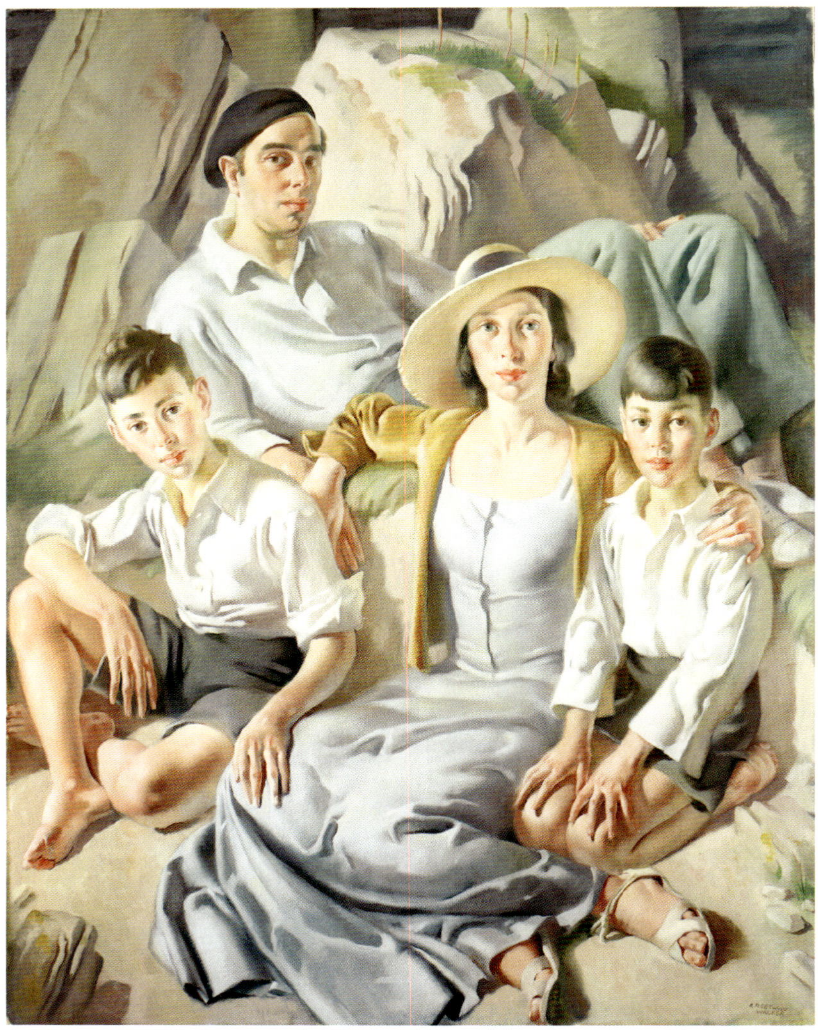

FIG 71

Bernard Fleetwood-Walker

The Family at Polperro 1934–36 (cat. 12)

In the 1936 Royal Academy, this large painting was rather overshadowed by Fleetwood-Walker's painting of two nudes. It was much more than a makeweight, however, showing the artist attempting a marriage of portrait and modern subject-picture.

Holidays

Cornwall, more than any other part of Britain, had a particular association with open-air painting which dated back to the 1880s and the first espousal of Impressionist principles by British artists. While the founder of the 'Newlyn School', Stanhope Forbes, had chosen subjects from the working life of the local community, later generations of artists had concentrated more on leisure. Cornwall's beaches, coves and cliffs had become familiar to London exhibition audiences through a succession of painters, including Henry Tuke, Laura Knight, Harold Harvey and Dod and Ernest Procter (fig. 72; cat. 19).[31] Ernest Procter went to Newlyn from Northumberland in 1907 to study with Forbes. He remained in the south-west (at least for part

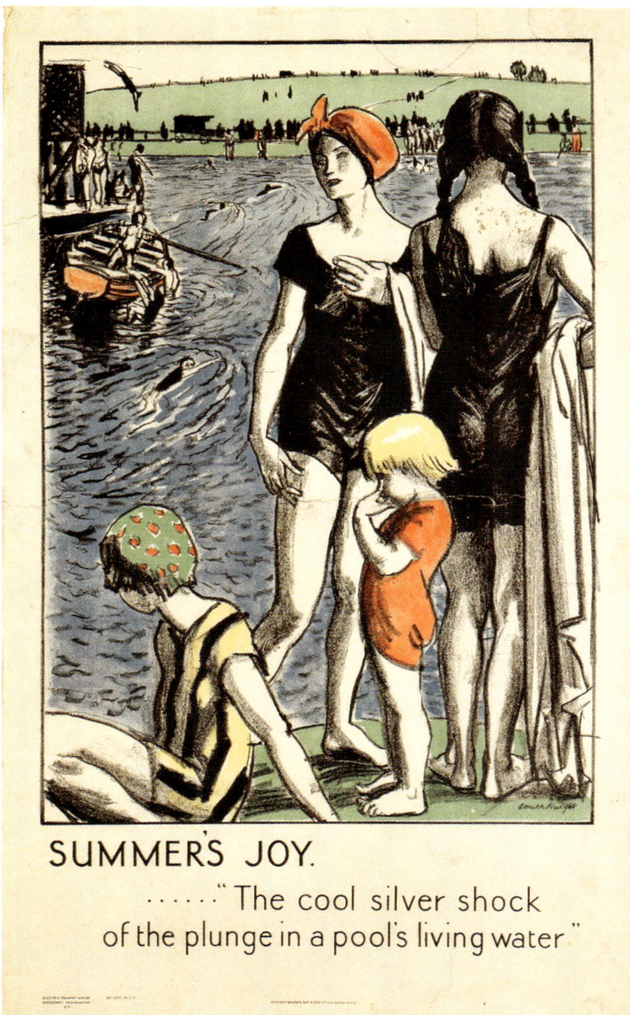

FIG 72

Laura Knight
Summer's Joy 1921 (cat. 19)
These statuesque bathers still display the female virtues of modesty and motherhood, to counter any sense they may be going too far along the route of physical liberation.

of the year), and after the war produced a number of lively canvasses depicting popular amusements. *Summer Holidays* (fig. 73; cat. 27) is the last and also the largest; the beaches which had earlier been celebrated as the haunt of sparsely scattered paddlers are now overrun by an almost bacchanalian profusion of bodies. Nonetheless, the cottages on the skyline reinforce the suggestion that the chaos is part of what makes the scene enjoyable; this is still a homely, old-fashioned holiday compared to the quasi-industrial atmosphere of resorts like Blackpool (fig. 74).

Stanley Spencer's *Southwold* (fig. 75) is similarly nostalgic; typically for the artist, the location is overlaid with personal associations. He first visited the Suffolk seaside village in 1924 while courting his first wife, Hilda Carline. When he visited again in 1937, following the collapse of his second marriage, it was to recapture some of his earlier feelings. The shelving pebbly

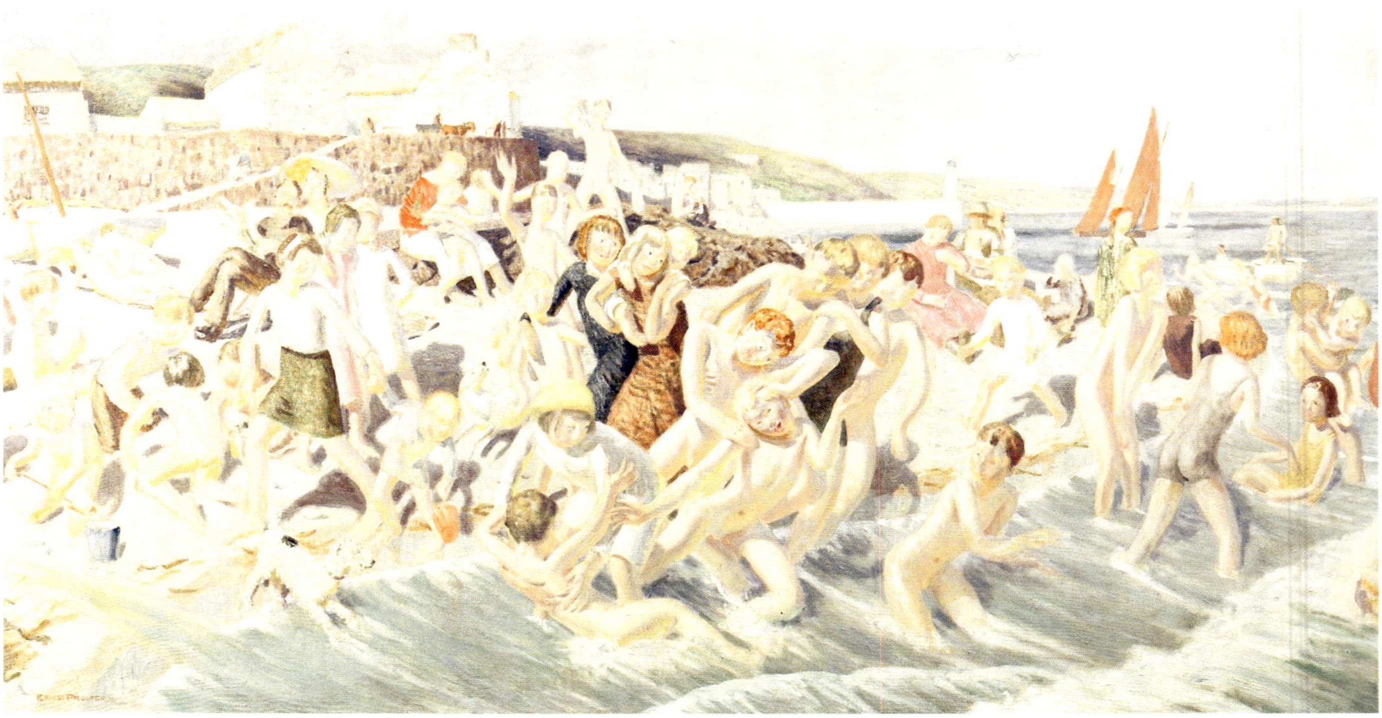

FIG 73

Ernest Procter

Summer Holidays 1934 (cat. 27)

Procter captures the sense of exhilaration and sheer physical abandon of the summer holiday. The break was savoured all the more when it was likely that for one week only during the year could a family travel together away from home.

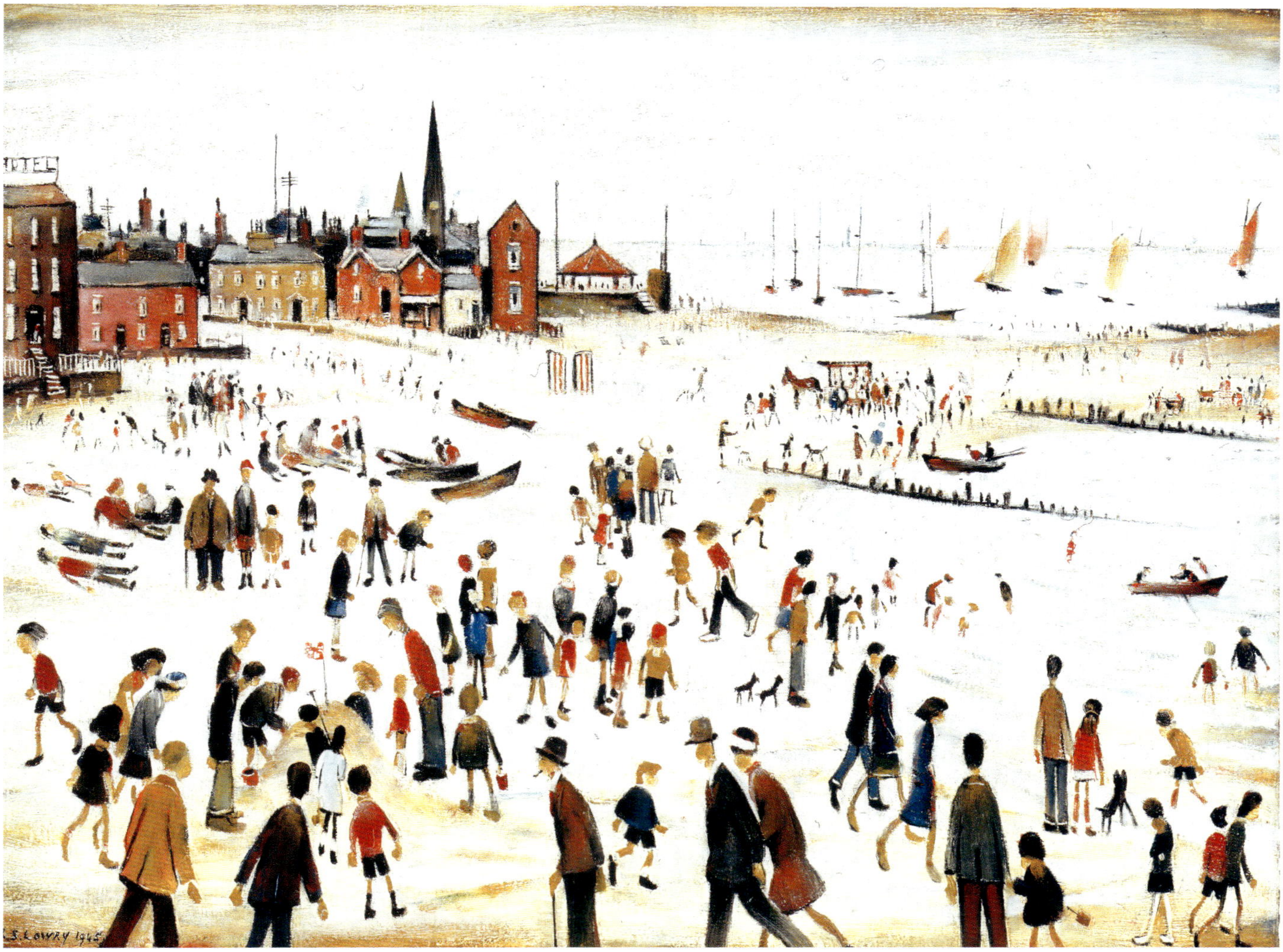

FIG 74

Lawrence Stephen Lowry
Beach Scene, Lancashire 1945

As a child, Lowry took regular family holidays at the more genteel Lancashire resort of Lytham St Anne's, rather than Blackpool. Here, he captures a sense of aimlessness and unfamiliarity; some people settle into an activity, but more are pacing to and fro, their bodies well covered, unable to yield fully to the pleasures the beach offers.

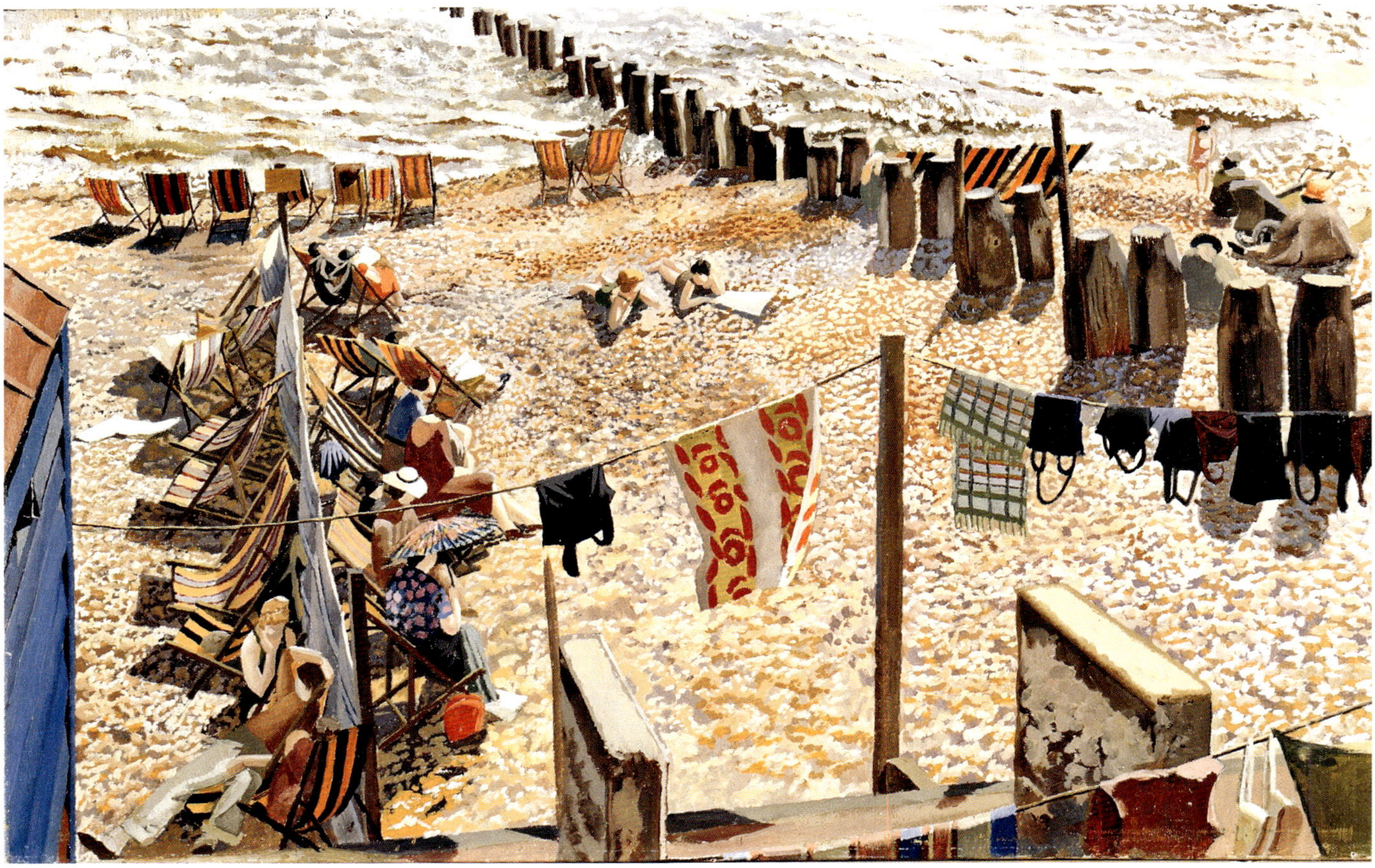

FIG 75

Stanley Spencer
Southwold 1937

The sheer brilliance of the dazzling sunshine in this painting is one aspect of its modernity. So too is the highly informal, almost random placement of the elements, suggesting Spencer wanted to portray the seaside very much as part of contemporary life, rather than as a well-worn, traditional type of recreation.

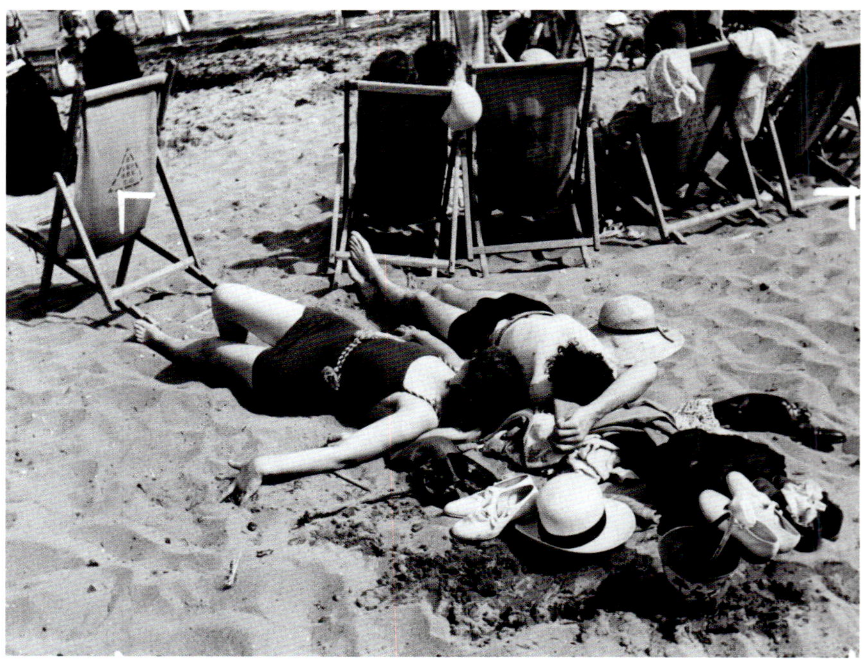

FIG 76

Sunbathing in the Sand 4 July 1936 (cat. 44)

The photographer captured the contrasting postures of the seated deckchair users and the sprawled sunbathers, but the crop marks reveal it was the latter that the editor chose to highlight.

beach, impromptu clothes line and tightly packed deckchairs arranged for protection from either wind or sun emphasise a personal experience of a specific place. Even the breakwater with its pairs of wooden stumps proclaims a quirky individuality, which can only be fully understood as a type of resistance to the prevailing trend of the periodic mass invasion of other East Anglian beaches such as Southend (fig. 76; cat. 44). Aberystwyth, like many other seaside towns, used a guarantee of sun as a selling point, along with the promise of acres of empty sand (fig. 77). Laura Knight was capable of updating her beach scenes to incorporate the more modern, athletic woman, and soon found echoes in the images captured by the press photographers. (figs. 78, 79; cats. 20, 49)

Edward Bawden's *By the Sea* (fig. 80), depicting one of the smaller resorts on the same stretch of coast (probably Walton-on-the-Naze), was

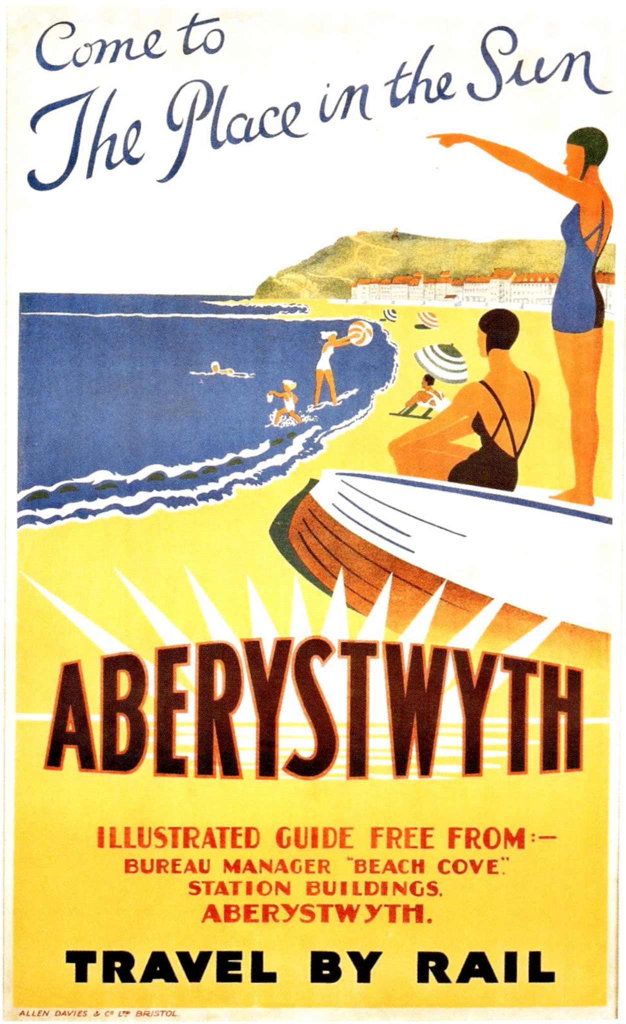

FIG 77

Come to The Place in the Sun. Aberystwyth
ca. 1938
Colour poster
Ceredigion Museum, Aberystwyth

Aberystwyth had been a popular holiday resort since Victorian times. In the 1930s, its advertising concentrated on the recent obsessions of sunshine, sleek bodies and acres of golden sand.

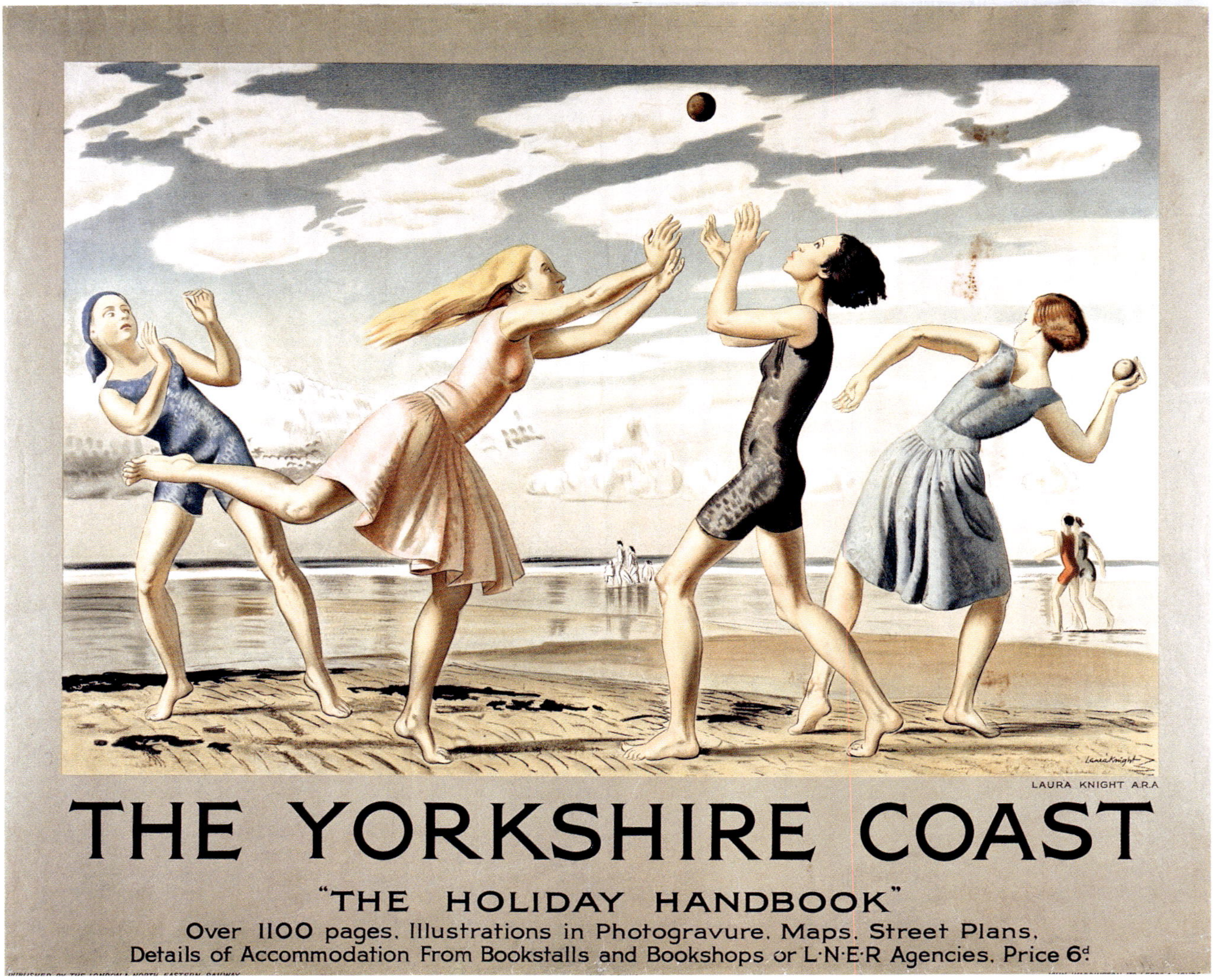

FIG 78

Laura Knight

The Yorkshire Coast c. 1929 (cat. 20)

Surely one of Knight's most startlingly modern images, portraying an almost unprecedented female physicality.

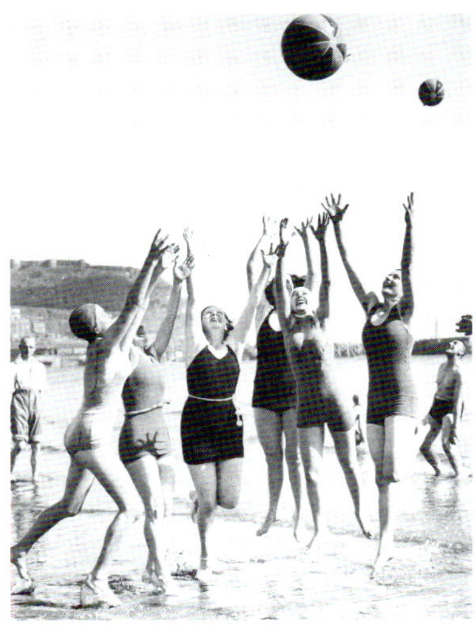

FIG 79

Holidays on the Beach 13 October 1937 (cat. 49)

A late-season photo on a similar theme to Knight's earlier poster. The active, energetic woman is, momentarily at least, in possession of her own destiny.

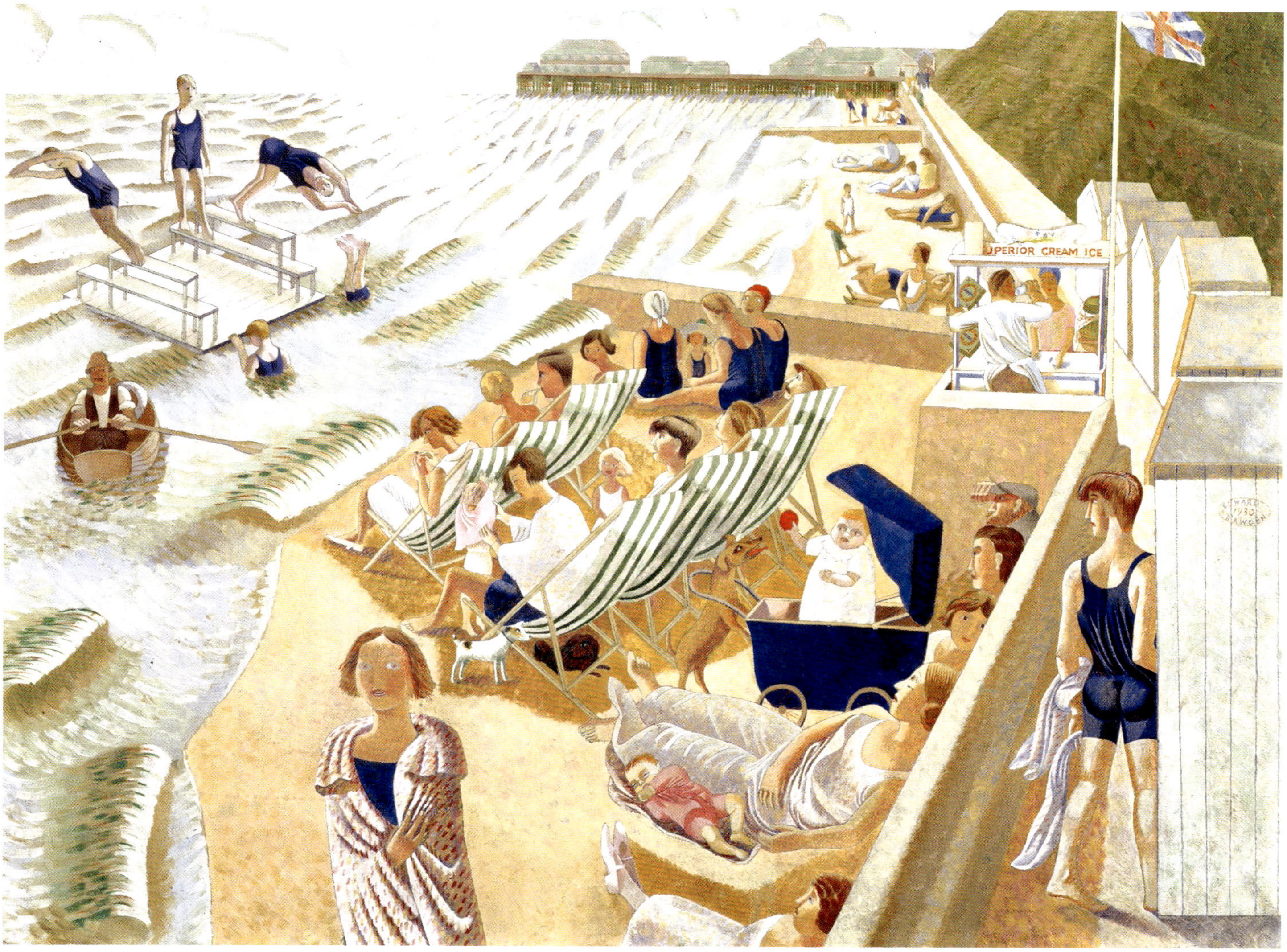

FIG 80

Edward Bawden

By the Sea 1929–30

Bawden produced a series of small engravings of seaside subjects in the late twenties. This early painting seems to grow out of that work, contrasting the rather severe architecture with the quirky individuality of the bathers.

painted very early in his career, around 1929–30. It is full of wry humour in its observation of the people – and dogs – on the beach; the angularity of the setting, the sea wall, diving platform and distant pier, is somehow unsympathetic to this human comedy (see also fig. 81). Whatever tensions Bawden may perceive in the changing nature of the seaside holiday is kept well at bay in the work of Maxwell Armfield and Joseph Southall (figs. 82, 83; cats. 6, 36). The sheer intensity of colour achieved through their use of tempera adds another level of unreality to these idealised images. Armfield's *At the Seaside* (fig. 84; cat. 7) is in some respects another fantasy picture, with the mother and children able to enjoy a secluded beach to themselves. The boy with the camera adds an element of modernity which is highly self-conscious; he may look like a new recruit for the snapshot generation, but his subject is posing with her towel draped like a classical statue (this was a

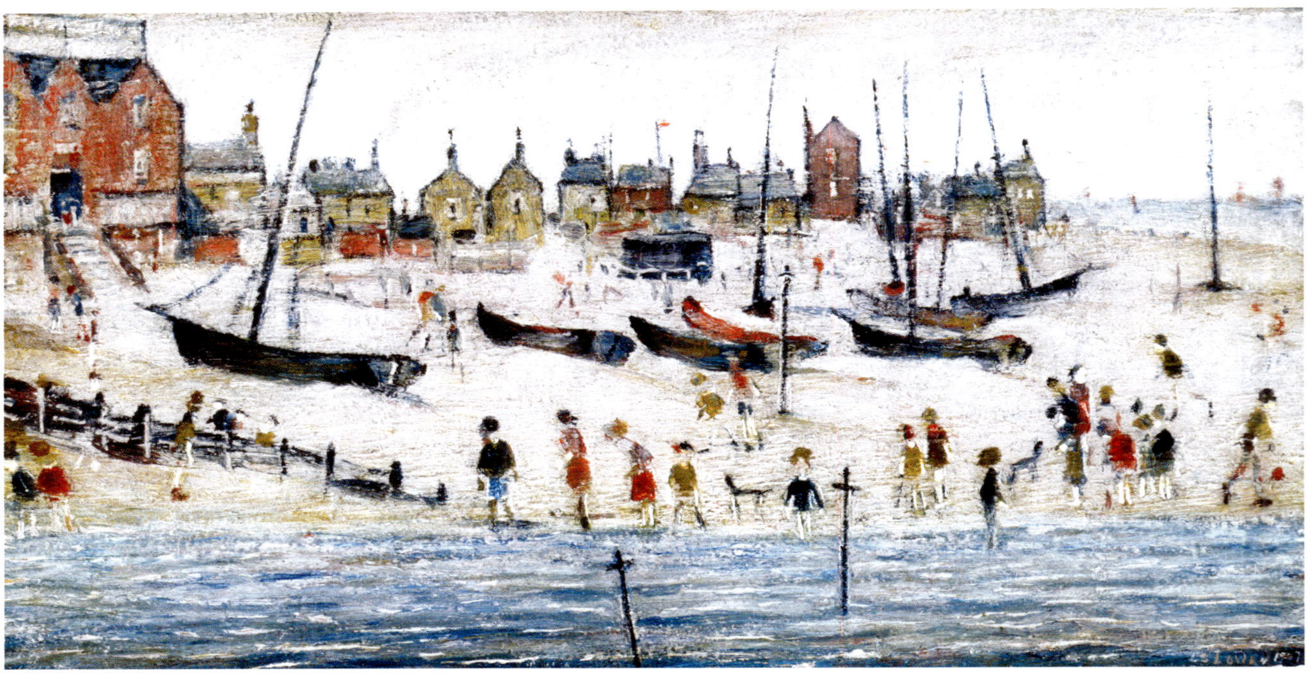

FIG 81

Lawrence Stephen Lowry
Deal Sands 1947

With scattered groups of children rather tentatively approaching the water, Lowry seems to want to recapture in this scene something of the experience of his own childhood, when a visit to the seaside was still an exciting novelty.

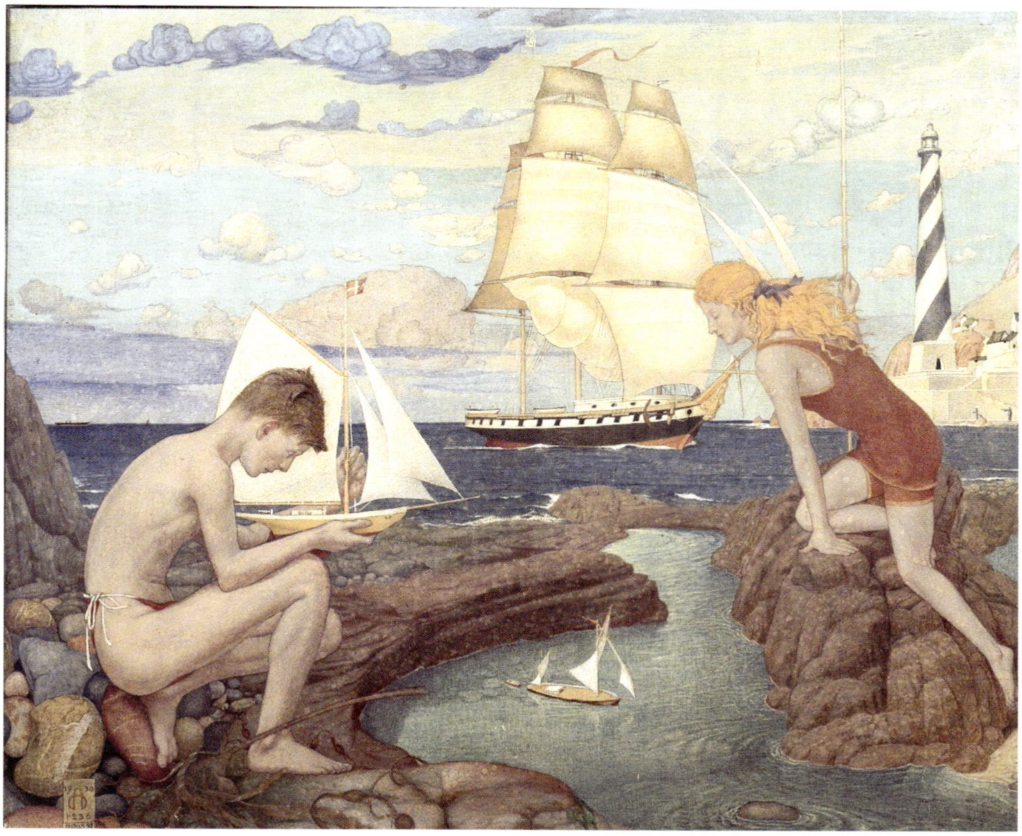

FIG 82

Maxwell Armfield

I Saw Three Ships 1930 (cat. 6)

Through the familiar imagery of seaside pleasures, Armfield creates a wistful commentary on the passing of youth, as the comfort of childish play gives way to the greater demands of adult seafaring.

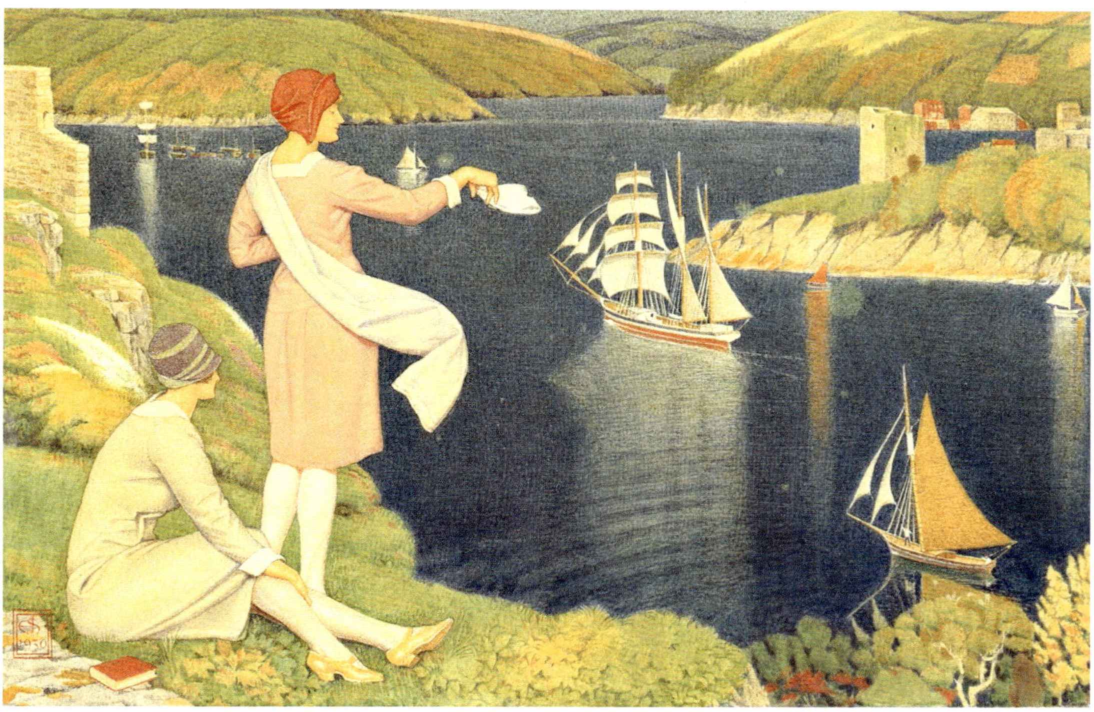

FIG 83

Joseph Southall

The Return 1930 (cat. 36)

Yachting was a recreation which remained the preserve of the well-to-do. Yet it seemed to project a seductive simplicity, a naturalness relying on technologies as old as European civilization itself.

strategy not without its parallels in press photography; fig. 85; cat. 46). Harold Williamson seems to have a similar idea in mind in his 1935 painting, *Summer Morning* (fig. 86); a print based on the pose of the female figure was entitled 'Modern Venus'.[32]

The provision of holidays with pay was one of the great social causes of the 1930s. It has been estimated that at the time of the passing of legislation in 1938, only 28% of the national workforce had been granted this right.[33] There were regional variations, with around 50% in London, according to a survey published in 1935. More extensive provision was neither immediate, nor universal and in many instances held up by the outbreak of war in 1939. A Saturday morning shift was still the norm in many industries; shop staff, who worked all day on Saturdays, had been granted a weekday half-day during the 1920s. There remained some ambivalence over exactly what was

FIG 84

Maxwell Armfield

At the Seaside 1932 (cat. 7)

The back-to-nature attitude of the girl playing with the seagulls, the classical pose of the mother and the up-to-the minute boy photographer provide a highly complex and intriguing essay on the cultural meanings of the beach holiday.

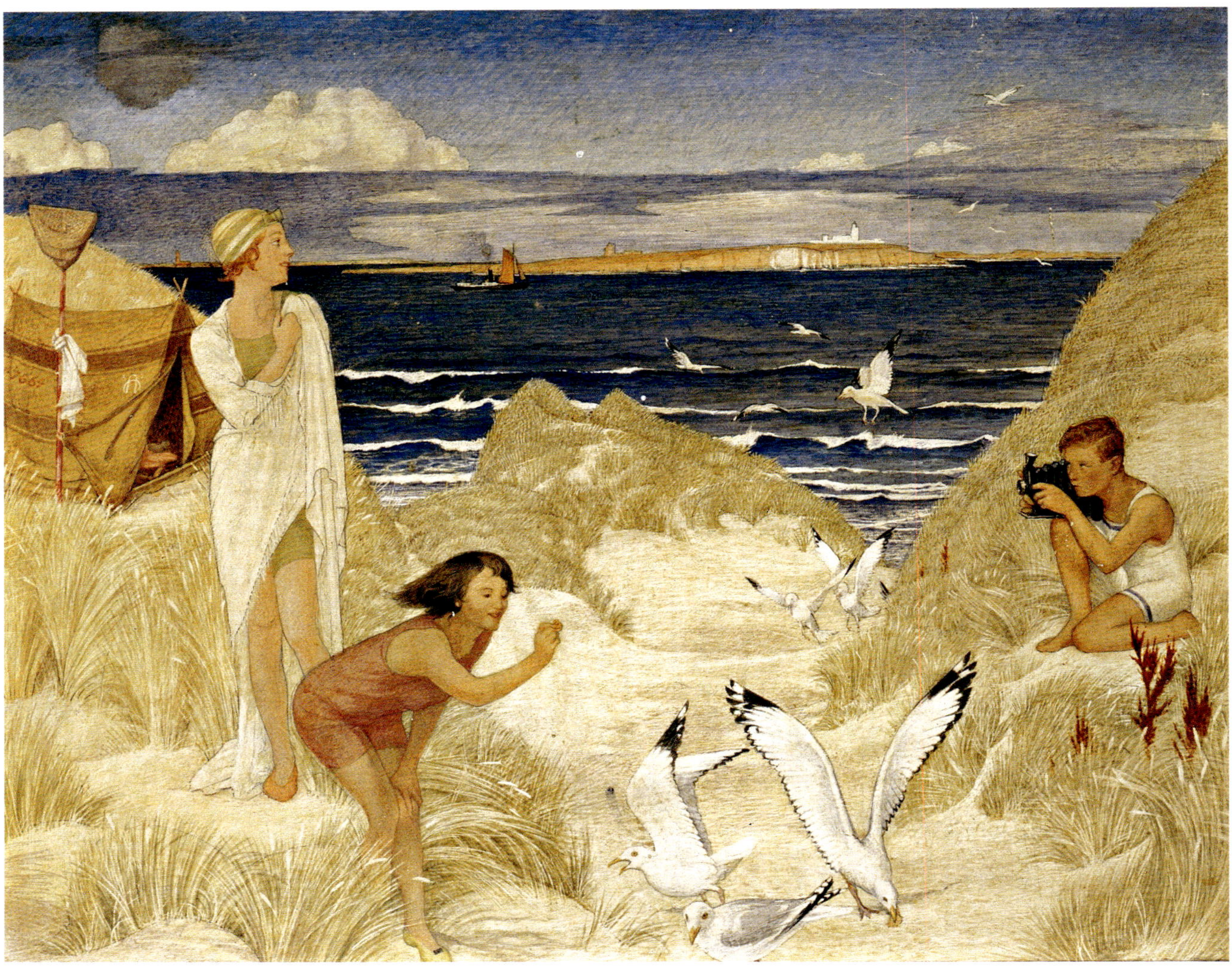

permissible on Sundays, and thus Bank holidays, especially the summer holiday on the first Monday in August, were events of major significance. Literally hundreds of trains brought day-trippers to Blackpool; Southend, Margate and Brighton were the favoured destinations for thousands of Londoners (figs. 87–90; cats. 52, 55, 15, 8).[34] Holiday camps existed before Butlins opened their first purpose-built facility at Skegness in 1937. They were either under canvas, or in other sorts of more or less temporary shelters. By the end of the decade, there were, according to one estimate, 30,00 places available each week. The poster advertising the camp at Clacton in Essex, opened in 1938, shows how the sophisticated visual and verbal techniques of sports photography and poetic quotations are being applied to the mass market (the central building is emblazoned with an adaptation of lines from Shakespeare's *A Midsummer Night's Dream*; fig. 91).

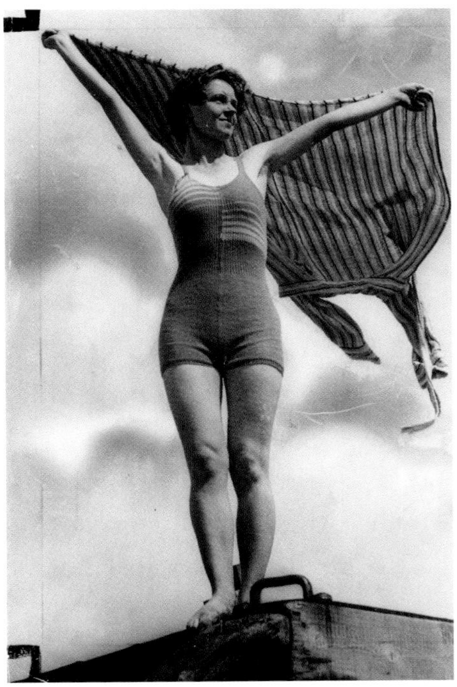

FIG 85

Holiday spirit at Barry Island 6 October 1937
cat. 46)

Printed with the caption, 'but the sea breezes at Barry Island bring health to the holiday makers, who, like this bather, make the most of them'.

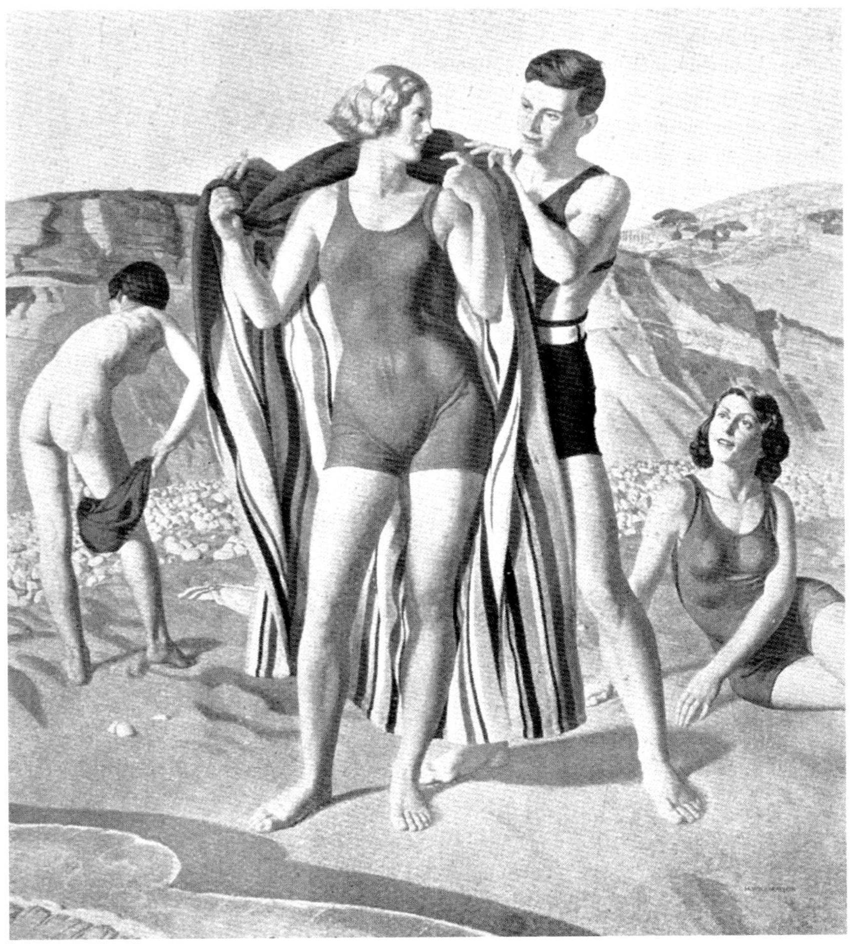

FIG 86

Harold Williamson
Summer Morning
(exhibited Royal Academy 1935)

Williamson's swimsuited female pays homage to Botticelli, a reference made more explicit in an etching based on the painting, which he entitled, 'Modern Venus'.

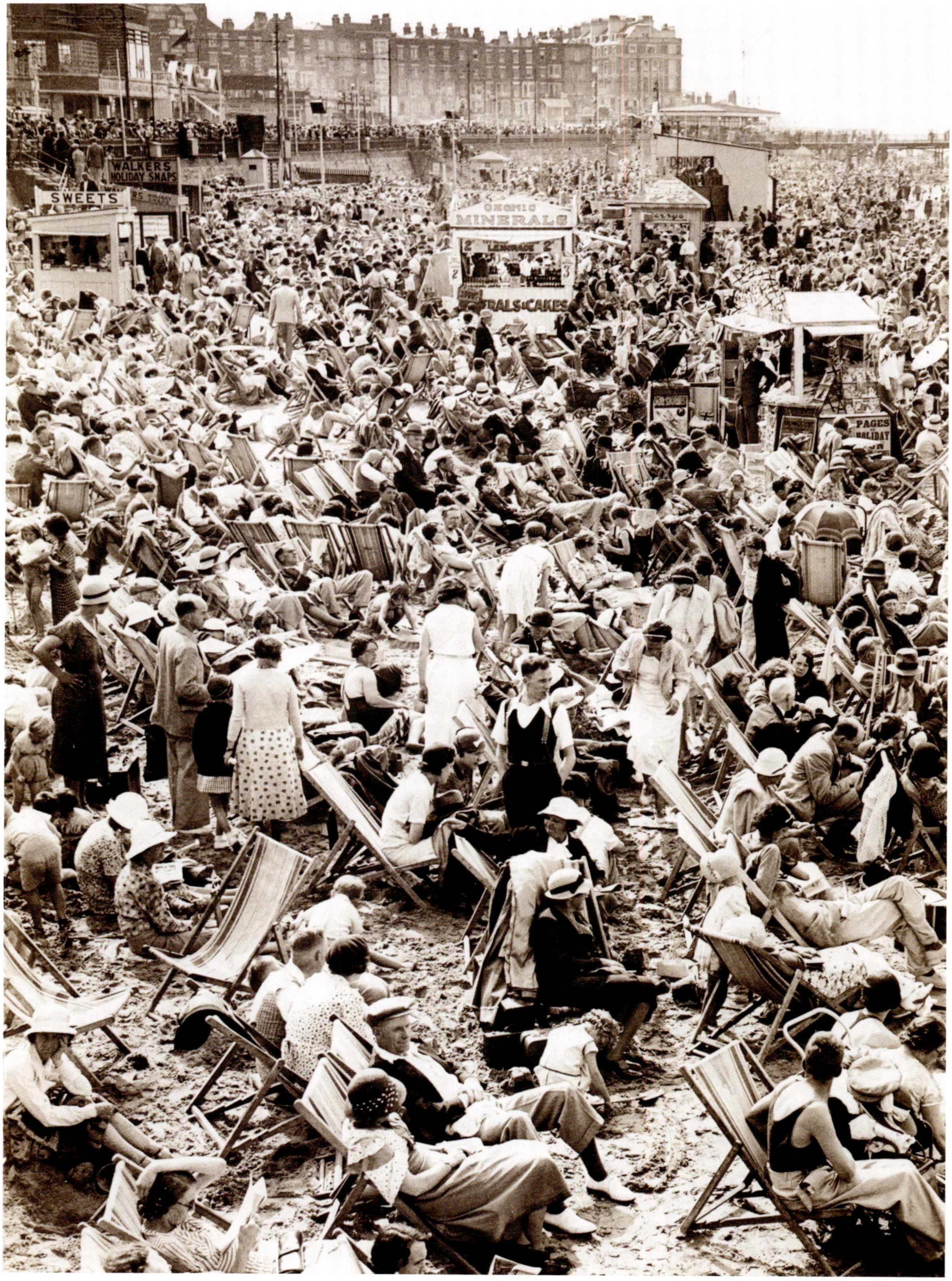
WALKERS
HOLIDAY SNAPS
SWEETS
MINERALS

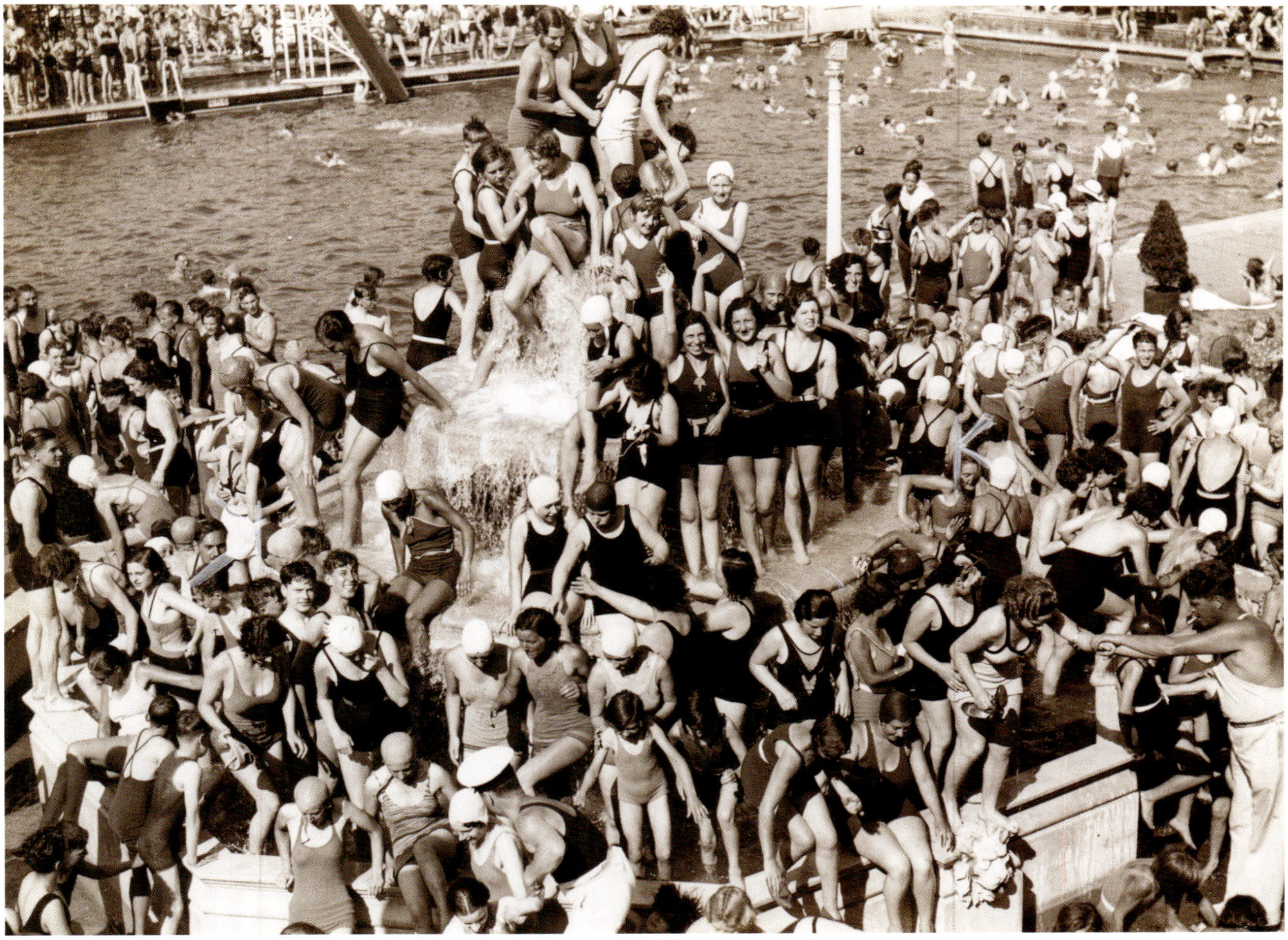

FIG 88

Sunday in the sun at the Enfield Pool
6 July 1934 (cat. 55)

The newspaper caption read: 'Part of the vast crowd at the Enfield pool yesterday. The baths were so full that many would-be swimmers were unable to even don their costumes.'

FIG 87

Margate 5 August 1935 (cat. 52)

A Bank Holiday view of Margate in 1935, to contrast with the more upbeat one of Brighton (fig. 9). Dozens of special coaches and trains brought the masses from London, but no overcrowding would deter them from enjoying the biggest holiday of the year.

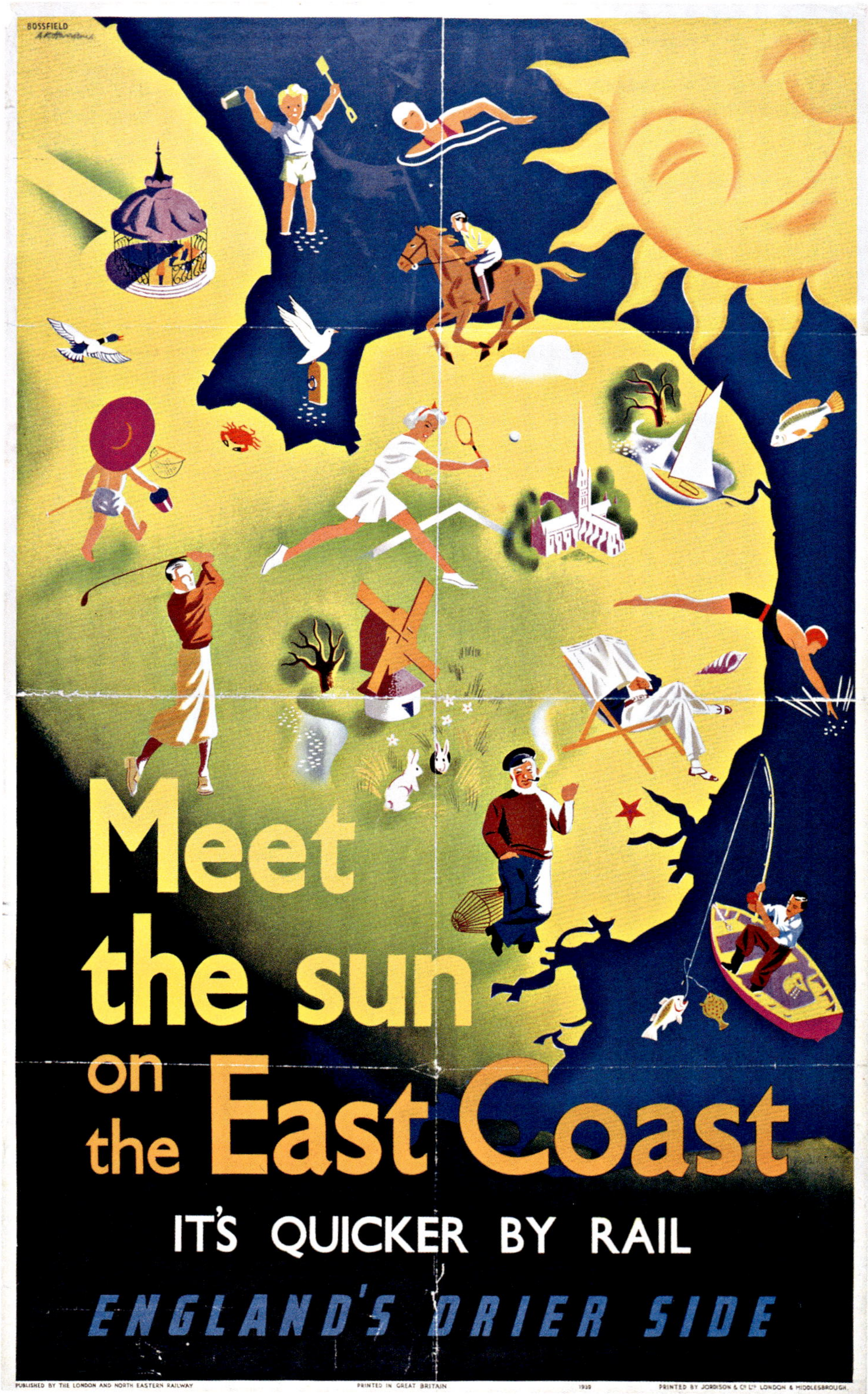

FIG 89

Arthur Harrison

Meet the Sun on the East Coast 1939 (cat. 15)

The railway companies vied with each other in their claims to the greatest amount of sunshine. The pleasures on offer here are little different to the beginning of the decade, but they are conducted in a more energetic way, reflecting a growing acceptance of recreational sport and the physical pursuit of leisure.

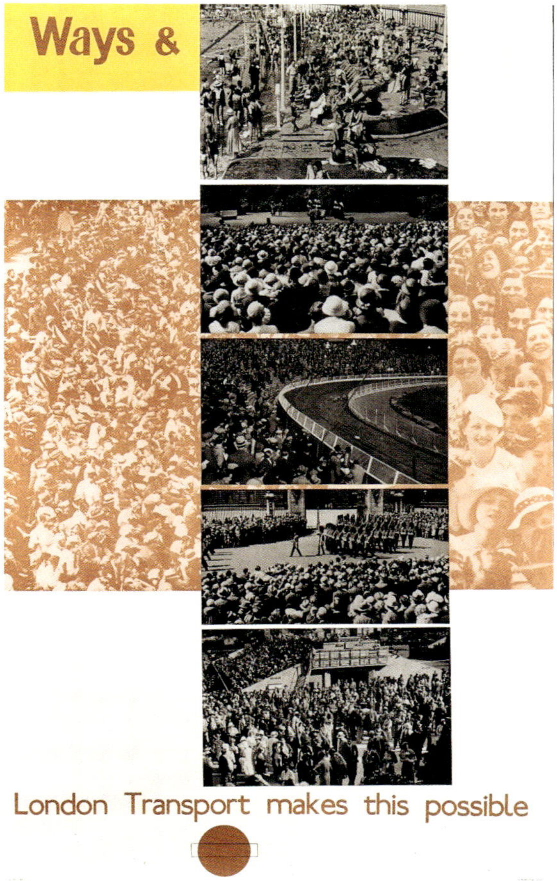

FIG 90

Richard Beck
London Transport Makes This Possible 1938
(cat. 8)

In contrast to the country idylls of ten years before, this London Transport poster unashamedly celebrates mass involvement in leisure. It relies primarily on the power of image rather than text, especially when the caption is itself so enigmatic.

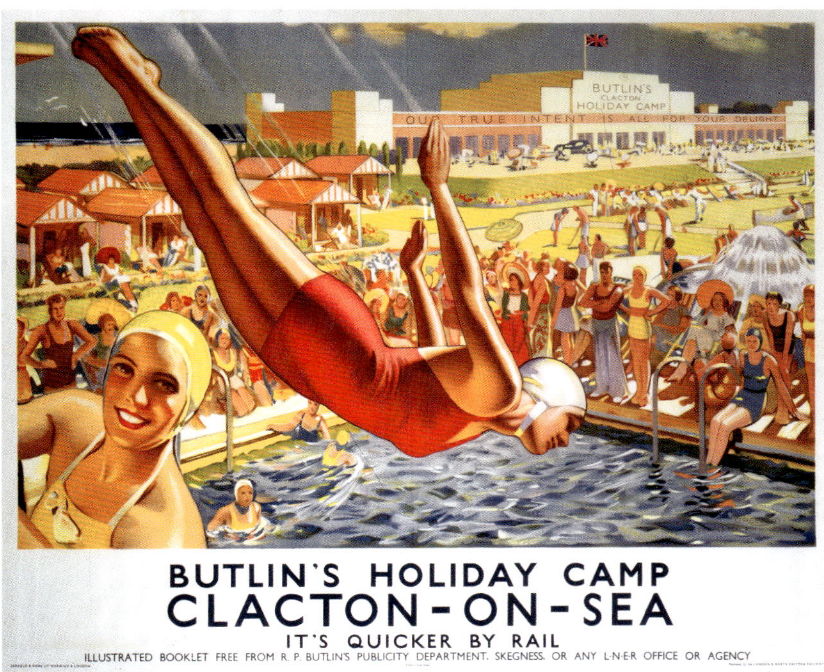

FIG 91

J. Greenup
Butlin's Holiday Camp, Clacton-on-Sea 1940
LNER poster

The airborne figure, complete with slipstream marks, brings into popular advertising a new vision of the sporting body first disseminated in photography of the 1936 Berlin Olympics.

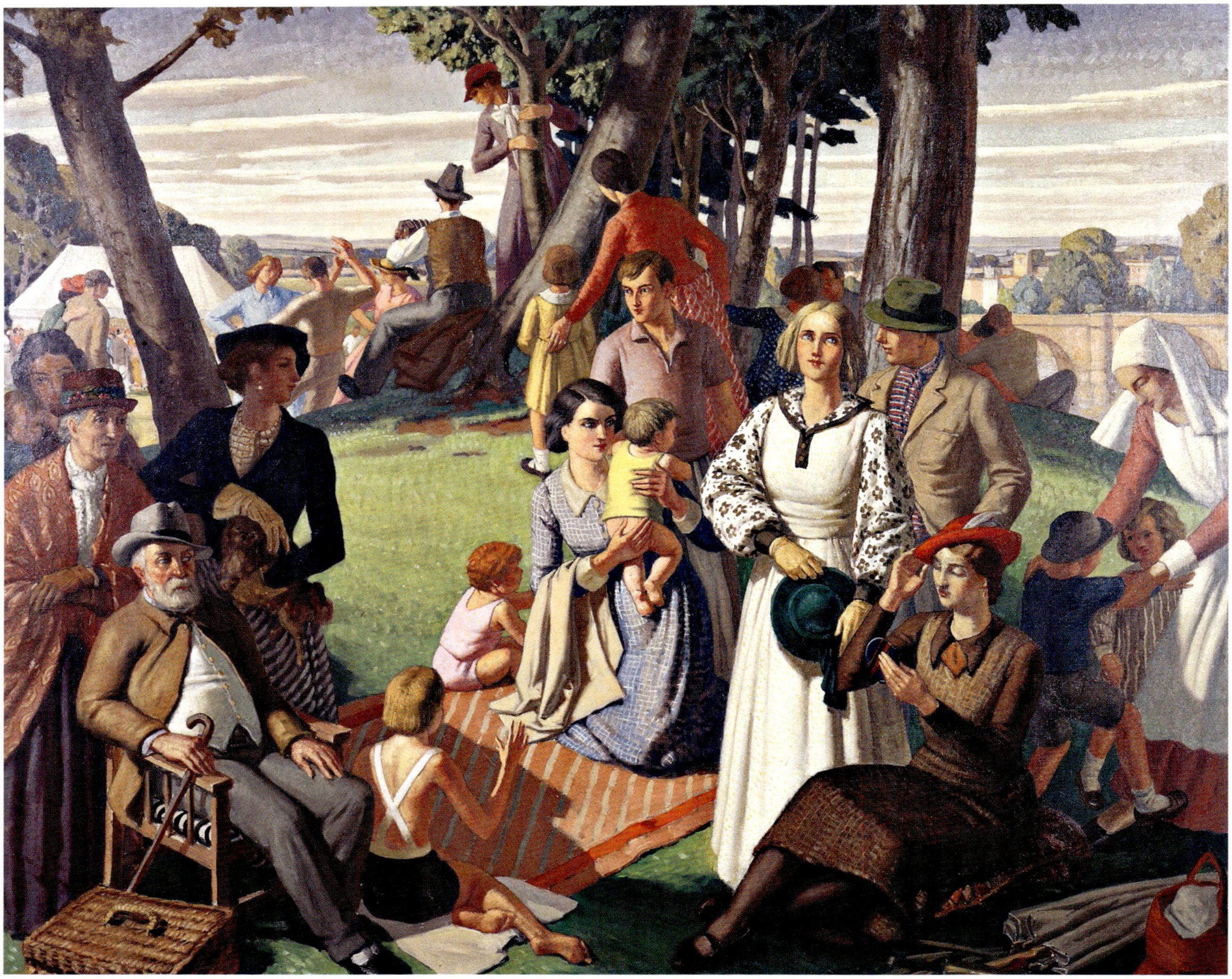

FIG 92

Harry Morley

Holiday 1935 (cat. 25)

At a riverside location, presumably somewhere along the Thames, a variety of well-dressed people enjoy a day's outing. The older generations are reserved and self-conscious; it is the children and young people who really make the most of the opportunity for relaxation.

The country festivals depicted by Harry Morley and Harold Harvey (fig. 92; cat. 25, fig. 93) are not modern, yet they have become interesting subjects for artists precisely because of contemporary debates about the nature and type of leisure society wanted and needed. While some of the London audience imagined themselves part of some nuclear village community, Lowry, in his 1931 painting of Peel Park in Salford understood a day out in an entirely different way (figs. 94, 95; cats. 21, 43).[35] 1931 was a landmark as the first-ever census which did not record an increase in the proportion of the population living in London, taken by one commentator as a sign that the pull from country to town was on the turn, and may even be reversed. The caption of Graham Sutherland's 1938 poster, 'Go out into the country', was addressed in the first instance to the large numbers of female typists who, with telephonists, were a new force in the labour

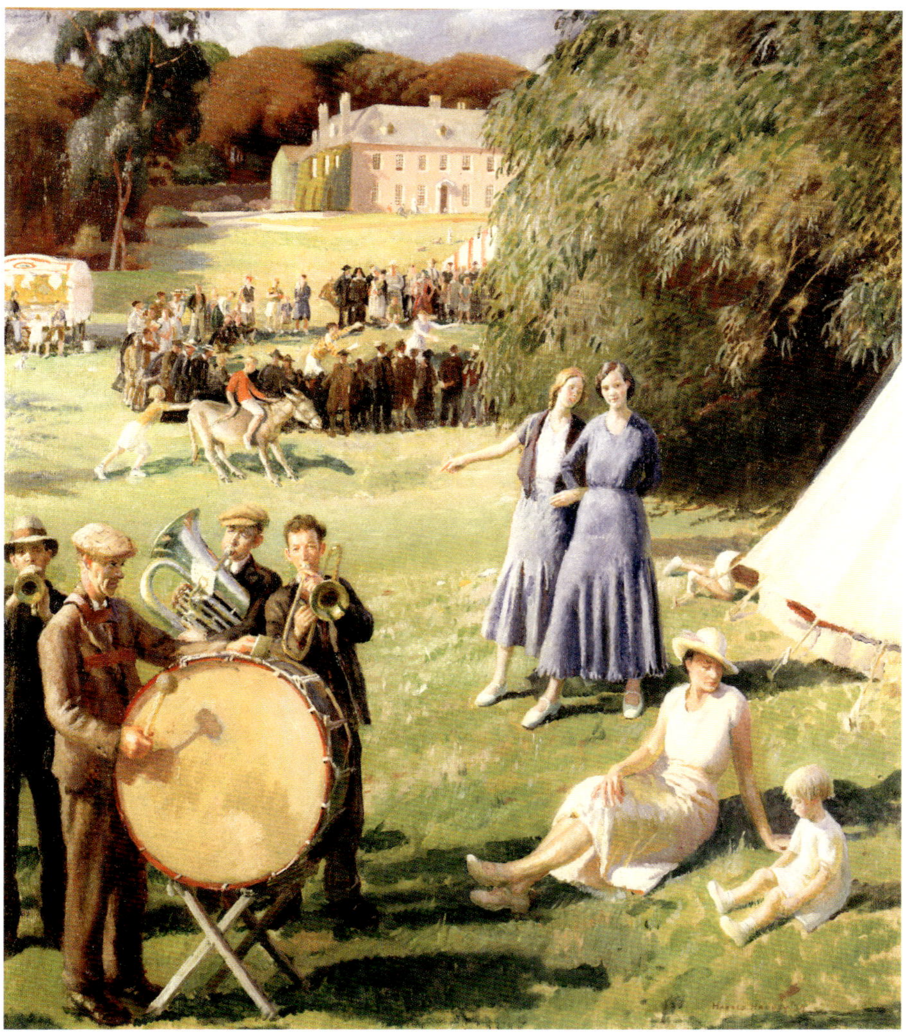

FIG 93

Harold Harvey

Fête Champêtre 1934

The cloth-capped musicians playing at a village festival in the grounds of a great house seem to suggest that summer fairs are an occasion when the population can join in common pleasures, regardless of class.

FIG 94

Lawrence Stephen Lowry

The Bandstand, Peel Park, Salford 1931 (cat. 21)

For the factory workers of Salford, an afternoon in the park listening to a band was a special occasion that would draw crowds. Lowry is almost unique in this period in depicting what leisure might mean for the mass of working families.

FIG 95

Fairground 9 August 1934 (cat 43)

In northern towns and cities, popular attractions such as travelling fairgrounds continued to provide entertainment for the masses.

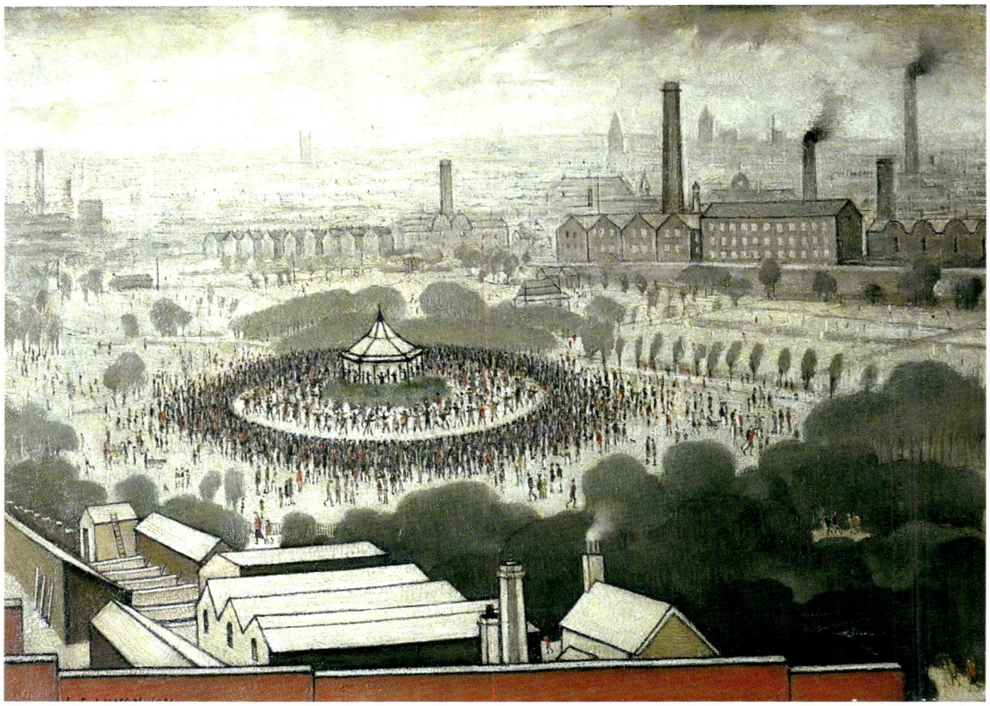

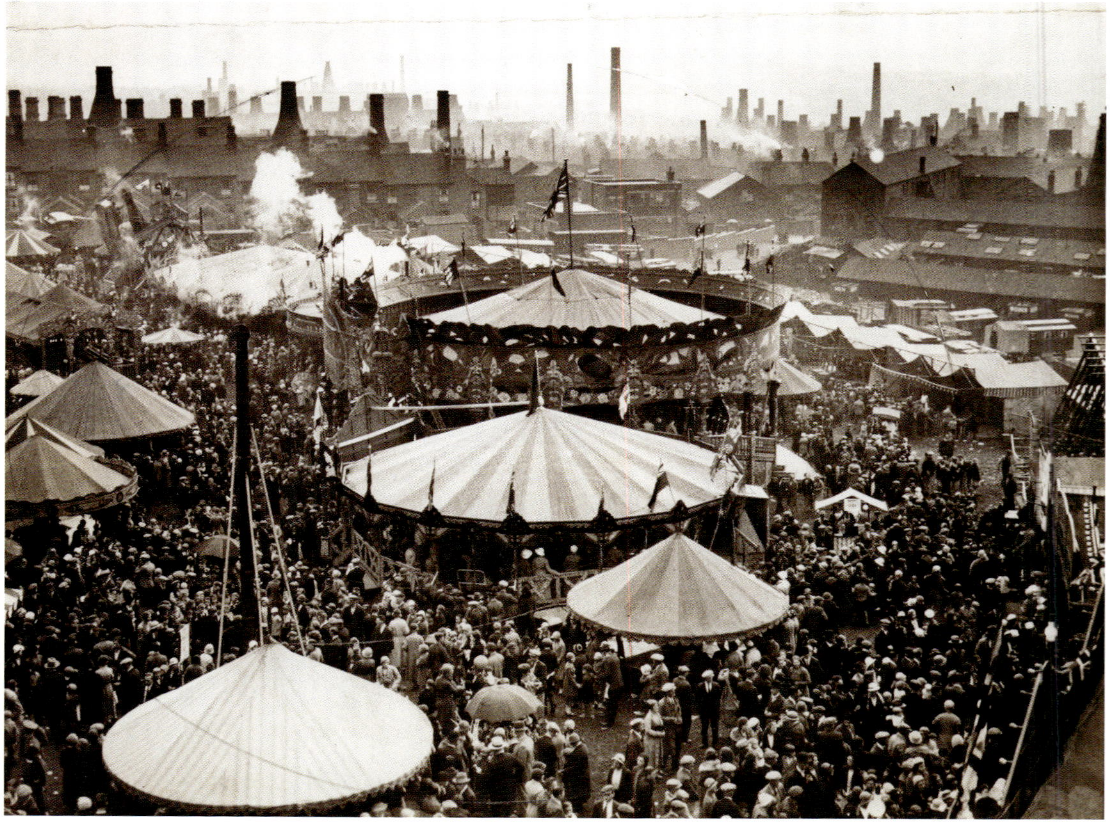

market, particularly in the south-east (fig. 96; cat. 39). But they were not alone in following its injunction, and this brought its own problems. As more people wanted to make the rural idyll enjoyed on occasional rambles and picnics a permanent reality, and as car ownership made this practicable, more of the professional classes, at least, moved to the country. Harry Allen's large panel, exhibited in 1935 (fig. 97), demonstrates how the idea of 'a day in the sun' was not an end in itself, but was triggering further social change. DeLisle Burns, the writer whose radio talks published in 1932 as *Leisure in the Modern World* have just been referred to, saw modern leisure as effecting a fundamental change in people's expectations: leisure now implied 'not merely a momentary relief from work, but a life outside the world of work.'[36] Was there ever a time when leisure was of such concern to the whole of society, when to discuss it touched the whole of the social

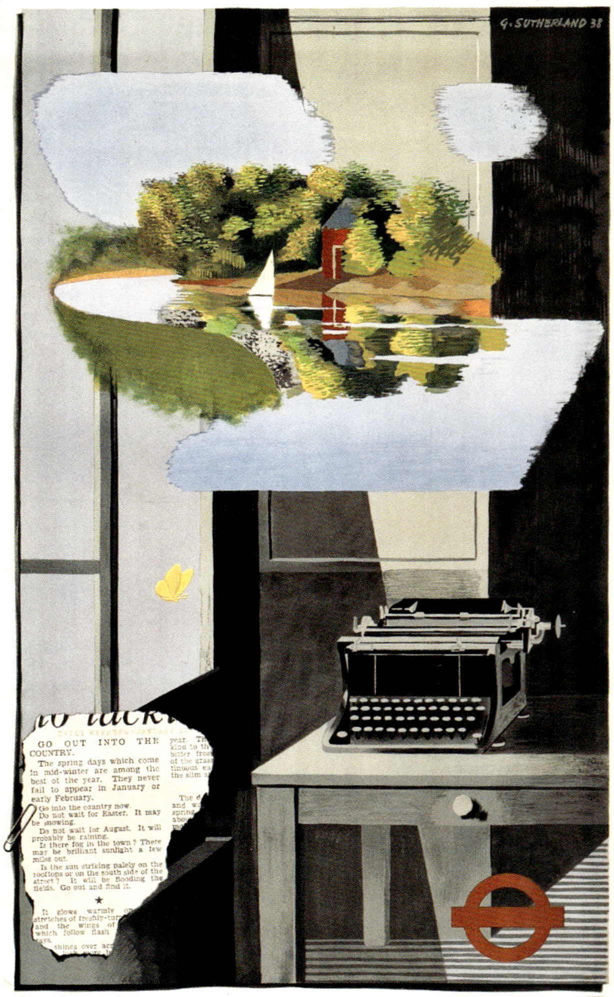

FIG 96

Graham Sutherland

Go out into the Country 1938 (cat. 39)

Typing and switchboard-operating were taken up particularly by women, and the mass of jobs concentrated in the south-east. This London Transport poster addresses itself primarily to a female audience, encouraging a spirit of fantasy and wish-fulfilment.

order? 'We feel', Burns concluded, 'that modern civilization is not a fixed point to be reached, but a process of which our own daily lives form parts. We are going on'.[37]

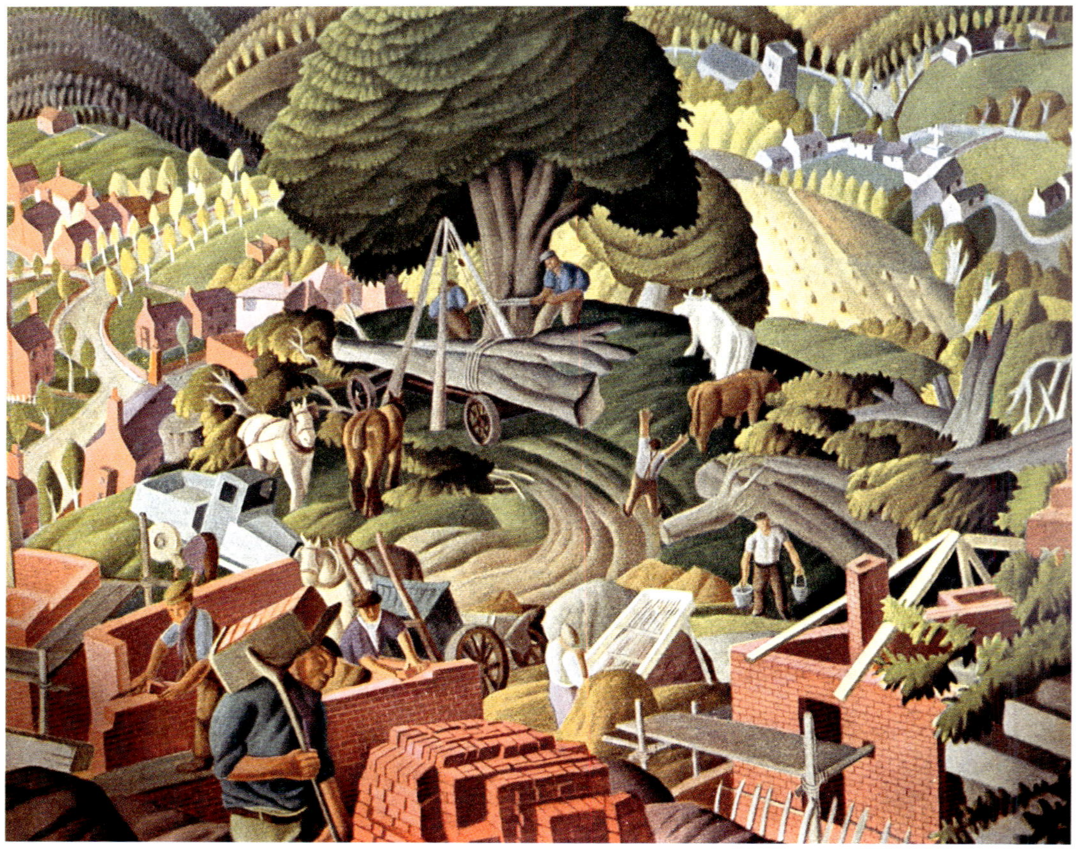

FIG 97

Harry Epworth Allen

The Countryside 1935

The painters who celebrated the open-air life were not unaware of the social and economic consequences of this mass movement. Here, Allen shows how short-term enjoyment was also a catalyst for permanent destruction; the countryside could not remain unscathed by the pressures of modern living.

NOTES

1 The meaning of the term 'leisure' in this period is highly problematic and would vary considerably according to the class, gender and geographical location of the person using it. For the purposes of this brief exposition, 'leisure' is used to refer to activities which are presented as such in the period, regardless of who by and who to. For a critical exploration of the concept, see J. Lowerson and A. Howkins, 'Leisure in the Thirties' in *Leisure and social control*, ed A. Tomlinson, Brighton 1981, pp. 70–92 and C. Langhamer, *Women's leisure in England 1920-1960*, Manchester 2000.

2 Quoted in the Annual Report of the Chief Medical Officer of the Board of Education; see P. McIntosh, *Physical Education in England since 1800* 1952, rev. ed. 1968, p. 222.

3 P. Nash, *Writings on art*, ed. A. Causey, Oxford 2000, p. 105. See also D. Mellor, 'British art in the 1930s: some economic, political and cultural structures' in *Class, culture and social change; a new view of the 1930s*, ed. F. Gloversmith, Brighton 1980, pp. 185–207.

4 F. Gloversmith, 'Defining culture: J. C. Powys, Clive Bell, R. H. Tawney and T. S. Eliot' in F. Gloversmith, *op. cit.*, p. 19.

5 Manchester City Art Gallery. See *Earthly delights: Mary Adshead 1904–1995*, ed. M.C. Clough and A. Compton 2005, p. 23.

6 *Birmingham Mail*; undated press cutting in the possession of the artist's descendants. The link between paintings of open-air nudes and modern naturism is made explicit in a cutting from the June 1936 issue of *Health and Efficiency* magazine, from the same source. It reproduces Fleetwood-Walker's painting *The Toilet*, showing two nude women in a woodland setting, under the heading 'Naturism at the Royal Academy'. The text observes a decline in the numbers of such paintings, commenting, 'the nudes are the merest handful'.

7 Unidentified press report, datable to 1957, in the possession of the artist's descendants.

8 R. Graves and A. Hodge, *The long week-end. A social history of Great Britain 1918–1939* 1941, p. 230.

9 The best account of this phenomenon, still awaiting a definitive study with an international perspective, is R. Golan's outstanding *Modernity and nostalgia. Art and politics in France between the wars*, 1995. See also *Les réalismes*, Musée national d'art moderne, Paris, and E. Cowling and J. Mundy, *On classic ground; Picasso, Leger, De Chirico and the New Classicism 1910-1930* [exhibition catalogue] Tate Gallery 1990.

10 J. Smith, *Liquid assets. The lidos and open air swimming pools of Britain* 2005, pp. 18–31.

11 *The Times* 25 January 1937, p. 9.

12 Capital investment in new facilities at seaside resorts in 1933 has been calculated at between £200-£300 million; S. G. Jones, *Workers at play. A social and economic history of leisure 1918-1939* 1986, p. 46.

13 S. K. Cahn, *Coming on strong. Gender and sexuality in twentieth-century women's sport*, New York 1994, p. 31.

14 *Spotlighting the sporting body* [exhibition catalogue], Musée Olympique, Lausanne, 2002, esp. pp. 98-109, tracing developments in 1930s sports photography from avant-garde experiments at the Bauhaus and in Russia during the 1920s.

15 K. Bell, *Stanley Spencer: a complete catalogue of the paintings* 1992.

16 P. C. McIntosh, op. cit (n. 2 above), p. 234.

17 Ibid., p. 239.

18 *The Tatler* 2 December 1932; *News Chronicle* 2 May 1932.

19 *Yorkshire Herald* 10 May 1932; *News Chronicle* 5 May 1932.

20 C. Dodd, 'Rowing', in *Sport in Britain. A social history*, ed. T. Mason, Cambridge 1989, p. 299.

21 'The feminine mind in sports reflects the general trend of feminine thinking of the day. The ideas and, along with them, the inhibitions imposed upon us by previous generations are being dispelled'; *Saturday Evening Post* 28 May 1932, quoted in S.K. Cahn, *op. cit.* (n. 13 above), p. 47.

22 D. Birley, *Playing the game; sport and British society, 1910–1945*, Manchester 1996, p. 272; H. Llewellyn Smith, *The new survey of London life and labour*, vol. IX, *Life and leisure* 1935, p. 58.

23. R. F. Wheeler, 'Organized sport and organized labour: the workers' sports movement', *Journal of contemporary history*, vol. 13, no. 2 April 1978, p. 196.

24 J. Huizinga, *Homo ludens; a study of the play element in culture*, 1949, p. 198. The commercialisation of sport during the inter-war years was felt to be changing its very nature; in *Brave New World*, published in 1932, Huxley refers satirically to games 'which do nothing whatever to increase consumption'.

25 J.-Y. Guillain, *Art et olympisme. Histoire du concours de peinture*, Anglet 2004 is the most thorough study of these exhibitions, but concentrates on the French.

26 D. Prynn, 'The Clarion clubs, rambling and the holiday associations in Britain', *Journal of contemporary history*, vol. 11 no. 2/3 July 1976, pp. 65–77; A. Holt, 'Hikers and ramblers: surviving a thirties' fashion', *The international journal for the history of sport*, vol. 4, no. 1, May 1987, pp. 56–67.

27 Motorised transport, for instance, expanded more than fourfold, from 3.5 million passenger miles in 1920 to 19 million in 1938; S. G. Jones, *op. cit.* (n. 12 above), p. 20.

28 Taylor, stressing the lengthy British tradition for rational leisure, warns, '[t]he influence of that wider contemporary milieu cannot be ignored, but does need to be kept in perspective'. H. Taylor, A claim on the countryside 1997, p. 228.

29 J. Stevenson, *British society 1914–45* 1984, p. 387.

30 Christie's, London 12 June 1998, lot 205.

31 See C. Fox, *Painting in Newlyn 1900-1930*, Penzance 1985.

32 *The Studio*, vol. 112, July 1936, p. 37. On 24 May 1932, *The Times* reported a lecture given by Sir Ernest Graham-Little in which the benefits of the exposure of the skin to light and air were a discovery attributed to the ancient Greeks and Romans, with no mention of Germany.

33 A. Howkins and J. Lowerson, *Trends in leisure 1919–1939* 1979, p. 9; S. G. Jones, 'Work, leisure and unemployment in western Europe between the wars', *The British journal of sports history*, vol. 3 no. 1 May 1986, p. 65.

34 J. Stevenson, *op. cit.* (n. 28 above), p. 393.

35 Jones notes that union-sponsored Bank Holiday fêtes, with a brass band providing music, were to be found all over the country. S. G. Jones, *op. cit.* (n. 12 above), p. 145.

36 C. DeLisle Burns, *Leisure in the modern world* 1932, repr. 1975, p. 208.

37 Ibid., p. 72.

Catalogue

All measurements are in centimetres

Mary Adshead (1904–95)

Mary Adshead was the only daughter of an architect and professor of town planning. She studied at the Slade School from 1921 to 1924, winning the composition prize in her final year. Over the next few years, she received commissions, sometimes through her father, for murals for several public and private locations, and began to show in London exhibitions. She married Stephen Bone in 1929 and the following year held a one-woman show at the Goupil Gallery in London. Her paintings were seen at the Royal Academy, the New English Art Club and the Artists' International Association. Adshead continued to be in demand as a painter of murals for the rest of her working life, producing colourful, engaging schemes for international exhibition pavilions, shops, churches and large country houses.

1. Country Joys on London's Undergound 1927 (fig. 4)
Colour lithograph 101.6 x 63.5
London's Transport Museum © Transport for London

Harry Epworth Allen (1894–1958)

Born in Sheffield, the son of a skilled mark-cutter in the cutlery trade, Allen spent more than half his life in a variety of occupations before concentrating full-time on painting as a result of being made redundant in 1931. As a young man, he attended art evening classes while working as a clerk in the steel works of Arthur Balfour. During the First World War, he was badly injured and lost a leg, but returned to work as a policy advisor to Balfour. He had started to exhibit locally, and in 1933 three works were accepted for the Royal Academy. After that, he showed there almost every year. Most of his paintings are landscapes near his home in Sheffield, executed in tempera.

2. *The Caravan* 1935 (fig. 64)
Tempera on board 37 x 50
The Trustees of Homerton College

3. *The Hikers* (fig. 53)
Oil on board 56 x 35.5
Elizabeth and Paul Thornton

Adrian Allinson (1890–1959)

Allinson was the son of a doctor and nutritionist whose campaign for brown bread led him to found the company which still sells wholemeal flour. He initially planned to follow his father into the medical profession, but gave this up to enter the Slade School in 1910. He was a keen skier and mountaineer; many of the paintings he exhibited at the Royal Academy from 1921 were of mountain scenes. Allinson taught at Westminster School of Art for most of his working life, and worked as a designer for the railway companies and for the theatre.

4. *Windsor Castle* 1934 (fig. 43)
Colour lithograph 101.6 x 63.5
London's Transport Museum © Transport for London

5. **Anonymous**
It's a Pleasure 1938 (fig. 2)
Colour lithograph 101.6 x 63.5
London's Transport Museum © Transport for London

Maxwell Armfield (1881–1972)

Armfield entered Birmingham School of Art in 1899, where he encountered Southall and other artists active in the tempera revival, who taught him the technique he was to practise for the duration of his career. He visited Italy then spent some time studying in Paris. Returning to London in 1905, he held the first of a number of successful one-man exhibitions, first at the Carfax Gallery, then at the Leicester Galleries. In 1915, he left for America with his wife, the writer Constance Smedley, and remained there until 1922. On his return to England he became a regular exhibitor at the Royal Academy and elsewhere up until his eightieth year. He published the *Manual of Tempera Painting* in 1930 and was a prolific illustrator, designer for the theatre and writer on a wide variety of topics.

6. *I Saw Three Ships* 1930 (fig. 82)
Tempera on wood 50 x 60
Derby Museums and Art Gallery

7. *At the Seaside* 1932 (fig. 84)
Tempera on board 36 x 46
Private Collection

Richard Beck (1912–85)

Born in Hampshire, Beck studied at the Slade School and in Munich. He established a successful design studio, creating posters for London Transport, for Shell and for the Orient Line, before emigrating to Australia. He served in the Australian forces during the Second World War, then returned to work in Australia, eventually becoming Head of Graphic Design at Prahran Technical College until his retirement in 1972.

8. *London Transport Makes This Possible* 1938 (fig. 90)
Colour lithograph 101.6 × 63.5
London's Transport Museum © Transport for London

Jean Dupas (1882–1964)

Dupas was born in Bordeaux. He studied at the Ecole des Beaux-arts in Paris and was active in a wide range of the fine and applied arts, producing ornate panels for some of the most luxurious transatlantic liners in the latest Art Deco style. He won a Gold Medal at the Paris Salon in 1922. He produced a total of six poster designs for London Transport between 1930 and 1933.

9. *'Where is this bower beside the silver Thames?'* 1930 (cat. 41)
Colour lithograph 101.6 × 127
London's Transport Museum © Transport for London

Bernard Fleetwood-Walker (1893–1965)

The great-grandson of the artist and inventor Cornelius Varley, Fleetwood-Walker was born in Birmingham. He worked in the city's silver industry before studying at the School of Art, and subsequently in London and in Paris.

Following war service, he was for ten years an art master in Birmingham, then in 1929 was appointed to the Birmingham School of Art. He later became Assistant Keeper at the Royal Academy Schools, under another Birmingham artist, Henry Rushbury. Fleetwood-Walker's exhibits at the Royal Academy alone totalled nearly 150, and he also showed regularly in Birmingham, at the Royal Watercolour Society and the New English Art Club. He enjoyed great success for his figure compositions, and as a portrait painter.

10. *The Family* 1932 (fig. 70)
Oil on canvas 100.5 × 92
The Potteries Museum & Art Gallery, Stoke-on-Trent

11. *Amity* 1933 (fig. 69)
Oil on canvas 101.3 × 94.7
National Museums Liverpool, The Walker Art Gallery

12. *The Family at Polperro* 1934–36 (fig. 71)
Oil on canvas 127.6 × 101.9
Birmingham Museums and Art Gallery, presented by the artist in memory of his wife, 1939

Lancelot Glasson (1894–1959)

Glasson was born in west London, the son of a barrister. During the First World War, he was an officer in the Royal Fusiliers, and lost a leg. Only then did he take up painting seriously, and attended Heatherley's School and the Royal Academy Schools. His exhibits at the Academy and elsewhere rapidly attracted notice, crowned by the widespread enthusiasm for *The Young Rower* in 1932. Soon afterward, Glasson became Chairman of the family firm of beer bottlers in Cumbria, and his output as a painter understandably declined.

13. *Repose* 1929 (fig. 7)
Oil on canvas 90.9 × 110
Royal Pavilion, Libraries and Museums, Brighton and Hove

14. *The Young Rower* 1932 (fig. 38)
Oil on canvas 102 × 76
Touchstones Rochdale Art Gallery

Arthur Harrison

15. *Meet the Sun on the East Coast* 1939 (fig. 89)
Colour lithograph 101.8 × 63
Victoria and Albert Museum

George Henry (1858–1943)

The earliest of the artists represented in this exhibition, Henry was born in Irvine, Ayrshire, the son of a brewer. He began his working life as a clerk, then in 1882 enrolled at Glasgow School of Art. He had also been to paint at Brig o' Turk, a haunt of the Glasgow Boys, Guthrie and Walton. Henry may have travelled to France; he certainly became aware of Gauguin's Pont Aven painting, which influenced *The Druids*, the large canvas he painted with E.A. Hornel, and which was shown in London and in Munich. Henry travelled with Hornel to Japan in 1893-4. After 1900, Henry settled in London, and gradually became part of the artistic establishment there, a reputed portrait painter and regular exhibitor at the Royal Academy from 1905. Elected RA in 1920, he painted a long series of brilliant, airy landscapes of the South Downs which began in 1930 and continued until his death in December 1943.

16. *Hikers at Goodwood* 1937 (fig. 56)
Oil on canvas 102 × 127.5
Sheffield Galleries and Museums Trust

Walter Hutton (active 1888–1952)

Very little is known about Hutton, beyond his exhibiting career, which began in 1888, when he was living in London. During the 1890s he went to Italy, and on his return lived in Bedford and in Liverpool before settling first in Salisbury and finally at Parkstone in Dorset. His final exhibit at the Royal Academy in 1952 was a landscape entitled *A Lane in Little England*.

17. *They See an Oread* 1933 (fig. 8)
Oil on canvas 103 x 197
Grundy Art Gallery, Blackpool

Andrew Johnson

18. *The South Coast is the Sunny Coast* 1933 (fig. 28)
Colour lithograph 102.2 x 62
Victoria and Albert Museum

Laura Knight (1877–1970)

Knight was born in Long Eaton, Derbyshire, but grew up in Nottingham, where her mother was a school art teacher. She attended Nottingham School of Art, and met there a fellow student, Harold Knight (1874-1961), her future husband. She became a member of the artistic community in Staithes, on the Yorkshire coast, from 1895 until 1907, when she settled in Newlyn. Scenes of the beaches and coasts of Cornwall, often painted in vibrant colour, became a mainstay of her work. Based in London after 1918, she was elected ARA in 1927 and RA in 1936; she became a Dame in 1929. During the latter part of her long career she concentrated on paintings of the itinerant life of gypsies and the circus.

19. *Summer's Joy* 1921 (fig. 72)
Colour lithograph 101.6 x 63.5
London's Transport Museum © Transport for London

20. *The Yorkshire Coast* c.1929 (fig. 78)
Colour lithograph 100 x 125.2
Victoria and Albert Museum

Lawrence Stephen Lowry (1887–1976)

Lowry was born in Manchester. On leaving school, he entered an accountancy firm, then became a rent collector, retiring in 1952 as a chief cashier. From 1905, he attended evening classes at Manchester School of Art, under the French painter of urban scenes, Adolphe Valette. After ten years, he transferred to Salford School of Art, and began to paint the local industrial landscape. He was exhibiting his work locally, and also in London, but was 'discovered' in 1939 and given a one-man exhibition at the Lefevre Gallery.

Lowry was elected ARA in 1955 and RA in 1962. He was awarded the freedom of the city of Salford in 1965.

21. *The Bandstand, Peel Park, Salford* 1931 (fig. 94)
Oil on canvas 43.2 x 62.2
York Museums Trust (York Art Gallery)

Miguel Mackinlay (1895–1958)

Mackinlay was born in Spain, the son of a Scottish engineer father and a Spanish mother. Following his mother's death in 1909 his father took the family to Australia. Proceeds from exhibitions in Perth enabled Mackinlay and two friends to travel to England in 1914. On the outbreak of war, he joined up, but was discharged wounded and in 1916 went to study at the Slade School. He married, and moved out to Hertfordshire, settling in Bushey in 1928, where he joined a thriving artistic community. Much of Mackinlay's work was in advertising, but he produced numerous large and eye-catching paintings for the Royal Academy.

22. *Tête à Tête* 1930 (fig. 45)
Oil on canvas 202 x 237.5
Mackinlay Collection, Bushey Museum and Art Gallery

23. *Summer* 1933 (fig. 26)
Oil on canvas 167.5 x 200.5
Mackinlay Collection, Bushey Museum and Art Gallery

André-Edouard Marty (1882–1974)

Marty studied at the Ecole des Beaux-Arts in Paris. Active as a designer and illustrator, he was particularly associated with drawings of the latest fashions for luxurious magazines such as the *Gazette du Bon Ton*. Marty designed posters for the opening season of the Théâtre du Champs Elysees in 1913. In 1925, he was a member of the jury at the Paris International Exhibition of Decorative Art that launched the Art Deco style. He designed 17 posters for London Transport in the years 1931-3.

24. *Picnic: 'Come on wings of joy we'll fly'* 1931 (fig. 66)
Colour lithograph 101.6 x 63.5
London's Transport Museum © Transport for London

Harry Morley (1881–1943)

Born in Leicester, Morley studied at the School of Art there and at the Royal College of Art, intending to become an architect. A scholarship to study in Italy for two years led him to change course towards painting, and in 1908 he spent six months at the Académie Julian in Paris. A series of mythological scenes, exhibited from 1915, show a great admiration for the artists of the early Renaissance and a lively spirit of fantasy. Popular and highly successful, he mounted numerous one-man exhibitions in London galleries. He joined the Tempera Society in 1923, and in 1930, affected by the downturn in the market, took a teaching post at St Martin's School of Art in London. Only in the 1930s did he turn to modern subjects with any frequency.

25. *Holiday* 1935 (fig. 92)
Oil on canvas 101.6 x 127
Geffrye Museum, London

Dod Procter (1892–1972)

Born Doris Shaw, Procter received early encouragement from her mother, who had studied at the Slade. She settled in Newlyn in 1907, in order to study with Stanhope Forbes, and met there her future husband, Ernest Procter. The two studied in Paris in 1910. They married two years later and in 1913 held a joint exhibition at the Fine Art Society in London. Procter exhibited at the Royal Academy from 1913, and also at the regular mixed exhibitions of the Leicester Galleries, where she and her husband held their second joint exhibition in 1926. In 1919-20 they were invited to Burma to paint murals; thereafter her studies of Burmese women made a distinctive strain in her art. Procter was elected ARA in 1934 and RA in 1942, at the time the only woman Academician apart from Laura Knight.

26. *The Orchard* 1934 (fig. 12)
Oil on canvas 101.6 x 127
Tate. Presented by the Trustees of the Chantrey Bequest 1937

Ernest Procter (1886–1935)

Procter was born on Tyneside, the son of an eminent Quaker scientist. He arrived in Newlyn in 1907 to study with Forbes. He studied at the Atelier Colarossi in Paris from 1910 and returned to France during the war as an ambulanceman. As a student in Paris, he was encouraged to concentrate on his brilliant landscapes, but he retained a predilection for fantasy scenes with figures, which rivalled Harry Morley's. During the 1930s, he produced painted decorations for several churches, in Cornwall and elsewhere. He was appointed to a senior position in Glasgow School of Art in 1934, but the demands of the post, on top of his already heavy workload, may have contributed to his early death.

27. *Summer Holidays* 1934 (fig. 73)
Oil on canvas 99 x 191
Private collection

Tom Purvis (1888–1959)

Purvis was born in Bristol and studied at Camberwell School of Art. He worked in advertising before setting up his own studio at an early age. His numerous clients included food and drink manufacturers as well as the railway companies and the outfitters, Austin Reed. His poster designs of swimmers and divers were included in the Painting section of the 1928 Olympic Art exhibition in Amsterdam. He became Vice President of the Royal Society of Arts and was a member of the organising committee of the exhibition of British Art in Industry at the Royal Academy in 1935. He was an official war artist for the Ministry of Supply during the Second World War.

28. *East Coast Joys: Sunbathing* c.1925 (fig. 29)
Colour lithograph 100.5 x 63
Victoria and Albert Museum

William Roberts (1895–1980)

Roberts was born in Hackney, London, the son of a carpenter. Evening classes at St Martin's School of Art led to a scholarship to the Slade School in 1910, where he was a contemporary of Wadsworth, Spencer and Bomberg. Roberts was a member of the Vorticist group and shared their enthusiasm for Cubism, verging at times on abstraction. Commissions for large-scale paintings as a war artist for Canada and for Britain led him back towards a more figurative style, incorporating simplified, almost geometric figures, which he retained for the rest of his life. In 1923 Roberts held a one-man show at the Chenil Galleries and in 1925 began to teach part-time at the Central School, where he remained until 1960. He held regular exhibitions throughout the 1930s and in 1932 a group of paintings was shown at the Venice Biennale. Only in 1948 did Roberts begin to show at the Royal Academy, being elected ARA in 1958 and RA in 1966.

29. *Going to Swim* 1930 (fig. 32)
Oil on canvas 48 x 39
Richard Burrows

30. *Les Routiers* 1931 (fig. 60)
Oil on canvas 101.7 x 76.3
Collection Ulster Museum, Belfast

31. *Sunbathing* 1936 (fig. 13)
Oil on canvas 91.5 × 112
Jonathan Marland

32. *Parson's Pleasure* 1944 (fig. 14)
Oil on canvas 40.5 × 51
Samantha Frank

Frederick Cayley Robinson (1862–1927)

Robinson was the son of a stockbroker and had a lengthy artistic education at the St John's Wood Academy and the Royal Academy Schools followed by three years at the Académie Julian in Paris. He spent the years 1899-1902 in Florence, studying tempera technique and also the fresco paintings which would imbue his later symbolist compositions with a unique sense of calm and clarity. He lived for a time at Newlyn then again in Paris before settling finally in London in 1914. As well as exhibiting regularly at the Royal Academy and Society of British Artists, he was a member of the Society of Painters in Tempera, the New English Art Club and the Royal Watercolour Society. His sets for a production of Maeterlinck's *The Blue Bird* in 1909 were greatly admired and formed the basis to an illustrated edition of the text, published in 1911. He was also active as a painter of murals, most notably for the Middlesex Hospital, completed in 1920.

33. *Summer: A Day in the Country* c. 1923–24 (fig. 5)
Colour Lithograph 101 × 249
Victoria and Albert Museum

Percy Shakespeare (1906–43)

Shakespeare was born in Dudley, the fourth of eight children. He attended the local art school, then, from 1923, the Birmingham School of Art. He continued to teach there part-time until called up in 1941. He exhibited in Dudley, and in Birmingham, and first showed a painting at the Royal Academy in 1935 (*On the Rhine*). He made a particular speciality of paintings of local sporting events, tennis, boating or swimming. He was killed by a stray flying bomb on the cliffs near Brighton in May 1943.

34. *Morning Exercise* 1934 (fig. 37)
Oil on canvas 76 × 63.5
Private Collection

35. *On the Rhine* 1935 (fig. 52)
Oil on canvas 77 × 65
Dudley Museum and Art Gallery

Joseph Southall (1861–1944)

Southall was born in Nottingham, to a Quaker family. He attended Birmingham School of Art, and came into contact with Ruskin, Morris and Burne-Jones. He exhibited with the Birmingham Society of Artists from 1887, at the Royal Academy from 1895 and also with the Arts and Crafts Exhibition Society. In 1901 he was a founder member of the Society of Painters in Tempera, the technique he preferred and which he did much to promote. Southall held a successful one-man show in Paris in 1910, and, after the war, two at the Leicester Galleries in London, in 1926 and 1931.

36. *The Return* 1930 (fig. 83)
Tempera on silk 37.5 × 58.4
Nottingham City Museums and Galleries: Nottingham Castle

Stanley Spencer (1891–1959)

Spencer was born in Cookham, the setting for much of his later work. From 1908, he studied at the Slade School, in a generation that included William Roberts, Mark Gertler and Paul Nash. After war service in Bristol then in Macedonia he returned to Cookham. Spencer held a one-man show at the Goupil Gallery in 1927, including his large *The Resurrection, Cookham*, and that year was given the commission to decorate the Sandham Memorial Chapel at Burghclere. Elected ARA in 1932, he resigned in 1935, following the rejection of two works. He was re-elected RA in 1950. From 1942-4, he painted the series *Shipbuilding on the Clyde* in Glasgow. A major retrospective was mounted by the Tate Gallery in 1955.

37. *Sunbathers at Odney* 1935 (fig. 34)
Oil on canvas 76.2 × 50.8
Stanley Spencer Gallery, Cookham

38. *Girls returning from a Bathe* 1936 (fig. 33)
Oil on canvas 76.2 × 50.8
Private Collection. On loan to the Stanley Spencer Gallery, Cookham

Graham Sutherland (1903–80)

The eldest of three children of a well-to-do civil servant in south London, at sixteen Sutherland became an engineering apprentice for the Midland Railway in Derby. In 1921 he overcame parental resistance, and entered Goldsmith's College of Art; he came to specialise in etching, one of a generation of young enthusiasts for the medium including Paul Drury and William Larkins. They revered Samuel Palmer, whose reputation was boosted by the major retrospective held in 1926. Sutherland was still only twenty-one when he mounted his first one-man exhibition in London, and was soon elected to the

Royal Society of Painter-Etchers. The Depression brought an end to the etching boom, and during the 1930s Sutherland worked as a teacher, illustrator and designer, for ceramics and glass as well as for posters, encouraged by Milner Gray, founder in 1930 of The Society of Industrial Artists. His work as a war artist took him into mines and iron foundries; promoted and patronised by Kenneth Clark, and other influential figures, he was for a time hailed as the most significant British artist of the post-war era.

39. *Go out into the Country* 1938 (fig. 96)
Colour lithograph 101.6 x 63.5
London's Transport Museum © Transport for London

James Walker Tucker (1898–1972)

Born in Wallsend, Northumberland, Tucker studied at Newcastle School of Art and the Royal College of Art. He won a travelling scholarship and returned to exhibit French and Italian landscapes at the Royal Academy in 1928. He spent his entire career as a teacher at Gloucester College of Art, exhibiting landscapes and the occasional figure subject, often in tempera.

40. *Hiking* 1936 (fig. 54)
Tempera on wood 51.2 x 60.3
Laing Art Gallery, Newcastle upon Tyne (Tyne and Wear Museums)

Harold Williamson (1898–1972)

Born in Manchester, Williamson began attending evening classes at the School of Art at the age of fifteen. He studied there full-time after the First World War, then in 1922 was taken on to teach drawing and painting, while also doing freelance work for wallpaper manufacturers Sandersons. In 1926 he became painting master at Bournemouth College of Art, then in 1947 returned to Manchester as head of the Department of Fine Art, where he remained until retirement in 1962. He first exhibited landscapes at the Royal Academy in 1916; his later submissions were largely figure compositions, temperas and etchings as well as oils.

41. *Picnic* 1938 (fig. 68)
Oil on canvas 116.8 x 91.4
Southampton City Art Gallery

42. *Spray* 1940 (fig. 30)
Oil on canvas 60.9 x 86.3
Russell-Cotes Art Gallery and Museum, Bournemouth

PHOTOGRAPHY

(All works on loan from the National Museum of Photography, Film & Television, [by courtesy of the Board of Trustees of the Science Museum]. Original prints approx. 23 x 25.4)

43. *Fairground* 9 August 1934 (fig. 95)
Gelatin silver print
Daily Herald Archive (1983-5236_10254)

44. *Sunbathing in the Sand* 4 July 1936 (fig. 76)
Gelatin silver print
James Jarche/Illustrated/Daily Herald Archive (1983-5236_01255)

45. *On the Sands of Waikiki Beach, Honululu* 14 August 1937 (fig. 16)
Gelatin silver print
Edward Mels/Daily Herald Archive (1983-5236_10256)

46. *Holiday spirit at Barry Island* 6 October 1937 (fig. 85)
Gelatin silver print
Saidman/Daily Herald Archive (1983-5236_10257)

47. *Young man with two women on a picnic* September 1939 (fig. 67)
Gelatin silver print
Studio Lisa/Daily Herald Archive (1983-5236_10258)

48. *Caravan by water* 23 June 1934 (fig. 63)
Gelatin silver print
Daily Herald Archive (1983-5236_01259)

49. *Holidays on the Beach* 13 October 1937 (fig. 79)
Gelatin silver print
Saidman/Daily Herald Archive (1983-5236_10260)

50. *Sun seekers at Enfield* 6 June 1937 (fig. 17)
Gelatin silver print
Daily Herald Archive (1983-5236_10261)

51. *Sunbathing at Brighton* 3 August 1935 (fig. 9)
Gelatin silver print
Fox Photos/Daily Herald Archive (1983-5236_10262)

52. *Margate* 5 August 1935 (fig. 87)
Gelatin silver print
Planet News/Daily Herald Archive (1953-5236_10263)

53. *Catching the sun in the open air baths at Blackpool* 1930s (fig. 35)
Gelatin silver print
Saidman/Daily Herald Archive (1983-5236_10266)

54. *New swimming pool in Geraldine Mary Harmsworth Park, Lambeth Road, Southwark* 6 August 1938 (fig. 18)
Gelatin silver print
James Jarche/Illustrated/Daily Herald Archive (1983-5236_10267)

55. Sunday in the sun at the Enfield Pool 6 July 1934 (fig. 88)
Gelatin silver print
Edward Malindine/Daily Herald Archive (1983-5236_10268)

56. Record crowd of the year at Serpentine Lido 20 August 1939 (fig. 24)
Gelatin silver print
Sayer/Daily Herald Archive (1983-5236_10269)

57. 'The Blue Lagoon' 11 April 1935 (fig. 27)
Gelatin silver print
George Woodbine/Daily Herald Archive (1983-5236_10270)

58. London's famous open spaces being fully appreciated by her citizens. A typical scene at the Serpentine Lido 21 June 1937 (fig. 22)
Gelatin silver print
Associated Press/Daily Herald Archive (1983-5236_10271)

59. Heat wave scene at Hyde Park Lido 6 August 1937 (fig. 23)
Gelatin silver print
Sayers/Daily Herald Archive (1983-5236_10272)

60. Scenes at the Serpentine Lido 23 June 1935 (fig. 21)
Gelatin silver print
George Woodbine/Daily Herald Archive (1983-5236_10273)

61. Under canvas – after a swim, a cup of tea, for holidaymakers in camp at Branscombe, South Devon 1 August 1938 (fig. 58)
Gelatin silver print
Roper/Daily Herald Archive (1983-5236_10274)

62. P.T. classes for workless. Unemployed men under instruction at Nottingham 19 December 1934 (fig. 36)
Gelatin silver print
Fox Photos/Daily Herald Archive (1983-5236_10275)

MODERN COPY PRINTS MADE FROM ORIGINAL GLASS NEGATIVES

63. Sun bathers at the lido 14 September 1934 (fig. 19)
Edward Malindine/Daily Herald Archive (1983-5236_10264)

64. Scenes at the Serpentine Lido. Sunbathers 23 June 1935 (fig. 20)
George Woodbine/Daily Herald Archive (1983-5236_10265)

65. Hikers enjoying the sunshine at Box Hill 9 April 1935 (fig. 55)
George Woodbine/Daily Herald Archive (1983-5236_10276)

66. Hikers at Box Hill 20 March 1932 (fig. 51)
Harold Tomlin/Daily Herald Archive (1983-5236_10277)

67. Ramblers Association West of England Rally at the White Horse, Westbury. Professor R J Brocklehurst, Vice President of the Federation addressing the rally 20 June 1937 (fig. 48)
Saidman/Daily Herald Archive (1983-5236_10278)

68. Epsom Racecourse. Derby Day. Finish of the course 2 June 1932 (fig. 62)
George Woodbine/Daily Herald Archive (1983-5236_10279)

69. Civil service girls. Rowing girls at Barnes 30 September 1932 (fig. 40)
Harold Tomlin/Daily Herald Archive (1983-5236_10280)

70. Tennis and lunch in the open at Lincolns Inn Fields 3 July 1934 (fig. 44)
George Woodbine/Daily Herald Archive (1983-5236_10281)

71. Girl cyclists rally, starting from Green Street Green 10 June 1934 (fig. 59)
George Woodbine/Daily Herald Archive (1983-5236_10282)

72. The Kent Rally of Out Door Folk at Mote Park, Maidstone. The crowd listening to the Health Minister Sir Hilton Young 26 May 1935 (fig. 49)
Woodbine/Daily Herald Archive (1983-5236_10283)

73. Cyclists studying maps before proceeding from Box Hill 15 April 1938 (fig. 61)
Malindine/Daily Herald Archive (19683-5236_10284)

EX CATALOGUE ILLUSTRATIONS

Fig. 1 Stephen Bone (1904–58)
Mural Painting in Piccadilly Circus Station 1928

Fig. 3 1933 Woman as Seen in the New Academy
Daily Sketch April 29 1933

Fig. 6 Laura Knight (1877–1970)
Daughters of the Sea
(exhibited Royal Academy 1928)

Fig 10 Lancelot Glasson (1894–1959)
Déjeuner sur l'herbe
(exhibited Royal Academy 1931)

Fig. 11 Francisco Vidal
Summer

Fig. 15 John Lavery (1856–1941)
Sun-Bathers
(exhibited Royal Academy 1937)

Fig. 25 Dermot Patrick Fitzgerald (died 1985)
Hoe Bathing Pool c. 1960
b&w photograph 21.5 x 16.5

Fig. 31 William Roberts (1895–1980)
Water Wings 1938
Oil on canvas 40.5 x 51
Private collection

Fig. 39 Lancelot Glasson with Freda Walker
Reproduced with kind permission of William Glasson

Fig. 42 Harry Morley (1881–1943)
Riverside
(exhibited Royal Academy 1937)

Fig. 46 Eric Ravilious (1903–42)
Tennis 1932-3
Oil on Wood 3 panels, each 82 x 49.5
Bristol Museum and Art Gallery

Fig. 47 James Stroudley (1906–88)
The Games ca. 1930
Oil on canvas 167.6 x 279.4
Private collection

Fig. 50 Anonymous
Hike for Health 1931
Southern Railway poster

Fig. 57 Nowell Edwards
Camping Sites in Southern England 1935
Southern Railway poster

Fig. 65 E. Dean
Little Orme Picnic 1935
Getty Images. Collection Hulton Archive

Fig. 74 Lawrence Stephen Lowry (1887–1976)
Beach Scene, Lancashire 1945
Oil on canvas 45.7 x 61
Private collection

Fig. 75 Stanley Spencer (1891–1959)
Southwold 1937
Oil on canvas 57.9 x 89.9
Aberdeen Art Gallery & Museums Collections

Fig. 77 *Come to The Place in the Sun. Aberystwyth* c. 1938
Colour poster
Ceredigion Museum, Aberystwyth

Fig. 80 Edward Bawden (1903–89)
By the Sea 1929–30
Oil on linen laid on panel 63.5 x 86.4
Private collection

Fig. 81 Lawrence Stephen Lowry (1887–1976)
Deal Sands 1947
Oil on board 26 x 51
Private collection

Fig. 86 Harold Williamson (1898–1972)
Summer Morning
(exhibited Royal Academy 1935)

Fig. 91 J. Greenup (died 1946)
Butlin's Holiday Camp. Clacton-on-Sea 1940
LNER poster

Fig. 93 Harold Harvey (1874–1941)
Fête Champêtre 1934
Oil on canvas 102.4 x 91.5

Fig. 97 Harry Epworth Allen (1894–1958)
The Countryside 1935
Tempera on board 46.9 x 59.8
(exhibited Royal Academy 1935)

Further Reading

Place of publication is London unless stated otherwise:

D. Birley, *Playing the game; sport and British society, 1910–1945,* Manchester 1996
D. P. Corbett, *The modernity of English art 1914*–30, Manchester 1997.
C. Fox, *Painting in Newlyn 1900-1930*
R. Golan, *Modernity and nostalgia. Art and politics in France between the wars* 1995
R. Graves and A. Hodge, *The long week-end. A social history of Great Britain 1918–1939,* 1941
R. Holt, *Sport and the British; a modern history*, Oxford 1989
J. Hill, *Sport, leisure and culture in twentieth-century Britain* 2002
S. G. Jones, *Workers at play. A social and economic history of leisure 1918–39* 1986.
P. McIntosh, *Physical Education in England since 1800* 1952, rev. ed. 1968
R. D. Mandell, *The Nazi Olympics*, Chicago 1971, repr. 1987
T. Mason, ed., *Sport in Britain. A social history*, Cambridge 1989
D. Matless, *Landscape and Englishness,* 1998
J. A. R. Pimlott, *The Englishman's holiday,* 1947, repr. 1976.
J. Smith, *Liquid assets. The lidos and open air swimming pools of Britain,* 2005
Spotlighting the sporting body [exhibition catalogue], Musée Olympique, Lausanne, 2002
J. Stevenson, *British society 1914–45,* 1984
H. Taylor, *A Claim on the Countryside: A History of the British Outdoor Movement,* Edinburgh 1997
Thirties. British art and design before the war [exhibition catalogue], Hayward Gallery 1979
J. K. Walton, *The British Seaside: Holidays and resorts in the twentieth century,* Manchester 2000

Acknowledgements

As with all exhibitions, the greatest thanks must go to the many lenders, both institutional and private, who have generously supported the show.
I would particularly like to thank Caroline Collier for her initial support of the idea, and Julius Bryant and Julia Findlater, both previously of English Heritage, for their encouragement. Also, Nicholas Alfrey for keeping a friendly eye on the project all along. Of the many others who have given generous help and assistance, I would especially like to thank Ruth Artmonsky, Janet Barnes, Hannah Bennett, Toni Booth, Lindsay Brooks, Michael Child, David Cleall, Roger Dodsworth, Harriet Drummond, Monika Flacke, Brendan Flynn, William Glasson, Anne Goodchild, Irving Grose, Melissa Hardy, Alan Hobart, Tracey Isgar, Melanie Lenz, Brian Liddy, Paul Liss, Michael Mackinlay, Johanna McDonald (Christie's), Philip and Betty Miles, Susan Morris, Simon Murphy, Jane Peterson, Susannah Pollen (Sotheby's), Alan Powers, Jan Reynolds, Jonathan Riddell, Marie-Thérèse Russell, Richard Shone, Peyton Skipwith, John and Ruth Snow, Penny Thompson, Stuart Tulloch, Alex Voice, Tim Walker, Winfred Walker, Heather Watkins, Bryen Wood.
TW

Credits

Photographic Credits

All catalogue works reproduced by kind permission of the owners. Images were supplied by the lenders with the following exceptions:
3, fig. 81 Sotheby's Picture Library; 16 © Sheffield Galleries and Museums Trust/The Bridgeman Art Library; 27 David Messum Fine Paintings; 37 © Stanley Spencer Gallery, Cookham, Berkshire/The Bridgeman Art Library; 38 © The Bridgeman Art Library; fig. 75 Aberdeen Art Gallery & Museums Collection; 41 © Southampton City Art Gallery/The Bridgeman Art Library; 42 © Russell-Cotes Art Gallery and Museum, Bournemouth/The Bridgeman Art Library; fig. 74 © Christie's Images Ltd 2002; fig. 47 © Christie's Images Ltd 1993; fig. 25 Plymouth Library Services; fig. 80 © The Fine Art Society, London/The Bridgeman Art Library; fig. 93 © Richard Green Gallery, London/ Bridgeman Art Library; fig. 77 Ceredigion Museum, Aberystwyth; fig. 39 Lancelot Glasson with Freda Walker Reproduced with kind permission of William Glasson

Additional Credits

1,4,5,8,9,19,24,39 London's Transport Museum © Transport for London; 2 Image reproduced with the kind permission of Homerton College, Cambridge and The Hamilton Kerr Institute, University of Cambridge; 6,7 © Courtesy of the Artist's Estate/Bridgeman Art Library; 15, 18, 20, 28, 33 © V&A Images/Victoria and Albert Museum; 10,11,12 © Courtesy of the Estate of the Late Peggy Fleetwood-Walker; 13, 14, fig. 10 © Courtesy of the Estate of the Late Lancelot Glasson; 22,23 © Courtesy of Michael Mackinlay; 26 © Tate, London 2005; 27 Courtesy of the Procter Estate/ Bridgeman Art Library; 29, 30, 31, 32, fig. 31 © Courtesy of the Estate of John David Roberts. Reproduced by permission of the William Roberts Society; 30 Reproduced with the kind permission of the Trustees of the National Museums and Galleries of Northern Ireland; 34,35 © Courtesy of the Artist's Estate; 36 © Courtesy of George Harrison Barrow; figs. 50, 57, 91 National Railway Museum/Science & Society Picture Library; fig. 80 © The Estate of Edward Bawden; fig. 15 © By courtesy of Felix Rosenstiel's Widow & Son Ltd., London, on behalf of the Estate of Sir John Lavery; 37, 38, fig. 75 © Estate of Stanley Spencer 2005. All Rights Reserved, DACS; fig. 46 © Estate of Eric Ravilious 2005. All Rights Reserved, DACS; fig. 6 © The Estate of Dame Laura Knight 2005. All Rights Reserved, DACS; 43-73 The Daily Herald Archive at the National Museum of Photography, Film & Television; 25, fig. 42 © Courtesy of the Artist's Estate, Julia Baron; fig. 65 Getty Images. Collection Hulton Archive; fig. 3 © Daily Sketch/Associated Newspapers; fig. 47 © The Artist's Estate. Courtesy of Jake Stroudley; 21, figs. 74,81 © courtesy of The Lowry Estate; fig. 1 © The Artist's Estate. Courtesy of Sylvester Bone.
We have been unable to trace the copyright holders of works by Harry Epworth Allen, George Henry, Walter Hutton, James Walker Tucker, Harold Williamson, Dermot Patrick Fitzgerald and Francisco Vidal and would be grateful to receive any information as to their identity.

Lenders

Belfast, Ulster Museum
Birmingham Museums and Art Gallery
Blackpool, Grundy Art Gallery
Bournemouth, Russell-Cotes Art Gallery and Museum
Bradford, National Museum of Photography, Film & Television
Brighton and Hove, Royal Pavilion, Libraries and Museums
Richard Burrows
Bushey Museum and Art Gallery, Mackinlay Collection
Cambridge, The Trustees of Homerton College
Cookham, Stanley Spencer Gallery
Derby Museums and Art Gallery
Dudley Museum and Art Gallery
Samantha Frank
Liverpool, The Walker Art Gallery
London, Geffrye Museum
London, Tate
London's Transport Museum
London, Victoria and Albert Museum
Jonathan Marland
Newcastle upon Tyne, Laing Art Gallery
Nottingham Castle
Private Collections
Rochdale Art Gallery
Sheffield Galleries & Museums Trust
Southampton City Art Gallery
Stoke-on-Trent, The Potteries Museum & Art Gallery,
Elizabeth and Paul Thornton
York Museums Trust (York Art Gallery)

This catalogue has been published in conjunction with the exhibition organised by the Djanogly Art Gallery, Lakeside Arts Centre, Nottingham in collaboration with The Lowry, Salford

A Day in the Sun
Outdoor Pursuits in Art in the 1930s

Curated by Timothy Wilcox and organised by Neil Walker, Visual Arts Officer, Djanogly Art Gallery

Djanogly Art Gallery 18 February – 9 April 2006
The Lowry 29 April – 25 June 2006

First published in 2006 by
Philip Wilson Publishers
109 Drysdale Street, The Timber Yard
London N1 6ND

ISBN 1 900809 36 2 (softback)
ISBN 0 85667 619 5 (hardback)

Designed by Peter Ling
Printed in China by Everbest Co

Djanogly Art Gallery
Lakeside Arts Centre
University Park
Nottingham NG7 2RD

LAKESIDE

THE LOWRY
ART & ENTERTAINMENT